What the Experts Are Saying About *How to Avoid Falling in Love with a Jerk*

"I have never read a book with more practical wisdom for finding real love and a healthy marriage."
—WILLIAM J. DOHERTY, PH.D., AUTHOR OF
TAKE BACK YOUR MARRIAGE

"Eye-opening and practical, *How to Avoid Falling in Love with a Jerk* is for anyone who's tired of dating and wants to finally find 'the one.'"
—JOHN GRAY, AUTHOR OF
MEN ARE FROM MARS, WOMEN ARE FROM VENUS

"*The* tool for finding the love of your life. John Van Epp and his RAM model make it possible for you to assess the five key areas when picking a partner."
—JON CARLSON, PSY.D., ED.D., AUTHOR OF
TIME FOR A BETTER MARRIAGE

"An insightful and creative contribution to managing the complexity of choosing a life partner. I heartily recommend it."
—HARVILLE HENDRIX, PH.D., AUTHOR OF
GETTING THE LOVE YOU WANT AND
KEEPING THE LOVE YOU FIND: A PERSONAL GUIDE

"Don't be part of the 'where-was-this-book-when-I-needed-it?' crowd. It's not too late—read it now!"
—PAT LOVE, ED.D., AUTHOR OF
THE TRUTH ABOUT LOVE AND HOT MONOGAMY

"The best way to avoid walking on eggshells in your marriage and living with resentment, anger, or emotional abuse is to choose your partner well. This book will help any serious-minded person to pick well."

—STEVEN STOSNY, PH.D., AUTHOR OF
*YOU DON'T HAVE TO TAKE IT ANYMORE: TURN YOUR RESENTFUL,
ANGRY, OR EMOTIONALLY ABUSIVE RELATIONSHIP INTO
A COMPASSIONATE, LOVING ONE*

"Follow John Van Epp's road map and create the lifelong marriage of your dreams. This is an important book that easily wins the Smart Marriages seal of approval."

—DIANE SOLLEE, FOUNDER AND DIRECTOR,
WWW.SMARTMARRIAGES.COM

"John Van Epp will teach you everything you need to know about picking a loving partner and getting your marriage right from the start."

—MICHELE WEINER-DAVIS, AUTHOR OF
DIVORCE BUSTING

HOW TO AVOID FALLING IN LOVE WITH A JERK

The Foolproof Way to Follow Your Heart Without Losing Your Mind

JOHN VAN EPP, Ph.D.

New York Chicago San Francisco Lisbon London Madrid Mexico City
Milan New Delhi San Juan Seoul Singapore Sydney Toronto

Library of Congress Cataloging-in-Publication Data

Van Epp, John.
        How to avoid falling in love with a jerk : the foolproof way to follow your heart
    without losing your mind / John Van Epp.
            p.   cm.
        Rev ed. of How to avoid marrying a jerk, 2007.
        ISBN 978-0-07-154842-7 (alk. paper)
        1. Mate selection.   I. Van Epp, John. How to avoid marrying a jerk.   II. Title.

    HQ801.V275   2008
    646.7'7—dc22   2007035668

1 2 3 4 5 6 7 8 9 10 11 12 13 14 15 16 17 18 19 20 21   DOC/DOC   0 9 8

ISBN 978-0-07-154842-7
MHID   0-07-154842-4

Interior design by Think Design Group LLC

McGraw-Hill books are available at special quantity discounts to use as premiums and
sales promotions or for use in corporate training programs. To contact a representative,
please visit the Contact Us pages at www.mhprofessional.com.

The case histories and personal stories presented in this book are real. However, names
and other details have been changed to protect privacy.

This book is printed on acid-free paper.

To four women who have shaped my life and taught me about love and marriage.

To my mother who longed to be a writer but was cut short in the prime of her life by cancer.

To my wife who has battled cancer during the last year of writing this book, yet has been a pillar of strength, always giving more than what she takes, and a constant source of unwavering belief in me.

To my two daughters who have graced my life with love, joy, pride, and friendship.

Contents

Acknowledgments

This book would have only remained wishful thinking had it not been for many who impacted my life, supporting me and opening doors of opportunity. First and foremost, I want to thank Diane Sollee, founder and director of Smart Marriages, who built public platforms for me to present my "no jerks" program, introduced me to almost every major contact I have, and has been an endless supporter and good friend over these last ten years.

I am grateful for the many men and women who have become certified in my program and diligently teach the concepts of pacing relationships that empower singles to make confident and fulfilling relationship choices. Some of you go way back to the beginning of this venture, before any teaching manual was designed, like Don Rossbach, Marlene Peterson, Bill Donaldson, Marisa Girman, David Toom (who was brainstorming titles with me ten years ago when the title of this book popped out, instantly detonating us with uncontrollable laughter), Thom and Linda Coney, and Don and Cathy Poest.

Then there are those who have devoted so much of their time and energy to bringing marriage programs to their regions and states, and have included the PICK program in their selections like Bob and Dianne Ruthazer, Kathy Schleier, Julie Baumgardner, Mark Eastburg, John Jauregui, Beth and David Miller, Dick and Carol Cronk, Bob and Anne Funkhouser, Dennis Stoica, Carolyn Rich Curtis, Vicki Larson, Richard Marks, James Sheridan, Rita DeMaria, Lawrence Compter, Aaron Larson, Bill Bailey, and the many others whom I have neglected to name.

I also want to thank those in the military who have become certified and now teach the PICK program, particularly the Army Chief of Chaplains office that has provided certification training for more than five hundred chaplains this past year;

your work continues to be invaluable. I have been more than fortunate to serve you and enjoy your friendships, especially Chaplains Glen Bloomstrom, Mike Yarman, Ronald Thomas, and Peter Frederich.

I am indebted to Tom Zitkovic for his friendship, tremendous talent, and selfless investment in developing and maintaining our nojerks.com website and likewise to my long-standing friend Tom Mohoric for his diligent development of the Love Thinks software.

I want to express my appreciation to my agent, Jim Levine, who skillfully led me each step of the way in proposing and marketing this project. I would also like to thank Hara Marano for lending her expertise to the editing of my manuscript; my daughter Morgan, for her vast research in dating and relationships and her contributions to this work; and to Deb Brody at McGraw-Hill for believing in my material and making the editing project easy and so much fun.

And last but certainly not least, I want to thank my family. My wife, Shirley, has been my best friend, never complaining, always willing to read and edit my writing, discuss endless topics, create new designs, and share in my dreams and always quick to say the most complimentary and encouraging words. My daughters, Morgan and Jessica, have constantly stayed excited and involved, even in the midst of their hectic academic responsibilities. My siblings and their spouses, Barb, Margie, Patty and Tom, and Steve and Rose have never grown tired of asking about my program and writing, regularly inquiring and expressing their interest. My dad and step-mom, Betty, have frequently told me how proud they are of me, giving me an irreplaceable gift of love. And my mother-in-law, Lois Newman, was always supportive and willing to type the initial drafts.

June 23, 2005, will forever remain a very meaningful date for me. At 4:00 A.M. my father breathed his last breath on this earth, and at 11:45 A.M. the proposal of this book was accepted by McGraw-Hill for publication. I like to believe my dad had something to do with it.

PART I

Your Heart Matters, but So Does Your Head

This book is divided into three parts. The first part consists of three chapters that are your orientation to the overall concepts of the book. The second and third parts are the core of what you will come to know as the Relationship Attachment Model (RAM) plan for building a relationship and confidently choosing a partner.

For the past ten years, the ideas of the RAM have been taught and researched in a program called PICK a Partner (Premarital Interpersonal Choices and Knowledge). Chapter 1 describes the reasons why this program was developed and its successful impact on singles.

Chapter 2 introduces you to the RAM, a simple interactive picture of the complex forces of love. Love is exceptionally difficult to define. However, the RAM portrays the major bonding dynamics of love in a clear and understandable way. Keeping the areas of intimacy in balance maximizes your emotional safety and clarity of judgment with dating partners.

Being the best person you can be and dealing with any of your own issues is the first step toward finding a good match. Chapter 3 addresses several areas that need to be worked through for people to build healthy relationships.

Follow Your Heart Without Losing Your Mind

How Did Something So Right Go So Wrong?

Meet Charlotte, twenty-five, who has just ended a two-year relationship:

> *When I first met James [twenty-seven] at the insurance company where I worked, he was easygoing, charming, and funny—he turned out to be all that and more. He moved in with me after seven months of spending almost every free moment together. I would have sworn that I knew him better than anyone in the world. But then he changed; he went out with his friends more and became less interested in me. When I tried to talk with him about*

*keeping balance in our relationship, he would become
defensive and detached, as if he just didn't care. I kept
trying for the next year and a half, thinking that he
would change, but he only became worse. Looking back,
I wonder if I ever* really *knew him.*

Then there's Marc, thirty-eight, at the end of a three-year
relationship:

*I felt sorry for Jenell the first time we talked. She was
going through a divorce from a real jerk who cheated on
her. I wondered how any guy could do something like
that to her; she was so beautiful and nice. She told me she
had never been treated or loved in the ways that I took
care of her. When I heard about her screwed-up family,
I realized why she seemed to feel
so "at home" with jerks. It felt
great to give her love, something
she said she never really had.
Around the fourth month of
dating, however, Jenell became
moody and picked fights with me,
as if she wanted to be mad. I kept trying to make things
better, and they were, for a while, but then she would go
back into her shell. I should not have stayed with her so
long. Why do I always get into relationships where I am
the giver?*

> It is easy to get
> fooled when you
> are feeling in love.

Listen to Tasha, twenty-eight, at the end of a five-year
relationship:

*The thing that impressed me most when I met Duane
[thirty-one] was that he was so good with my six-year-
old son. He always talked to him, horsed around and
played with him, and would even bring him surprises
when he came to my apartment to see me. Being a
single mother, I easily fell in love with the father my son*

never had. I was bothered by the way Duane became harsh sometimes with me, but I wrote it off as just a bad mood. And anyway, you've got to take the bad with the good. We married on our first anniversary of going out, but from that time on he was never the same. He had frequent rages and treated me just like his father had treated his mother. I never thought he would act like that; he had been so different before we married. How did I miss the signs of what he was going to be like in marriage?

What do Charlotte, Marc, and Tasha have in common? All three ended up with something different than what they thought they had originally. They minimized incidental problems that became damaging patterns, not recognizing the signs. It is easy to get fooled when you are feeling in love.

The problem is *not* that you are unsure of what you want. According to a recent national survey by researchers at Rutgers University, 94 percent of singles stated that they want to marry their soul mate.[1] However, many of them acknowledged a lack of confidence in being able to achieve this goal. You're probably reading this book because you've noticed a pattern in your own relationships—a pattern you want to break—and you're asking yourself this: I know what I want, so what am I doing wrong?

You know what you want, but

- Why are you always attracted to jerks?
- Why do you keep picking partners who have the same problems?
- How can you really *know* what someone will be like as a marriage partner?
- Why are you so desperate?
- How can you see so clearly what you want in a soul mate but be so blind to a realistic view of what your partner is really like?
- Why does your partner change so much in just three months?

- Why do you think more clearly, feel more confident, and act more assertively when you are *not* in a relationship?
- You were told that the ex was such a jerk . . . but now you wonder?
- Why did you overlook so many signs of problems?
- Why do you always end up trying harder than your partner to make the relationship work?
- What are you supposed to do to protect yourself from trusting too much?
- How long does it take to really know someone?
- How can you feel so loved and yet so betrayed by the same person?
- How can you love and hate the same person?
- Why did your partner change as soon as you married?
- Is this as good as it gets?

Can you relate to some or all of these questions? If so, then you are not alone.

My Ten-Year Courtship

I have been dating this book for almost ten years. My friends and family begged me to take the plunge and *get* published. But I kept telling them I needed to test things; I was not quite ready—just a little more time, maybe next year. Am I starting to sound like a commitment-phobe?

This book presents the successful and scientifically proven PICK program that, if followed, guarantees you won't marry a jerk.

In my defense, this ten-year courtship has paid off. It allowed me the time to test the ideas in this book in my clinical counseling practice. Even more important, it allowed me to turn those ideas into a curriculum, the PICK a Partner program (or PICK for short) that has been validated with research conducted at Ohio State University and road tested in seven countries, forty-eight states, and by thousands of instructors in military bases, churches, and social agencies. This book presents the successful and scientifically proven PICK program that, if followed, guarantees you won't marry a jerk.

Love Is Blind

It all started with a collection of comments by my hurt and dismayed patients who thought they had the best partners, only to discover later that they had either overlooked or minimized significant problems. I was in the habit of asking them to look back on the early stages of their relationships and tell me if they could see any signs of these problems. Invariably, they said yes.

Haven't you wondered why so many people overlook issues and differences in their dating relationships only to have these problems plague their marriages years later? You are dumbfounded when your friend forgives her boyfriend (or his girlfriend) for that destructive and repeating pattern of behavior that everyone else can see . . . but then it happens to you. You become struck by love and everything blurs. Not until after a breakup (or sometimes after the wedding) does the lightbulb come on, and then you feel really stupid because all those warning signals you ignored in the beginning of the relationship seem so clear in hindsight. Why is it that love *is* blind?

Two reasons emerged when I asked my disillusioned patients why they did not pay attention to those early warning signals. Combined, they capture the essence of what causes the love-is-blind syndrome.

You become struck by love and everything blurs.

First, many of these patients said, "If I only knew then what I know *now*." They lacked the *head knowledge* of what to look for in a prospective partner. It is not surprising that most of us are greatly misinformed about the characteristics that predict marriage material, seeing that few of us have ever been formally taught about relationships. Our classrooms have been our families, friends, romantic movies, trashy novels, and our own trial-and-error experiences. While some of you gained clarity on this subject from these real-life courses, most have become more confused and apprehensive.

As my curiosity deepened, I started digging through the annals of research on love, romance, dating, mate selection, and predictors of satisfaction in marriage. I read more than a thousand articles, dozens of self-help books, and endless writings from popular magazines. I had taught advanced marriage and family graduate courses and was well aware of the plethora of research on the premarital predictors of marital happiness. I pored over these studies and found that most of the predictors grouped into five categories:

1. *Compatibility potential*—the balance between the similarities and differences of personality, values, and interests between you and this person—in other words, how you "fit together"
2. *Relationship skills*—communication, openness, and conflict management and resolution
3. *Patterns from other relationships*—relationship patterns from both romantic and nonromantic relationships
4. *Family patterns and background*—the quality of the parental marriage and the family's expression of affection and emotion, development of roles, and interaction patterns
5. *Character and conscience traits*—the emotional health and maturity of conscience

The first two categories are fairly obvious and likely to be identified and understood early in a new relationship. The other three, however, are more subtle and usually remain hidden for much of the premarital time. These three categories were most often overlooked according to my dissatisfied and reflective patients.

The second reason that these patients minimized crucial signs of problems was summed up in a phrase I most often heard them say while sighing, "I guess I was just too much *in love*." Rather than lacking an understanding of their partners, they experienced an overdeveloped emotional attachment that resulted in severing their heads from their hearts. Embedded in this latter reason were thoughts like "things will get better" and "I know this is a problem but he (or she) loves me, and that is all that matters." I refer to this as a lack of *heart knowledge*. We can laugh when we see this kind of overattachment in popular television programs about singles because we relate to them. But the sobering reality is not funny at all, especially if you've been in a series of relationships that felt like true love but ended up as anything but.

It's Just Not Working

It became convincingly clear to me that conventional dating practices simply are not physically or emotionally safe. Nor do they lead to satisfactory partner choices. The need to provide a user-friendly guideline to balance the head with the heart is fundamental to the development of a healthy relationship and the choice of a partner. But no one had ever designed a road map for an individual to use when choosing a life partner for marriage. A wealth of research was not being translated into a practical and useful tool for singles to use in dating relationships and their quests for a marriage partner.

Can it be done? Should it be done? Why hasn't it been done before? I wondered about these questions and more. The longer I studied, the more I realized that I had it all backward. I was wondering if the world of singles could handle a plan for choosing a marriage partner when I realized that the world had *always* followed a plan for choosing a marriage partner. What it cannot handle is *not* having a plan to follow.

Singles had never been completely on their own in this venture. In the past, the plan for choosing a marriage partner had involved families, communities, and traditions. Eighty percent of all cultures throughout all history practiced some form of *planned* marriages: arranged marriages and forced marriages. These marriages were designed to maximize a rational approach to marriage: bringing together a couple who were similar in cultural, religious, and ethnic backgrounds; compatible in social status and family values; and beneficial for not just the two who were marrying but also the extended families involved. This historical approach to the choice of a partner was not really about love, romance, attraction, or intimacy. It was a practical arrangement that was directed by a rational plan. You could sum it up in just one word: *think*.

Not until the last few centuries were planned marriages replaced by marriages where individuals chose partners based on romantic attraction and feelings of love. Family and community guidance gave way to individual pursuits. The importance of similar backgrounds, values, religious beliefs, and cultural traditions was overthrown by passionate love and romance. This was such a new concept that in the early 1900s romantic love as a reason for marriage was considered a "pathological experiment" by most sociologists and marriage educators.[2] The famous sociologist and family researcher Ernest W. Burgess wrote in 1926 that "the presumably irrational, arbitrary and fleeting nature of a romantic choice of spouse is diametrically opposed to the serious, prudent and responsible undertaking which it should be."[3] In other words, don't follow your heart—use your *head*.

However, Burgess's warning was not heeded, most likely because the public assumed you can only do one or the other—so Western society revolted against reason and embraced the emotion of love. The twentieth century raised romance to heights it had never previously known. Singles were led to think love and only love. From music to movies to literature, love and romance dominated the charts. The classic Beatles song "All You Need Is Love" captured the culminating sentiment of the entire century.

The trouble with the approach is it didn't recognize that the head and heart were made to work together. The old world of arranged marriages focused on a rational approach to compatibility of family background, status, individual character, religion, culture, and family values. It was an era where the head led in the choice of a mate. The new world of the twentieth century focused on love, attraction, chemistry, devotion, sex, needs, intimacy, and loyalty. Love could be irrational but beautiful.

However, I believe that it is possible to have the best of both worlds. The twentieth-century motto "Think love" needs to be replaced with a new, twenty-first-century motto "Love thinks." *It is possible to combine the resources of your mind with the passions of your heart.* Doesn't it make sense to use them both?

Not until the last few centuries were planned marriages replaced by marriages where individuals chose partners based on romantic attraction and feelings of love.

Too often people act on the belief that being in love entitles them to stop taking in and analyzing information about their partners. The assumption is that love itself will take care of all that is to come, including maintaining the relationship. Love is conceived as an either-or phenomenon. You either are in love, or you are not. And if the love switch is thrown on, the brain switch is turned off. You leap into an exciting pool of pure emotion and willfully choose to stay there until you are about to drown in bad feelings.

Charting the Course of Love

So what is the alternative? How can you chart your course of love? You need a plan, a road map, a model that joins the head and heart in a harmonious whole so that they work together to guide you through the building of a relationship.

I spent years developing the RAM. It summarizes massive amounts of theory and research on love, attachment, intimacy, and bonding into just one interactive picture. It portrays the amazing forces of love and how they interact with the discerning powers of the mind. The RAM is simple, yet it respects the complexity of love; personal, yet universally applicable; and rational, yet open to the mystery of love. I will completely explain the RAM in the next chapter, but at this point it is important to say that it provides everything you need to choose a partner: a plan to guide you to know what a partner really will be like as a spouse, to stay emotionally and physically safe while the relationship is growing, and to make healthy choices that will lead to a fulfilling marriage.

The first time I presented the RAM publicly was in the summer of 1996. I titled the seminar "How to Avoid Marrying a Jerk." I had invited sixty colleagues from various fields—educators, counselors, ministers, social workers, and divorce experts. I taught the five-lesson curriculum in an all-day format. The response was overwhelmingly positive. From that group alone I received over a dozen invitations to present the program in other settings. In a short amount of time, I had stopped all my other seminar presentations and was teaching only this. A year later I had a film crew videotape one of my live presentations so that others could use it with their respective groups and classes. I wrote a discussion workbook that students and group participants could use along with the videos and formally titled it *PICK a Partner*.

It became evident that videos were not enough. PICK had crossed cultural and generational boundaries, and a diversity of instructors needed to be trained and certified to teach the program without the videos. I wrote an instructor's course with detailed lesson plans and made the certification training program available online. Before I knew it, instructors were teaching PICK in almost every state and requesting translations in other languages.

Military chaplains and family advocacy managers were becoming certified in larger numbers than any other professional group. They raved about the benefits PICK offered to military singles. The U.S. Army officials at the Pentagon responded with strong support, and a research study was funded in conjunction with the Ohio State University to evaluate the effectiveness of the PICK program on the dating practices of single soldiers and cadets. We trained instructors at two military academies and two military bases: the U.S. Military Academy at West Point, the Defense Language Institute at the Presidio of Monterey, Fort Jackson, and Fort Benning. The conclusions were impressively positive. As a result of attending the PICK program, participants:

The RAM is simple, yet it respects the complexity of love; personal, yet universally applicable; and rational, yet open to the mystery of love.

- were more critical in assessing their past relationship experiences based on what they learned from the PICK program about pacing a relationship
- placed greater importance on each of the five areas the PICK program deems crucial for getting to know one's partner, or FACES: **F**amily background, **A**ttitudes and actions of the conscience, **C**ompatibility potential, **E**xamples of other relationships, and **S**kills in relationships
- reported less influence from myths such as "Love alone is a sufficient reason to marry," "Cohabitation improves the odds of a lasting marriage," "Opposites always complement," and "Choosing a mate should be easy or happen by matter of chance or accident"
- had a stronger understanding of the importance of taking one's time to really know his or her partner and whether the relationship was ready for marriage
- were more likely to recognize the influence of family of origin on their relationships
- were more aware that changes in a relationship should be worked on prior to marriage and that those changes

will be more easily accomplished before rather than after marriage

- understood more clearly that definite, identifiable indicators (e.g., previous relationships) foreshadow what a person will be like in a marital relationship
- believed more deeply that early experiences in a premarital relationship are often misleading and only with time can a person learn what a prospective partner will really be like in marriage
- felt more knowledgeable about developing a healthy relationship that leads to a healthy marriage and more confident in their abilities to use the skills learned to develop a healthy relationship

Furthermore, 98 percent of the program participants agreed to follow the RAM and stated that they would recommend it to others.

This book is built on the foundation of the last ten years of successful and effective use of the RAM. Contrary to many conventional dating practices, the RAM exposes jerks, protects you from a blinding love, and provides you with a map for pacing your relationship while exploring the key target areas that foreshadow your future with a partner.

I will close this chapter with one last word of introduction: I have attempted to present a fair representation of the many scientific studies on love, sex, and marriage. These studies are difficult to find for the average person because they are dispersed among the millions of journal articles in our university and college libraries. To make matters worse, these studies can be tedious and somewhat boring. However, they offer a wealth of insight and guidance in the journey of choosing a partner and building a relationship. Therefore, I have chosen

The RAM exposes jerks, protects you from a blinding love, and provides you with a map for pacing your relationship.

the studies that are the most representative of each topic area and done my best to make them interesting and practical for your use. My hope is that the ideas of this book accurately translate the world of research into the language of the average person.

DON'T FORGET

- The love-is-blind phenomenon results when one of two areas is lacking—head knowledge or heart knowledge.

- The bulk of research on what someone will be like in marriage boils down to five key areas you need to get to know about a partner.

- The PICK program has been proven successful in helping singles avoid problem partners.

2

The RAM Plan

∞

Jerks

Jerks have no gender. The only difference is the package they come in.

No one earns the right to be called a jerk from merely acting like one once or twice. If we are honest, all of us act like jerks now and then. However, the most fundamental identifying feature of true jerks is their persistent resistance to ever changing their core jerk qualities. No matter how many times they have been confronted by you or others, they still persist in their hurtful pattern. If it is possible to reform a jerk, it will almost always require a major life crisis or life-transforming event. But the longer the jerk's track record, the lower the likelihood for improvement.

The first criterion for identifying a jerk is the habit of breaking boundaries. Boundary breakers come in many forms. One common type is the *player*. Players have an insatiable appetite for attention and the intoxicating excitement of infatuation.

For a player, living within the fences of one relationship is both boring and unfulfilling. Players feel trapped by any sense of commitment and are addicted to the frequent fix of new love. But don't expect them to immediately extinguish the old flame. The irony of players is that they often try to keep one relationship burning while they ignite another.

> The most fundamental identifying feature of true jerks is their persistent resistance to ever changing their core jerk qualities.

Another common type of habitual boundary breaker is the *space invader*. The space invader's motto is, "What is mine is mine, and what is yours is mine." Space invaders have a never-ending entitlement to your attention, interest, money, time, and emotional support. But a relationship with a space invader is never a two-way street. You must conform to their agenda or you will be left behind. Count yourself fortunate if you are ever left behind.

The second diagnostic trait of a jerk is the utter inability to ever see anything from anyone else's perspective. Did you ever have a relationship with someone like this? You may not know it at first, because the deflection of your perspective seems trivial. You feel a bit selfish and would most likely not bring it to their attention. Why? Because you are a good-hearted person who is more inclined to overlook and forgive a shortcoming than hold it over someone's head.

Good-hearted people, by the way, have the greatest risk for staying in a relationship with a jerk, because good-hearted people so quickly forgive, overlook problems, minimize short-comings, and give second chances (and third, and fourth, etc.). "Give 'em the benefit of the doubt," you think, "everyone makes mistakes."

But after a person fails to recognize your perspective several times, a pattern emerges, and you realize the occasions of oversight are actually related in a long strand of similar self-absorbed omissions. This pattern is what becomes so difficult to handle in a long-term relationship. You feel a void of never being understood or validated. In time, you realize that you are invisible to your partner.

The third identifying feature of a jerk is a dangerous lack of emotional controls and balance. Failure to express feelings appropriately immobilizes one's ability to build healthy relationships and relate intimately. People afflicted with this characteristic most likely are either immature and emotionally turbulent, or emotionally flat and unexpressive.

The range and fluctuation of emotion can be described as a pendulum. The midpoint, or area of rest, represents emotional calm. A swing to the right side indicates extreme emotional reactions. A swing to the left represents little to no emotion.

Emotionally unstable people live on either the extreme right or the extreme left of center. Those on the right are the overreacting, explosive personality types. Those on the left are the flatliners. They have no emotional pulse. At first they appear easygoing, but later you realize that they are cold and detached.

Emotionally unstable men and women typically have their best showing in the initial stages of a relationship. Overreacting types are often the life of the party. They are known for their enthusiastic and entertaining personalities. They are addicted to captivating, fast-paced romances that mask their deeper problems under a shroud of attentiveness and passion. Yet with time and exposure, their dark side emerges.

Good-hearted people have the greatest risk for staying in a relationship with a jerk, because good-hearted people so quickly forgive, overlook problems, minimize shortcomings, and give second chances.

If you've been involved with an emotionally unstable person, be careful about swinging on the pendulum from one side to the other. In other words, if you have been with someone on the right, overreactive side, then the left side, marked by emotional detachment, will feel like a safe haven—but not forever. Eventually you will feel empty and unloved, as if you escaped from an emotional hurricane only to end up in an emotionless desert.

If you swing from the left to the right, you will feel rocketed out of your mundane world right into a world of chaos. The swing effects most likely occur when people overlap relationships. That's why it's necessary to end one relationship and take some time to regroup before beginning the next.

If you're like most people, you have, at one time or another, dated a true jerk. The worst part is that you probably didn't realize that the person was a jerk until it was too late. The medical and especially the dental professions have learned the importance of prevention. Most people know that regular checkups and daily brushing lower cavities. Our family doctors remind us months ahead of time to get our names on the list for the flu shot. Yet the prevalent love-is-blind virus that infects so many young (and old) lovers continues to plague our relationships with still no preventive help. Without a plan for building safe relationships and determining the true character of the partner you picked, you can easily find your emotional immune system compromised and your vulnerability to unhealthy relationships heightened.

On the Fast Track to Getting Involved with a Jerk

One of the most common ways people are set up to get involved with a jerk is by accelerating the pace of a relationship. You run an extremely high risk of *thinking* that you know your partner deeply, when actually you only know that person in superficial ways. The initial and overwhelming feelings of closeness and connection cloak the problems that eventually will turn you off. Because of your accelerated relationship, you become infected with the love-is-blind syndrome and run the high risk of making a commitment to someone you later realize is a jerk.

If attachment is the glue in relationships, then an accelerated attachment is like superglue. It activates a willingness to overlook and minimize obvious problems; it blinds your vision so that you see only the part, never the whole; and it intoxicates your emotions and hormones so that you feel safe and secure in this newfound love. It is crucial to realize that your ability to form strong and loving bonds can betray you *if you do not intentionally pace a new relationship.*

Emotional bonding is intrinsic to relationships, and an understanding of how you bond provides a practical guide for pacing your relationships. This is the way to be immunized against the love-is-blind infection.

Can Love Be Defined?

I have spent much of my professional life teaching couples *how* to improve their relationships. But what actually comprises this feeling of love? Is it just a "secondhand emotion" as Tina Turner sings, or is it a complex blend of many sources? One of the difficulties with the subject of falling in and out of love is that the experience has no clear definition. How can we exercise any volition or control over that which we do not even understand?

In the arena of relationship research, there are scores of studies but few definitions that describe this mysterious force. I do not pretend to have an exhaustive or perfect definition of love, but I do have an empirically derived model that summarizes and categorizes from research the forces that contribute to the feelings of closeness and love. This model has been successfully used by singles to clarify their confused feelings of love and connection.

A Picture Is Worth a Thousand Words

More than twenty years ago, I created an interactive model that portrays the different forces that create bonds in relationships. This model is now referred to as the *Relationship Attachment Model*, or *RAM*. I have used this conceptual picture countless times in my counseling practice to clarify the abstract and often contradictory forces of love. I received such positive feedback from my clients that I decided to sneak this model in when I taught graduate courses on marriage and family relationships. I presented it as a tool to assess relationships and as a way to visualize the dynamic, changing bonds in intimate relationships. In order to gain accurate feedback from the students who might have only said what their professor would want to hear, I waited until the end of the course before revealing that I developed this model. Before I disclosed the origins of the RAM, I had students anonymously fill out an evaluation of the course materials; the RAM was almost always rated the most helpful and practical assessment instrument.

I tend to be a big-picture thinker and naturally try to find ways to visually represent abstract concepts. Few subjects are as abstract and as big as love and attachment. Relationship bonds include concepts such as trust, reliance, commitment, affection, emotion, love, needs, and intimacy. Each of these is the subject of endless volumes. However, I believe that they are all related and are the product of only five universal human dynamics working together. The five fundamental dynamics are the depth to which you *know*, *trust*, *rely on*, *have a commitment to*, and *have sexual involvement with* another person. The RAM portrays these five dynamics in a way that explains their unique contributions to the bond developed in a relationship, as well as the interactions they have with each other.

Picture a sound system's equalizer with five up-and-down sliders evenly placed across the face of the board (see Figure 2.1). The slider on the far left represents the extent to which you really *know* a person. As you move the bar on this slider up over time,

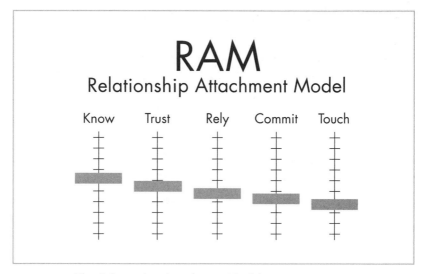

FIGURE 2.1 The Relationship Attachment Model

you signify a richer, fuller, and more personal knowledge of the other. The next slider represents the range of *trust* you have for that person. This bar rises to denote a deeper, more positive, confident trust in your partner. The third slider represents the extent to which you *rely* on this person. Moving this bar up indicates the greater ways you depend on this person to meet your most significant needs. The fourth slider represents the range of *commitment* you have established with this person. The slider for this dynamic rises to signify greater levels of commitment expressed within your relationship. The final slider, on the far right, represents the degree of sexual *touch* and chemistry that exists between you and your partner. Elevating this slider signifies increases in the passionate chemistry and sexual contact with your partner.

As you reflect on this portrayal of relationship connections, you will realize how bonding these five dynamics are in your own relationships. For example, your best friend likely knows you better than just about anyone else. This knowledge creates attachment. To the degree that you have opened up and shared yourself, you have become bonded to your best friend. An even stronger bond results from a reciprocal exchange in each of these areas. In other words, the bond doubles when the two of you know each other better than anyone else.

The same is true for trust. The deeper and more positive the trust you have in someone, the stronger your feelings of connection to him or her. When that person also fully trusts you, then this mutual trust generates even greater feelings of oneness. Depending on someone who also depends on you to meet personal and emotional needs intertwines the feelings of both in a powerful union. There is little doubt that mutual commitment and sexual passion also are intensely bonding dynamics that contribute to the mystical experience of attachment.

Not only do these dynamics stand on their own as channels of bonding in your relationships, but they also interact with each other to produce a mix of the overall attachment in a relationship. As soon as you imagine some of the sliders up and some down, you immediately gain a sense of the mixed nature of love and attachment. In the same way that the controls on your equalizer affect the different tones of the overall sound of your music, the blend of the different levels of these five bonding relationship dynamics produces the "sound" of your attachment.

When all five are at the top level, the feelings of attachment are strongest. But when even one is low, attachment is weakened and your feelings of closeness become mixed. You are easily confused, hurt, and doubtful. The *balance* of all five bonding dynamics determines the healthiness of your relationship and the clarity of your perspective on your partner.

Here lies one of the most important keys to building a healthy relationship: *keep a balance among the five relationship dynamics*. Whenever the relationship dynamics shift out of balance with each other, you will feel unsafe, experiencing feelings of hurt, betrayal, confusion, mistrust, unfairness, anger, loneliness, or any combination of these. But when you keep these five dynamics in balance with each other so that you are not moving further ahead in one area than in any of the others, then you are securely planted in the safe zone.

Safe Relationships

The balance of all five bonding dynamics determines the healthiness of your relationship and the clarity of your perspective on your partner.

There is one basic rule for guarding the safe zone: *never go further in one bonding area than you have gone in the previous*. This rule is based on the view that the five bonding dynamics have a specific order and logic to them: what you *know* about a person determines the degree you should *trust* him or her; this trust directs you in choosing what personal needs you can *rely* on him or her to meet; you should become *committed* only to the extent that you know, trust, and depend on that person; and finally, any degree of *sexual involvement* is safest when it matches the context of the overall intimacy reflected in the levels of the other four dynamics.

Slipping out of the safe zone explains the most common mistake people make in relationships: when the levels of the five dynamics are out of balance, then the emotional bond becomes unhealthy, and you tend to overlook crucial characteristics of the other person that should be exposed and explored. Thus, your love becomes truly blind. Or without knowing why, you wind up rationalizing characteristics and experiences that create a vague sense of unease.

Luanda always had a thing for the bad boys. Her romance with Anthony took off fast and furious. True to form, Anthony made Luanda feel drenched in his love; he convinced her that she was his breath of life and that without her he was nothing. They didn't hold back sexually, believing that their passion was unrivaled and that they would be together forever.

In time, though, Anthony started becoming extremely jealous. Almost as if some emotional switch had been flipped, he would become critical and insulting when she wore sexy outfits, went to particular places, or talked to certain people. Even though his behavior became a predictable pattern, she never failed to be surprised and angry. His rages intensified, and nothing she would say or do helped. She tried making promises and following his demands, but Anthony always found something more. In the height of his attacks he would resort to one of several threats: walk out, end the relationship, or find someone better. Luanda would invariably cry, being obsessed with losing him, and beg him to stay.

Relying on someone beyond your level of trust hooks you emotionally in a dangerous relationship addiction.

When Luanda sat down in my office and described her relationship with Anthony, I was perplexed by the contradiction between her head and heart. She could describe his pathological pattern as accurately as any professional but still could not stop dating him or assert any ultimatums. What kept her stuck on him?

What became apparent as our sessions continued was that Luanda had made Anthony the center of her world. She totally relied on him to be her source of emotional security and personal identity. He made her feel needed—even possessed, in some warped way.

Luanda was a lot like a child in this relationship. A child wants to feel like she belongs to her parents and her parents belong to her. This "belonging" is at the core of feeling secure. Parents express their "ownership" in many ways: "That's my girl," "We love you more than anyone in the whole wide world," or "You're my pride and joy." Children need this sort of exchange. When they don't get it, they can end up looking for the feeling of being *owned* in some adult relationship. This always leads to overdependence on someone in search of his or her approval, which usually comes at too great a cost to one's sense of self.

Luanda was fixated on wanting to be lovingly owned. She was trying to gain what she had never received from her father. She found "normal" guys boring. It was the overly controlling man that consistently caught her eye. But it was these same men who never assuaged her need; they just temporarily drugged it with their own paranoid controls. Relying on someone *beyond* your level of trust hooks you emotionally in a dangerous relationship addiction.

Safe Relationships Prompt Healthy Choices

Ultimately, Luanda's knowledge should have determined the boundaries of her reliance and trust. If she had set boundaries based on self-respect and an understanding of her boyfriend's problems, then she would not have panicked at his threats. She needed to lower the level of her reliance to match her reluctance of trusting Anthony. Then, and only then, would she have been able to stay healthy in the relationship, maintain a clear perspective, and have the strength to either push for change or break up with him.

When the safe-zone rule is followed, then your relationship grows in healthy and stable ways and the potential for making a lasting marital choice is maximized. The need to maintain balance among the bonding dynamics is central to keeping an objective perspective and avoiding overattachment. You must keep an equal involvement of your heart *and* mind. A healthy premarital relationship and a choice of a partner you won't regret require input from both the head and the heart.

The heart and mind were made to work together, each one making a vital contribution to the experience of love and attachment. When the safe-zone rule is not followed, the heart and mind are not in harmony. The attachment of the heart overrides the insights of the mind. Unhealthy love is blind because the mind disengages in order to maintain the imbalanced attachment of the heart. Healthy love is not blind, because the heart and mind are in sync with each other.

Scientists have now found evidence to support the old adage that love is blind. Through brain-imaging studies, researchers at University College London found that "feelings of love lead to a suppression of activity in the areas of the brain controlling critical thought. It seems that once we get close to a person, the brain decides the need to assess their character and personality is reduced."[1] Romantic love *suppresses* the neural activity associated with your ability to judge correctly a partner whom you have negative feelings about. In addition, massive releases of oxytocin, dopamine, and other hormones and neuropeptides in the brain create euphoric feelings that further cloud analytic judgments, masking those repeating offenses that should be obvious warning signals of problems to come.

Of course, there may be times when an imbalance among the five bonding dynamics is needed, and this is especially the case in a marriage. Ideally, married couples should work through conflicts in ways that strengthen all five of the bonding dynamics. However, sometimes sex is used to heal the wounds of an argument, because loving affection can be so effective in dampening grievances and rekindling closeness. Other times trust is compromised, and you need a heightened commitment to steer you through the rough waters. Under these circumstances, persevering commitment empowers you to lovingly stand your ground while facing a crisis.

Marriage Benefits Can Be Dating Detriments

Nevertheless, what is beneficial in marriage can be detrimental in dating. In marriage, the persevering forces of attachment and commitment are essential to overcoming the challenges and shortcomings partners face. But in a dating relationship, the stronger your feelings of affinity and loyalty, the more likely you will overlook the shortcomings and failures in a potential partner. The danger of any imbalance among the bonding dynamics is that it leads to tolerating or even encouraging serious problem areas that should be addressed once they are exposed. Although this same imbalance may be needed at some points in marriage, it is exactly what you do *not* want to happen in your search for a partner.

DON'T FORGET

- A jerk can be either a man or a woman.

- The most fundamental quality of jerks is their *persistent resistance* to ever changing their core jerk qualities.

- Three identifying features of jerks is their habit of breaking boundaries, their inability to see others' perspectives, and their dangerous lack of emotional controls and balance.

- One of the most common ways you become set up to get involved with a jerk is by accelerating the pace of your relationship.

- It is crucial to realize that your ability to form strong loving bonds can betray you if you do not intentionally pace a new relationship.

- The RAM comprises five dynamics—know, trust, rely, commit, and sex—that all contribute to the bond you develop in a relationship.

- Remember the safe-zone rule: never go further in one bonding dynamic than you have gone in the previous.

3

Healthy People Make Healthy Choices

Being the best person you can be is the first step in building a healthy relationship. For the most part, healthy people make healthy choices. In the same way, unhealthy people tend to build unhealthy relationships. Being a healthy individual is the prerequisite to being a healthy partner. There may be some serious personal issues you have never even acknowledged that will greatly influence both your choice of a partner and your ability to relate in that role.

When you think about the average age at which men and women marry for the first time (twenty-six and twenty-four, respectively), it makes you wonder how many personal problems have really been addressed or even recognized. The best time to review and alter the effects of your childhood is the period of time just after your independence—somewhere between eighteen and twenty-five years old. Yet the majority of people in this age bracket are consumed with gaining an education or becoming established in a job or career. Few ever take the time to reconstruct the influencing forces of the past. It is even more unsettling to consider the amount of dating that occurred *prior* to this period, as well as the patterns that were set. Unfortunately, personal issues are usually not dealt with until two or three decades into adulthood, long after they have shaped much of a person's marriage and family. Although plenty of self-improvement books have been written, it is essential to devote at least one chapter to some common, unhealthy emotional needs that can lead you to make unhealthy relationship choices and patterns.

Get Healthy and Get Smart

A clarification, however, is necessary before we delve into this topic. Some have taken personal healthiness as the only necessary quality and believe that if you just get your act together, then you will have everything you need to pick a partner. I disagree. Yes, getting healthy is the *first* step, but I have watched healthy people turn unhealthy after becoming involved with someone who has severe problems.

Curt came to me for counseling because he needed to sort things out after his divorce. He had been deeply hurt by his wife and her choice to leave him for another man. He worked hard in the healing process, reading self-help books, joining a divorce recovery group, and meeting me regularly for therapy. He gained a new sense of confidence, resolved the pain of his first marriage, and even worked through some previously overlooked issues from his childhood.

After completing his counseling, he decided to start dating again and became involved with Maria. At first, she was everything his first wife wasn't. After several months, however, it became clear that she was manipulative and controlling. Even though Curt managed to break off the relationship before it became too serious, he still experienced a serious setback.

Unfortunately, Curt's story is a common one. I have found that many good people are in danger of becoming involved with an unhealthy partner. Why? Because good people often give too much, accept too much, and overlook too much in a relationship. They believe people can change and that everyone usually deserves second and even third chances. As a result, good people often stay in a relationship too long, becoming more and more damaged while never seeing any genuine change in their partner. If this sounds familiar, then you need to reconsider the notion that all you need to do is get healthy. You need to get healthy *and* get smart about relationships.

On the other hand, you may be someone who has deep-seated troubles that have never been dealt with. These unresolved areas of your past produce unhealthy needs that lead to unhealthy relationship patterns. If you keep involving yourself with partners who all turn out to have the

I have watched healthy people turn unhealthy after becoming involved with someone who has severe problems.

same problems, then you may be compelled by unhealthy needs. If so, then it is crucial that you do the work to correct these problems so you can be ready to choose a healthy partner.

Unhealthy Needs

What exactly are unhealthy emotional needs? Simply put, unhealthy emotional needs are normal needs taken to extremes. We all need to be loved. Taken to an extreme, this normal need becomes dependency. We all need to give. Extend this normal need to the point of enabling somebody's problem and it becomes codependency. We all need to trust. But trusting to the extreme makes a person *naive*. We all need to test trust. Yet when a person cannot stop testing, then that person borders on paranoia.

Needs are natural and innate to the human experience. When you stop needing, you stop being alive. Think about a baby. Babies have physical, emotional, and relational needs, and they never require someone to teach them what they need. For example, imagine a newborn girl. She needs to be held, comforted, fed, and protected. When she needs something, she cries. For a time, her need is unfulfilled. During that time, she becomes more fearful and insecure, so she cries harder. She continues to cry as long as the need is unmet. Yet as soon as the parent attends to her, the need is resolved and she regains a feeling of contentment and safety.

Change requires insight into yourself.

The fulfillment of a need prompts growth in the child and stimulates the development of confidence that the next need will be successfully satisfied. This confidence forms the foundation for both the child's self-image (i.e., "I can accomplish what I set out to do") and the child's beliefs about his or her environment (i.e., "the world is a safe place that usually meets my needs" or "things usually work out in life").

However, when a need is repeatedly neglected, a different pattern emerges. The need intensifies into a demand. If this emotional demand is unfulfilled, then it continues to increase until it becomes an absolute necessity.

Psychologist Harry Harlow conducted a landmark study on newborns and the importance of being touched. He separated baby primates from their mothers immediately after birth and kept them in isolation. Although the primates were provided with food and warmth from a surrogate cloth mother, without any touch they all developed abnormal emotional needs. They were socially awkward, depressed, and unable to give affection normally.[1]

Although I have used primates to illustrate how normal needs can grow into unhealthy needs, this also can occur in human relationships. I have counseled many clients who have stayed in a relationship where their normal needs were starved. Like the primates, the needs of these clients escalated to unhealthy needs. Both adults and children develop coping mechanisms to handle this unhealthy situation. They may "stuff it," deny it, become depressed, or just channel the unhealthy needs in some way. Yet these unmet needs become the seeds for later relationship problems, setting up a person either to be *with* a jerk or in fact, *be* the jerk.

Keep the Good, Redeem the Bad

Although there is little from your past that will not influence your present, there is also much that can be altered and redeemed. This point is worth emphasizing. Change is possible, but not without four essential ingredients. First, change requires *insight* into yourself. It is very difficult to improve some area that you do not recognize as a problem. The Alcoholic Anonymous organization has acknowledged this for years. Until an alcoholic can break through denial and admit the addiction, there will never be any progress. (This process is true with any addiction—substance, physical, or emotional.) This insight can occur in many ways. Unfortunately, it often takes a rock-bottom experience to gain a clear view of yourself.

After you gain insight, you then need *new information* to direct the changes. In most aspects of life, we recognize the importance of training and experience. Every profession reveres those who have learned the most. When it comes to loving and relating, however, some think it is an insult to even suggest that they need to be taught how to get along with others.

Figure out what psychological defenses you commonly use. Ideally, healthy defenses soften a blow to the self so you can see and admit your shortcomings but not be overwhelmed with rejection or remorse. However, you may have such strong defenses that you deny your shortcomings. It will be difficult for someone to be in a relationship with you if you are overly defensive. Overdefensiveness leads you to feel that you are never wrong and usually limits your ability to change because you minimize or overlook your own problems.

Some people are more oriented toward personal growth than others. If you are one of these people, then you are probably more willing to look at yourself from the perspective of another, and your track record most likely supports this attitude. You have attended classes, listened to tapes, watched educational shows, read books, or pursued learning in some other way. Over the course of your relationships, genuine changes will be accompanied by insight, new perspectives, and new information.

Personal changes take concerted effort over time.

Two additional ingredients are involved when change occurs: *motivation* and *time*. Hard work is easy to observe and measure when you are engaging in a physical task. For example, if you were constructing an addition to your home, no one would doubt the hard work and labor required. No one would question the necessity of time in this endeavor. It would be ridiculous for someone to discuss renovating a home and expect it to be completed without time and effort. But consider how many times you have heard a person you are dating acknowledge a fault and promise to change, but then assume it is accomplished—if not immediately, then after only a week of improvement. As with physical construction, personal changes take concerted effort *over time*. Make sure you are putting forth the time needed to make lasting changes. The more significant the problem, the longer it usually takes.

Curt tried over and over to talk with Maria about her controlling behaviors but never saw any changes in her interactions with him. Only when he finally told her that he was going to break off the relationship did she change. She was much more willing to treat Curt like an equal, go along with things he was interested in doing, and be less argumentative and bossy when they had differences. These changes made Curt feel hopeful and optimistic, but celebration was premature. She continued for about a month and then slowly reverted back to her previous patterns. In this case, as in most other similar situations, Maria became defensive and even more resistant to change after she fell back into her old ways.

Changes like Maria's are only external and behavioral. Deep inside, Maria was not really motivated to change. No true effort was put into dealing with the core attitudes and beliefs that produced the problem behavior. Sometimes you can be motivated by emotions from a temporary situational state—for example, fear, panic, grief, or anger. But as soon as that state changes and the emotions dissipate, then so does the motivation. This is much different than the motivation that comes from a deep-seated conviction. The problem is that it is not always easy to tell which is which. The dust may have to settle before persistence and determination to change can be gauged. Time is the ultimate proof of a promise to change.

Think of pseudo-changes as a Hollywood set: an outward, convincing construction with no substance behind the scenes. If, like Maria, you have made a change like this, it was probably motivated by the fear of losing the person you love. However, as soon as your fear subsided, the set began to crumble and your prior landscape was revealed. Make sure that fear is not prompting your desire to change and that your new construction is not a new Hollywood set (which never takes long to build).

Time is the ultimate proof of a promise to change.

As with most rules, there are exceptions. To be fair, I want to mention the exception to the rule of the four ingredients required for genuine change. In rare occasions, a major life experience can lead to a lasting positive change. Crises, spiritual or emotional experiences, and physical or chemical changes can impact a person in life-altering ways. In these exceptions, as in all cases, time is the true measure of genuine change. Most often, however, personal growth requires an investment of insight, new information, and motivated hard work, over time.

Idealization: See No Evil

Unhealthy emotional needs lead people to develop one of three relationship patterns that attempt to *inter*personally resolve what can only be fixed *intra*personally. In other words, when you do not deal directly with your issues, they often become embedded in your relationships. At that point, you may no longer recognize them as your own issues, because they have become clouded by the dynamics of the relationship. You plunge forward to fix the relationship, all the while needing really to fix yourself. Regrettably, it does not work and your relationship continues to suffer. This will repeat until you identify your own problems and make the necessary changes within yourself.

The first pattern, *idealization*, occurs when you avoid feeling disappointment and pain by always looking through rose-colored glasses. A perfect example of this was a young woman, Ellie, who had grown up in a home where her mother died and her father subsequently remarried. During her adolescence, her father was tragically killed. His second wife favored her own children, leaving Ellie starved for love and attention. It was not surprising that Ellie soon met and married a man whom she had known only a short time. During their brief courtship, he lavished her with praise and adoration, calling himself Prince Charming.

Idealism always becomes dangerous when it blinds you to reality.

No doubt you know this age-old story of Ellie (her good friends knew her as Cinder Ellie, although most refer to her as Cinderella). She idealized everything! It was her way of surviving the atrocities of her family life. The beloved Disney version began with Cinderella waking up to the singing of the bluebirds and joining in with her own song, "No matter how your heart is grieving, if you keep on believing, the dream that you wish will come true."

I do not mean to tarnish the ending of this fairy tale, but seriously, don't you wonder whether Ellie looked at her prince through the lenses of overidealism? She wore clothes made from bluebirds, rescued trapped mice and dressed them in cute clothing, and never seemed to complain, even when she had to work all day and night! Maybe she was so determined to live her dream that she overlooked certain warning signals in order to fulfill her idealistic wishes. Idealism always becomes dangerous when it blinds you to reality.

Her prince was a wealthy, royal only child who was looking for the perfect woman. Men with the prince's profile usually turn out to be controlling, narcissistic, and emotionally abusive. They often have an extreme swing from infatuation to detachment as soon as some imperfection blemishes their ideal love. Ellie's idealism ultimately was leading her into the exact same family dynamic she experienced within her family of origin.

Your unhealthy need for idealistic love can be broken only by your *individual* efforts to face your pain and those who afflicted you, and to deal directly with the loss of having never been shown the love you needed, wanted, and deserved. Many times such efforts require courage to feel the loss as well as to face those who hurt you. A better blend of reality with idealism and the caution to test the one you trust over time will help distinguish an illusion from a genuine dream.

Rebounds and Crash Landings

Are you too trusting, always seeing the good and jumping to positive conclusions too quickly? Do you get into a relationship and immediately become swept away by the furious waves of attention and love? Do you find yourself enamored with this prince or princess, spending every free moment with that person, constantly conversing by phone or computer, or just talking to him or her in your head? If so, then you need to step back and look at your track record. If you have a history of these dreamy love attacks that end up spiraling into nightmares, then you may be avoiding some of your past pain by projecting your ideals onto a prince or princess who is nothing more than an ordinary frog.

Tonya had just ended a five-year relationship when she had her Cinderella nightmare. It began when she was approached by Will in a local club that she frequented. Will worked there and had talked briefly with Tonya in the past, but he had never engaged in any in-depth conversation with her. That night, however, Tonya started to tell Will, who listened intently, the tale of her long and rocky relationship. After an hour or so, Tonya remarked how understanding and attentive Will was and what a contrast this experience was from what she was used to. They went out that night and continued to talk until sunrise.

This began a romantic whirlwind that, after just thirty days, led Will to ask Tonya to marry him. She responded with an enthusiastic yes, having come out of a relationship with a commitment-phobe, and they made plans to move in together and save money for the wedding. Tonya confided in me that although Will had a long history of failed relationships, he had never truly been in love and no woman had ever made him feel so good. When I asked how many skeletons were actually in his closet, she blushed and disclosed that he had been with more than a hundred women. I warned her about the ways history repeats itself, but she acted hurt that I was not happier for her.

The day he moved in with her was both his first and his last. He brought a chair that Tonya did not think fit the decor of her home. When she tried to talk with him about this, Will snapped that it was his chair. Tonya retorted that it was her home. At this point, Will realized that she thought of the house as *hers* and not *theirs*.

Nothing was unusual about this kind of an argument. In fact, you would expect it to occur under the circumstances. But as a result, Will lost all feelings for Tonya and decided to move out the same day he moved in. Tonya was crushed (although I thought she was really spared). She couldn't understand how someone could feel so strongly in love one moment and then be so ice-cold the next.

Tonya encountered the unhealthy effects of idealization. How did this happen? It began when she was reeling from the rebound effect of her previous relationship and in her pain had concluded that no good men were out there, at least, none were *available*. You might think that this mentality would have made Tonya apprehensive about the sincerity of a man approaching her, but instead, it only ratcheted up her hopes for a perfect love. When Will treated her in ideal ways, she projected onto him all of her dreams of true love, and like a tightly wound spring, burst forward in her dependency and commitment to a man she really didn't know.

Will also suffered from idealization. He had a chronic and long-standing narcissistic condition, much like his father did. As the youngest, though, he did not overtly display his father's temper. Instead, he was a charmer. *Narcissists do not appear self-centered at the beginning of a relationship.* Will, for instance, craved ideal love, and his ego was inflated when Tonya looked at him as "the perfect lover who could meet her needs better than any other." This made Will feel like a god in Tonya's life during the first stages of their relationship.

Only after some time do narcissists reveal their extreme demands, a kind of "buy now, pay later" arrangement. Once one disappointment blemishes the relationship, the narcissist can never retrieve that fantasy feeling of true love. The benevolent god becomes depraved and angry, exacting obedient love while never feeling satisfied or fulfilled. This is why Will was so amazing in the beginning of a relationship but so quick to quit whenever something went wrong. Narcissism lacks resiliency; so when the first flaw appears, love begins to die.

Identification: Opposites Attract

Recall the Brothers Grimm story "The Fish and the Fisherman"? This story illustrates the second unhealthy relationship pattern, *identification*. Allow me to paraphrase. There once was a poor fisherman who caught a magical fish that talked. The fish promised any wish if the fisherman would just put him back in the sea. The fisherman was so amazed a fish could actually speak that he turned down the offer of a reward and swore not to harm it.

When he arrived home that evening, he told his wife about his astounding day. She was shocked that he didn't ask the fish for a wish, seeing that they were dirt-poor. She demanded that he go back, catch the same fish, and request a lovely cottage in place of their rundown shack.

He did as his wife requested. He apologized to the fish and humbly explained that his wife wanted a new home. The fish granted his request, and he gently placed it back in the ocean.

After some time passed, his wife was restless and told him to catch the fish again and demand a castle in place of their cottage. Although he was happy, he always tried to please his wife. So he followed her wishes, and they upgraded to a castle.

Eventually this no longer satisfied her, and she insisted that he again hook the fish and command it to appoint them rulers in their land. She had possessions, but now she wanted power. Not wanting to upset her, he obliged. They became the king and queen of the land.

Eventually, the wife became dissatisfied again. She told her husband to catch the fish and demand that he make them rulers of the universe. Even though he did not want to, he went fishing once again. This time, though, the fish was fed up with their continuous demands and sent them back to their old shack.

Now you may think that this tale is about greed. But you are wrong. It is really about *marriage*! It is about relationships where one imbalanced person becomes hooked up with an equally imbalanced person. Think about it, she was just as bossy as he was compliant. They both were imbalanced, but in opposite directions. You can represent this imbalance by a number line (see Figure 3.1 on the next page). If 0 represents a balance between the degree of aggressiveness (1, 2, 3, 4, 5, etc.) and submissiveness (−1, −2, −3, −4, −5, etc.), then she was a +5 and he was a −5. Both were equal distances from the center—but in opposite directions.

The problem with this kind of opposites-attract dynamic is that instead of fixing your emotional imbalance, you identify the opposite quality in someone else and think that *your relationship* will complete what is lacking. It doesn't! Instead, the relationship multiplies the problems and drives you further from center. The message is clear: fix yourself first, or your unresolved emotional problems will disrupt both your choice of a partner and the relationship you establish.

Don't confuse this problem pattern with complementary relationships, which also have the opposites-attract dynamic. In the complementary relationship, the opposite characteristics are in the *normal* range. Although differences in your partner can sometimes get on your nerves, for the most part, complementary differences help complete you and make your relationship more well-rounded. But unhealthy and extreme emotional needs cripple compatibility, especially when a person is linked with a partner with characteristics in the opposite extreme.

This was the case with Thom. He had been raised by an alcoholic mother who was more like a child than the mother in the family. Thom, being the oldest, would corral his younger siblings into a bedroom and keep them away from the battlefield.

Unhealthy and extreme emotional needs cripple compatibility.

SUBMISSION Partner 1   Partner 2 **AGGRESSION**

-5 -4 -3 -2 -1 0 1 2 3 4 5

FIGURE 3.1 Unhealthy Extremes of Opposites Attract

During the week it was not unusual for Thom to come home to his mother passed out on the couch. He would take care of the other kids, straighten up the messes, and even cook dinner most nights. He became so conscientious that he turned down activities with his friends, because he didn't want to take the risk of anyone in his family getting hurt while he was away.

When he started dating, he was quiet and reserved. But he was attracted to loud and flamboyant girls. In high school, he fell in love with Kara, who was strong willed and outspoken. They eventually married and had two children. Kara, anything but domestic, found it boring to sit at home with their two children. She frequently would stop off at friends' homes or local hangouts after work, leaving the care of the children to Thom. Whenever he would try to talk with her about the importance of spending time with the kids, she would become defensive and accuse him of nagging. He realized that ironically he was doing the same thing in his marriage and family that he had done all through his childhood. Kara's lack of conscience was the opposite "match" to his overdeveloped sense of responsibility.

So why did Thom find Kara so attractive? Because he unconsciously wished that he could be less conscientious and more carefree. However, because Thom and Kara were too extreme in their unhealthy patterns, they didn't learn from each other in some type of respectful, relational exchange; rather, they lived out their deficiencies vicariously through the other. Thom was Kara's conscience, and Kara was Thom's independence. If

Thom had worked on becoming more independent and adventurous prior to developing this relationship, he would have been attracted to someone who was not so extreme.

In Figure 3.1, "normal" would be defined as a range around the balance point, which is represented by 0. There are many types of healthy personalities, but all of them have characteristics that fall somewhere within a few points to the right or the left of 0. Some personalities are more easygoing, while others are quite driven. What makes a person unhealthy is to be outside the normal range in one or more areas. All personality needs and traits can be conceptualized on similar continua and used to define healthy ranges and unhealthy extremes. It is crucial that you recognize the areas of your personality or emotional makeup that are seriously outside of a normal range and work to balance them *within* yourself.

Incarnation: Repetition Compulsion

The third relationship pattern, *incarnation*, states that you are prone to re-create the dynamics of an unresolved relationship where your needs were not fulfilled. Sigmund Freud labeled this phenomenon *repetition compulsion*. It is as if you have the script of some unhealthy relationship pattern written in your head, and you keep playing out your part—only with different characters. Some refer to this as a self-fulfilling prophecy. The old story line keeps repeating and culminating in the same destructive ending. Naturally, you are shocked each time this happens, as if you never saw it coming. You promise yourself you will never get involved in this type of relationship again, only to arrange a new cast with the same old script.

You ask yourself, "Why do I engage in such self-defeating behaviors? Why do I keep choosing the same type of partner? Why do I get bored with the 'good' partners and feel so mesmerized by the bad?" The answer to your perplexing quandary is that your unconscious desire to *change the ending* of the original relationship drives this recasting phenomenon. You have never fully grieved the wounds of that disheartening relationship nor accepted the losses of your unmet needs.

Repetition compulsion is a defense mechanism used to avoid dealing with the grieving process. No one can change the past; yet repetition compulsion is an unhealthy attempt to do just that. You re-create the same dynamics with someone who has some of the same problems as the person from your past, only to find that this present partner, like the past offender, never really changes. You relive the pain of your past once again, with the wounds cutting deeper and wider, all the while hoping to bring closure to some unfinished phantom relationship. Significant relationships from your childhood that didn't meet your needs cannot be changed. The effects of those relationships, however, can be. It is over and done. Until you recognize and grieve this loss, it will drive you to reenact the script over and over with the hopes that the story will finally have a happy ending.

Humans are dynamic. Our bodies are locked in time, but our spirits are not. You find this to be true when you hear a favorite song from a time in your childhood or teenage years. It could have been decades ago, but all you have to do is shut your eyes and listen, and you are right back there.

I recall playing tennis with my father when he was in his seventies and starting to slow down a bit. We were partners in a doubles match, and one of our opponents shot the ball straight down my father's alley. He didn't move a muscle as he watched it whiz by. He looked at me and said, "You know, I brilliantly returned that shot in my head; the only problem was that my body just couldn't keep up."

Repetition compulsion is a defense mechanism used to avoid dealing with the grieving process.

After the match, he continued to share his observations of aging. He said, "It's funny, I don't feel any older than I did when I was twenty. But I know I am, because recently some twenty-year-old called me 'sir.' Sometimes the only way you know you are getting older is by the way others treat you."

As your body ages, the person within the body simply accumulates more experiences. These experiences can overlap and become lenses that alter your perspective on a present situation or relationship. The danger lies in those past experiences that have been left unfinished or unresolved. As a result, the past craves closure and drives you to repeat the same old pattern with the goal of finally gratifying your unmet needs.

Few situations exemplify this dynamic with such clarity as Jacqueline's affair. Jacqueline had been dating Sam since ninth grade in high school. He had everything her father lacked. Jacqueline despised her father's angry and domineering style. Sam, in contrast, was caring, empathetic, supportive, and faithful. She often wondered how she happened to be so lucky when she was so young.

It was when she was twenty-one years old, just one year before their wedding, that Jacqueline met Jeff, an older, divorced student who was in several of her classes. She struck up a friendship with him because he sat next to her and frequently initiated conversations. The first thing she noticed about Jeff was that he took charge of whatever situation he was in. She liked the fact that he was twelve years older, always confident and in control. She wouldn't admit it to herself in the beginning, but as time went on she found herself strangely caught up with him, almost as if he had some power over her. She was happy in her relationship with Sam and knew that any involvement with Jeff would be destructive, yet she could not resist the hypnotic effect Jeff seemed to have on her. The longer it continued, the more she regressed back into her childhood confusion and depression.

Jacqueline described her connection with Jeff like a trance similar to the one her verbally and emotionally abusive father had on her when she was young. He had been distant and demanding, never giving compliments, only criticisms. She desperately longed for his approval but always felt inadequate. Because she had never come to grips with the effects of her relationship to her father, it undermined her contentment with a partner who was healthy.

Oftentimes, the compulsion to replicate unhealthy patterns happens even if you are already settled with a healthy partner. Sam was able to offset most of those situations, and for the most part, their relationship remained healthy. However, this positive relationship did not heal her, because Jacqueline needed to grieve her losses from her father's problems *on her own*.

Jacqueline was able to break off the affair before it destroyed her future marriage to Sam. She had to deal with many aspects of her unresolved relationship with her father. First, she had to face and grieve what she did not have but always wanted. This grieving involved more than just a surface acknowledgment of her father's problems; she had to allow herself to feel both her sadness and anger toward her father. It culminated with Jacqueline letting go of her wish for a better father and accepting him with his shortcomings.

Second, she had to find something of value in her pain. Many times, the disconnected parts of our past keep intruding into our present. But these parts can also become sources of deeper character and commitment after you have worked through them. For Jacqueline, she used what she did not receive as a daughter as a driving force in her dreams of becoming a mother someday with Sam. She had turned her losses into determination. As a result, she felt more connected to her past and somewhat proud of all she went through. She also took steps to strengthen her relationship with her mother.

Resolving your emotional necessities is the first step to avoiding a marriage to a jerk.

Third, she redefined her comfort zone. Even though she was engaged to a much healthier man than her father, she still had some underlying discomfort and insecurity with her fiancé's love and approval. Deep down, she never fully believed the kind things Sam said to her. She felt she was different, not as good as him, and undeserving of his acceptance. However, as she reworked her self-image, she developed a more positive view of herself and became more receptive of her Sam's love.

Only You Can Save the Beast

Once again, it is not a relationship that changes a person, but the person *in* the relationship who changes him- or herself. After a personal resolution of some past unhealthy relationship, a new relationship becomes the stage for a new script. You may need to "practice" and get used to this new script, but once you do, you will never want to return to the old.

The fairy tale "Beauty and the Beast" depicts the importance of changing your inner self before you can establish the relationship of your dreams. The beast was once a handsome prince who was selfish and self-centered. When the witch came to his door dressed as a needy old woman, he sharply turned her away, refusing to offer her any care or assistance. In turn, she cast a spell on the prince that essentially turned him inside out. His outer beauty was replaced by his inner ugliness.

He was cursed to stay in that form until he developed a new character, one of compassion and genuine selflessness. Then a woman would have to recognize his change of heart and sincerely fall in love with him in spite of his outward form. He was doomed to a life of isolation unless he dealt with his problems. In the end, it was not Beauty that saved the beast, but rather the beast that saved himself by resolving his resentment and cultivating an inner beauty of selfless love.

Resolving your emotional necessities is the first step to avoiding a marriage to a jerk. It is also an indispensable step to avoid *becoming* the jerk in your marriage. The time and energy you put into self-improvement will remove the unconscious infectors of idealization, identification, and incarnation and provide you with the stability needed to use both your head and heart in choosing a life partner.

DON'T FORGET

- Healthy people make healthy choices; thus being the best person you can be is necessary for building a healthy relationship.

- Being healthy yourself is not enough; you need to get healthy *and* smart about relationships.

- Unhealthy emotional needs are normal needs taken to extremes. If not met, these needs can become the seeds for later relationship problems.

- Change is possible, but not without these four ingredients: insight into yourself, new information, motivation, and time.

- If you have unhealthy emotional needs, you may develop one of three relationship patterns that attempt to *inter*personally resolve what can only be fixed *intra*personally: idealization, identification, and incarnation.

PART II

Use Your Head . . .

This second part describes the five most important areas in a relationship that clearly foreshadow what a person will be like in marriage. Although the chapters move from the obvious areas to the more subtle, every area is layered with deep and rich material. At the surface, most people quickly acknowledge the importance of each of these areas. But as they explore them more deeply, they find a wealth of insight into understanding the heart of a partner.

First, Chapter 4 discusses the importance of truly knowing your partner. It is easy to *think* you know someone much more than you actually do. This chapter provides a formula for achieving a *true knowing* of a partner, as well as looks into the importance of timing and patterns that can protect you against the love-is-blind syndrome that infects so many relationships.

Chapter 5 describes the first of five areas to explore step-by-step in your relationship. Compatibility is determined by the level of your chemistry, the extent of your similarities, and the blend of your differences. As you begin to detect the compatibility potential in a relationship, you also can get to know a partner's ability to communicate and resolve conflicts. These two skills are described in detail throughout Chapter 6. Chapter 7 explains the importance of understanding the patterns or relationship scripts that a person practices in his or her relationships, from the most distant to the closest. Chapter 8 outlines the various influences that a partner's family background has on the attitudes and expectations that will be brought into a marriage. Chapter 9 pulls it all together with a description of the conscience and the vital role it plays in a long-term relationship.

Getting to know the compatibility, skillfulness, relationship scripts, family experiences, and depth of conscience in your partner will empower you to accurately anticipate your potential life together.

Hello, I Love You, Won't You Tell Me Your Name?

RAM Dynamic 1: Do I Really Know You?

I was having my hair trimmed when the stylist remarked that my ears are not level—just what I wanted to hear. "A lot of people have facial features that are imbalanced," she reassured me. I wasn't reassured. I kept thinking about that little word *imbalanced*.

I wondered to myself what it would be like if I were single and had to endure the *first-date scrutiny* where everything is examined under a microscope. I can just imagine it: I would be sitting at dinner chatting with my date. Yet every time she would look at my face, I would know exactly what she was thinking. "Is that one ear a little lower than the other? Do I want to wake up every morning for the rest of my life looking at his face and having to tilt my head to balance him out?"

Dating Scrutiny

In reality, you scrutinize much more than just superficial observations like appearance. It is common to watch everything early in a relationship and draw broad conclusions from single incidences. The irony of our scrutinizing is that most people conclude within a relatively short time that they really know the other person, and consequently they shut their investigative eyes. Yet the most significant patterns that influence long-term relationships are not even evident in the early stages of a dating relationship. Time is needed to expose these areas and accurately predict what these patterns mean for a future marriage and family. But all too often, these patterns don't surface until *after* your attachment has increased to the point of overlooking and minimizing problem areas.

This was Pauline's experience. Although she was not yet divorced, her coworker Anne encouraged Pauline to go on a blind date with Tom, Anne's new neighbor. He had just moved to her city, so she relented and offered to show him around the area. He was relaxed, easy to talk with, and easy to trust. She shared more with him in the first three weeks than she had with her husband in her three-year marriage. Although Tom traveled for his job, they talked daily and spent every minute together when he was around. She felt surges of excitement when she heard his voice, and her mind raced with thoughts of true love.

Most people conclude within a relatively short time that they really know the other person, and consequently they shut their investigative eyes.

It was a sunny, summer afternoon, and Tom surprised Pauline with a romantic picnic lunch at the park to celebrate their three-month anniversary. They ended up in his apartment after spending the perfect day together, when Pauline noticed an opened letter lying on his table. She knew better than to read it, but Tom was in the other room and her curiosity was getting the best of her. To her alarm, it was from his wife. In rage, she thrust the letter in Tom's face as he approached her. He explained to Pauline that he was, in fact, separated, but that he didn't tell her for fear he would lose her. He begged her to listen and cried as he disclosed that he had not been in love with his wife for years—it was as good as over.

Isn't it strange how the black and white of relationships often turns to gray when the feelings of attachment are stirred up?

Although she wanted to walk out the door, the bonds of her heart were stronger than the doubts in her mind. The longer he pleaded, the more believable he became. Pauline felt sorry for Tom and even a bit guilty for judging him when she, too, was not yet divorced. Anyway, she should not have read the letter and discovered this piece of Tom's life before he felt ready to share it with her. Isn't it strange how the black and white of relationships often turns to gray when the feelings of attachment are stirred up?

Twelve months later, Pauline sat in my office, perplexed by the love triangle that still paralyzed her relationship with Tom. She kept holding on to the hopes that Tom would soon finalize his divorce to his wife, but there always seemed to be one more delay. Also, she secretly wondered *who* she would have as a partner when his divorce was all over. Tom was cold and indifferent with his wife, and Pauline was concerned that that side of him might become directed toward her once his wife was no longer the target. As her session with me ended, she summed up her confusion in one penetrating question: "Do I really know this guy?"

At first, you may assume that you bond with someone *after* knowing him or her. Actually, it is within the *getting-to-know* process that a bond begins to form. A few years ago, on a flight

I was taking to Nebraska, a middle-aged woman sat down next to me. After we introduced ourselves, I asked her where she was heading. She explained that she was visiting her adult children and their families. She then asked me about my plans, and I told her I was presenting a program that I had designed to a class of graduate students at Concordia University. She was curious, so I went on to say that it was a program for premarital relationships and choosing a marriage partner titled "How to Avoid Marrying a Jerk." She laughed hard and shouted, "Where were you when I needed you? I've been married five times!"

Two hours and five marriages later, we arrived at our destination. As we stood in the aisle preparing to deplane, guess what she did? She gave me a great, big hug good-bye—as if we had been friends for years. She felt *bonded* because she had engaged in self-disclosure. She felt *known* and that produced a feeling of connection with me.

The cardinal bonding dynamic in all relationships is capsulated in the little phrase "to know." It involves the process of increasing your understanding of *and* union to the person with whom you are in a relationship. Everything flows from this dynamic. It has been used as a synonym for *intimacy*. For instance, it was used in reference to sexual intimacy in the Hebrew Scriptures in the passage, written thousands of years ago, "Adam *knew* Eve, and she conceived."

This historic definition of the word casts the idea of knowing another as an experience of the mind, heart, and body—in other words, two people knowing each other is something much greater than just a meeting of the minds. To fully know someone required the accumulation of many experiences over a long period of time. There were no shortcuts. It was considered the cornerstone of all of the other bonding ingredients (trust, reliance, commitment, and sexual touch) that made up the glue of love and attachment.

By reducing the meaning of this word to just an intellectual function, we have misrepresented the process of building a relationship. We have confused the ideas of merely knowing about someone with truly knowing that person. As a result, you can *feel* like you really know someone in a short amount of time because you have learned all kinds of things about that person. This is what happened to Pauline. Because she had talked so much with Tom and felt so known by him, she felt like she really knew him. This feeling can be very deceptive, leading you to make conclusions about a person that time will prove inaccurate. (For all that my traveling companion *really* knew about me, I could have been some deranged psychopath masquerading as a shrink.)

> *The cardinal bonding dynamic in all relationships is capsulated in the little phrase "to know."*

The Knowing Feeling

In a national study on dating and marriage, it was reported that singles in their twenties predominantly practiced two types of premarital relationships: "casual sex," which required "no commitments beyond the sexual encounter itself" and "no ethical obligation beyond mutual consent"; and "love relationships," referring to the pursuit of a more serious love interest that required higher ethical standards than casual sex. Trust, honesty, and sexual fidelity were expected in this second type of relationship.[1] The study continued to state that love relationships usually involved postponing sex until the couple really knew each other.[2]

The crucial unaddressed question about this second relationship type was, "How long does it take to *really* know each other?" Most of the respondents said that sex was postponed for only a couple of weeks. Some said that it was expected by the third date. "If you wait too long," said one, "they think you're not interested."[3] The current date-mate definition of what it means to *really know* each other in a new relationship is quite superficial because of the incredibly fast-paced process of involvement. The study highlighted the core of why accelerated relationships abound in our society—we have grossly misrepresented the fundamental relationship process of getting to know someone. There is a world of difference between feeling you know someone and truly knowing that person. Romantic relationships often begin in a whirlwind of excitement and passion. You see your heartthrob across a crowded room, you make that first connection when your eyes meet, and you feel electrified with the slightest touch. But the process of getting to know this person takes just as long as it would if there had been no connection at all. Once again, there are no shortcuts!

The Know-Quo

The know-quo, or the quotient for knowing someone, consists of three key components that take you much further than the feeling of knowing and make up the dynamic experience of truly knowing another. They can be conceptualized as a mathematical formula, $I = T + T + T$. Intimacy equals **T**alk (mutual self-disclosure) plus **T**ogetherness (diversified experiences) plus **T**ime. Although these three threads in the fabric of knowing someone may seem obvious, it is amazing how many people neglect one or more of them. The basic safe-zone rule for the five overall bonding dynamics also applies to the particulars of this one bonding dynamic: a balance is necessary between what you know about a person from talking and what you learn from your experiences in a new relationship. Sayings like "Talk is cheap," "Put your money where your mouth is," and "Walk the talk" have become popularized because of the established fact that talk alone can be misleading. It needs to be matched with actions. Therefore, to truly know another person, you must engage in a deepening openness that is matched with a variety of experiences in which you see the other person "in action."

Don't Tell All

Weaving disparate amounts of talk and togetherness can drive your relationship to either of two extremes. The first extreme is the tendency to tell *too much too soon*. In the sixties and seventies, countless books were written on the subject of communication, most of which emphasized the need for greater openness between couples. The irony is that many singles do too much of what many married couples do too little. In my marriage counseling I am frequently trying to help married couples find ways to talk more because they never seem to have time for meaningful conversations. On the other hand, many singles tell me about the nonstop, in-depth sharing they have with someone with whom they have just begun a relationship. Although the Internet is a useful tool for meeting prospective dates, it is *not* useful for building relationships. Internet relationships are one of the greatest culprits of creating a risky feeling of closeness through talking without the tests of togetherness.

A balance is necessary between what you know about a person from talking and what you learn from your experiences in a new relationship.

Two years ago I received an e-mail from Shelly describing a relationship she had developed with Steve, a man she met online. They had corresponded by e-mail and instant messaging for several weeks before they decided to talk by phone. Shelly told me that it was easier for her to open up through the computer because she could freely write her thoughts without feeling pressured by someone's presence. She described it as writing in her journal, except that *it* wrote back.

Shelly couldn't believe that she had shared as much as she had so quickly and how meaningful their relationship had become in such a short time. She didn't take lightly the act of opening up, yet she felt profoundly understood in Steve's lengthy and thoughtful responses. In fact, he identified with much of what she had written to him, comparing her experiences to similar ones he had encountered. Shelly wrote to me that in those three months she had talked more deeply with him than anyone she had ever known.

They wanted their first meeting to be extra special, so they both traveled to Las Vegas and reserved separate rooms in the same hotel. They figured it would give them the opportunity to do many different activities in a brief amount of time. Contrary to their plans, they spent most of their time in her hotel room. (Are you surprised?) When she returned home, she was certain she had found her soul mate. She poured out her heart in the longest e-mail she had ever written to him. The only hitch? He never wrote back.

Shelly wrote to me not long after her first and final encounter with her "soul mate." She was devastated. She asked me how he could have led her on for all that time. She felt deceived and betrayed by a man whom she had trusted more than anyone. She regretted telling him so much about herself and wondered what it was about her that had turned him off. She concluded her e-mail to me with a bitter promise to never let herself become that vulnerable again.

This story of Shelly's rendezvous underscores the damaging emotional risks that accompany this imbalance between talking and togetherness. It can sometimes be tempting to escape into a refuge of self-disclosure when beginning a new relationship. The discovery process is exciting and invigorating. Hearing stories from someone else's life is intriguing. As if watching a gripping miniseries, you can't wait for the next episode to answer all of the questions raised in the previous one. It is especially energizing when someone wants to know everything about you. A disproportionate amount of openness, however, will often lead to that knowing *feeling*, without any assurance that you have an accurate understanding of the *real* person you feel you know so well. You wind up jumping to conclusions and giving the person the benefit of the doubt because of the strong feeling of connection.

What You Don't Know Can Hurt

The second extreme is the tendency to share *too little too late*. Some dating relationships are overly focused on the activities you do together and not enough on what you share with each other. You may be in this kind of a relationship right now—a relationship where you are always busy, having loads of fun, and never discussing anything "deep." You may have even felt relieved by the nature of this romance because you didn't want a serious relationship at this time anyway. You really do like this person and have definitely *clicked* because of all you and this person have in common, so you figure you will enjoy yourself and postpone the "serious stuff" until later.

Be careful. This can become dangerous if your experiences together create a strong feeling of knowing this person and as a result you move too far ahead in any of the other bonding areas—trust, reliance, commitment, or sexual involvement. Such a relationship is one type of accelerated attachment. It is a by-product of the imbalance between talking and togetherness, but with a lopsided amount of togetherness. In this extreme, the *feeling* of knowing someone flows from the bonding effects of your many experiences together.

What's the Talk All About?

Mutual self-disclosure refers to the need for an expanding openness about your past and present experiences as well as future hopes and dreams. Talking is the ability to represent your unique, internal world in a common language that another can understand. It is the door that you open to allow access to your inner thoughts and feelings; it is the vehicle that unites two souls. Without language, you would be severely limited in knowing another person.

People long to be understood. The number one complaint in marital surveys is the feeling of not being understood by one's partner. Carl Rogers, a leading counseling theorist, built his entire approach to therapy, called nondirective counseling, on the core belief that people want to be understood. He mastered the technique of listening to the real meanings and feelings of what someone is saying, not just to their words. He believed that once someone felt safe in a relationship where that person could be completely open, understood, and accepted, then that person would naturally improve in his or her mental and emotional states. He was known for never asking questions or giving advice. He simply restated what the person was saying with poignant accuracy. Although the Rogers approach is not strictly followed by most therapists, nearly all mental health workers incorporate his empathetic listening technique.

The number one complaint in marital surveys is the feeling of not being understood by one's partner.

People in therapy are not the only ones who long to be heard—it is the cry of every person. Over time, this act of revealing broadens the scope of what you know about the person you are dating. Although we will discuss communication skills in much more depth in Chapter 6, knowing how to measure the degree of openness you should practice and expect is crucial when building a healthy relationship.

Sources of Information

Two areas of experience or domains provide sources of information to guide you through the talks and time you spend with another person in a relationship: the *situational* and *relational* domains. These two domains are distinguished by their unique contributions to your understanding of the other person. The primary focus of the situational source is the ways a person acts in various situations, and the primary focus of the relational source is the ways a person treats you throughout the course of the relationship.

Watch and Learn

By exploring the situational domain, you construct your understanding of someone from observations you make while watching how this person acts in different settings. Many times you are in the role of an observer. You are distant, almost like you are on the outside looking in.

Many romantic movies have followed this story line: the endearing boy who is always present but never the girl's choice—until the end. Both are in the position of observing how the other acts in different situations before they actually cross the line, finally discovering their mutual feelings for each other.

For instance, take my relationship with my wife, Shirley. At first, I watched her interact with others. I learned quite a bit about her personality from this vantage point. I also heard others talk about her, saying what they thought of her and how they were treated by her. This source of information formed my initial impressions of Shirley and set my expectations for how she would treat me. Even after we began dating, there continued to be plenty of observing in this situational domain.

The first time I visited Shirley at her parents' home, I noticed that she seemed to grimace while eating lunch. Later I asked if something had bothered her during that meal, and she told me that sometimes the way her father chews his food affected her like fingernails on a chalkboard. "His jaw," she continued, "seems to crack while he eats—it drives me crazy!"

I never recall Shirley feeling irritated by my chewing in the entire time we dated. But after we married, her sensitivity to sound amazingly returned. If someone had asked me back then which was more predictive of our future marriage, the situational or the relational info, I would have certainly replied that the way Shirley *treated* me (relational) most likely would predict our relationship in a marriage. It was the situational info, however, that actually foreshadowed our mealtime ritual of playing background music when we eat.

It is vitally important for you to be aware of any inconsistencies that appear between the situational and relational domains as you learn about the person you are dating. Most people are persuaded by the relational domain. You could be dating someone who treats his or her parents with contempt but makes you feel more loved than ever. Be careful. This person may do a 180-degree turn after you tie the knot. Unless there is clear evidence of change, situational information often has stronger predictive power than what you experience in the relational domain. We will examine this concept more specifically in Chapter 7 (getting to know the patterns practiced in other relationships) and Chapter 8 (getting to know someone's family background).

"The good doesn't always last, and the bad usually gets worse."

Listen to Your Feelings, but Don't Always Trust Them

As stated earlier, relational knowledge results from how you are *treated* in your relationship with someone. I am sure you are very familiar with this source of info; it is generated from the way a person makes you feel by the things he or she does or says. Relational information is one of the most powerful influences in your relationship choices. I am sure you have seen the familiar cartoon scene where the character literally transforms into rubber once intoxicated by love. When this happens to you, it is questionable whether or not you have a feeling or a feeling has you.

Feelings of love are powerful sources of intuition and prediction in relationships. No doubt, at one time or another you have had a really good feeling about someone. You couldn't explain exactly why, but you couldn't deny that you had that really good feeling. Whether you have near-psychic powers or an extensive collection of blinders, in either case, there is one cynical but true guideline of how the quality of the dating relationships translates into marriage. I refer to it as the "dating disclaimer," because it reminds me of the dialog boxes that appear on your computer screen when you download a program or order a product. You have to check "I agree" before you can proceed. Many of us check the "I agree" box even though we never read what we have just agreed to! Haven't you ever wondered if you just gave away your firstborn, retirement fund, or left kidney? In the same way, there is a dating disclaimer that most people rashly check off but few ever read. Therefore, I have edited it into a brief statement so you will thoroughly understand it and can test

The way you are treated and feel in the dating relationship usually sets the ceiling for your marriage to that person.

the signals you are receiving from your relational radar: "The good doesn't always last, and the bad usually gets worse."

This dating disclaimer can be broken down into several subpoints that provide some clarification and explanation. First, the way you are treated and feel in the dating relationship usually sets the ceiling for your marriage to that person. In other words, your dating experience with a particular partner is *as good as it gets* in a marriage with that partner. The quality of the dating relationship often establishes the potential of the marriage relationship. If you have a great premarital relationship, then you have great potential for your marriage.

Over the twenty-five years of my marriage I have reflected on the strong feelings and close friendship I developed when first dating Shirley. I don't think that those feelings ever really went away; they just became intertwined with many, many others. The accumulation of positive experiences in a good relationship brings about stronger bonds and deeper levels of satisfaction. In this way the good *does* gets better. I know I am fortunate to be in a relationship where I can still feel those vibrant emotions. You are not overly idealistic *or* unrealistic to want to fall in love and *stay* in love throughout the years of a marriage. It does take concerted effort, but it is definitely possible. The next chapter on compatibility looks closely at the role of chemistry in your romantic relationships.

What if you do not feel much chemistry? This is definitely something to pay attention to. In some relationships the chemistry does develop over time—either simultaneously with the process of getting to know that person or sometime after the relationship has been built. However, if you are dating someone and the chemistry just is not there, you need to take this lack of spark seriously.

Second, even though you are treated perfectly by your partner and feel a blissful satisfaction during your dating relationship, *everything may change after the wedding.* I have counseled many unhappily married, separated, or divorced women and men who described the strange phenomenon of having a partner completely change in one or more areas shortly after the marriage was sealed. This seems unfair, but typically a "good performance" in the dating relationship is a prerequisite but not a guarantee for a good performance in marriage.

A "good performance" in the dating relationship is a prerequisite but not a guarantee for a good performance in marriage.

A common example of this phenomenon is found in the transitory behaviors of men over the course of a premarital relationship. I had always been under the impression that women were the most likely to initiate the "love talk" in a new relationship—until my daughters started dating. I remember one of my daughters bringing us a note a boy wrote the day after his first date with her. It went something like this:

> *You are an angel, so perfect in every way. You are fun, beautiful, and smart, and I never knew I could feel this way about someone until I met you. I can't wait until tomorrow to see you again. Love always.*

My daughter thought his note was sweet but much too forward for only the first date. Later I came across a research study that established that men in their mid-twenties fall in love faster than women and frequently take the lead in saying words of love in the initial stages of a relationship.[4] Researchers found, in fact, that it was not uncommon for the woman to feel apprehensive when the man was attentive and expressive so early in the relationship. They coined the label *relationship manager* to refer to the person in the relationship who was the primary initiator of the couple's activities, affection, and words of fondness. The men consistently were in this role during the initial stages of a relationship.

What was disconcerting in this study was the conclusion that the job of the relationship manager changed hands by the time a typical couple was ready to marry. As the woman grew more secure in her feelings for her partner, she became more expressive and initiating. On the other hand, her partner became more comfortable and passive as his confidence in her commitment to him increased. The result was a complete reversal by the time of the wedding, which produced disappointment and unfulfilled expectations in the bride.

Perhaps you have seen a problem in your relationship but then doubted your judgment. If so, you are an example of the third point of this dating disclaimer: *and the bad usually gets worse.* Someone somewhere will come up with an exception to this—for example, a couple who had a tumultuous premarital relationship that completely smoothed out once they were married. But for the vast majority of married couples, the following point held true: the problems in the courtship became magnified in the marriage.

Deepening Your Communication

The key is to accurately and extensively get to know the person you are dating, delving deeper in your communication as the relationship grows. Openness in communication can be measured by four depths in the relational and situational domains. These depths range from shallow to deep, and most topics extend through all four layers. As a relationship grows and communication "deepens," the same topics are revisited time and time again but with greater depth. For instance, you can talk to someone about your experiences within your family of origin with minimal depth. However, as time goes on and more is shared, a greater depth of openness occurs.

The problems in the courtship became magnified in the marriage.

There are many descriptions for the different depths of openness. I use a simple acronym, OPEN, to characterize these four levels.

1. **O**bservations and facts—these refer to the type of communication where you relay current events, established facts, and things you've heard and seen. "I have four siblings in my family" is an example of communicating on this level.
2. **P**erspectives and opinions—they describe the type of communication where you add interpretations and opinions to your facts. "I think my entire family was deeply affected by my mother's death."
3. **E**xperiences and emotions—these convey more of the subjective, personal, and emotional content about your facts and opinions. "I grieved alone many times during the first three years after my mother died."
4. **N**eeds and relationship responses—this deepest level of communication occurs when you put your deepest feelings into words. Both refer to a here-and-now experience where you convey feelings you are having *at that time* about either something very personal or some way you feel toward the person you are with. "Even though I feel lonely while talking about my mother's death, I also feel really understood by you."

Healthy relationships continue to cycle through the same topic areas from the situational and relational domains, yet with more meaning and depth each time. Pacing both what you share and the depth of your openness protects you from "baring your soul" to someone who doesn't truly care. Your openness should match what you see in the other person, although you should be leery of the person who shares too much too soon.

Mixing It Up

Be careful of ruts. In order to get to know someone fully, your experiences need to be diverse. Going out to eat and watching a movie reveal only so much. Enjoy as many different activities as you can. If you are unable to be creative while dating, what will your marriage be like? If possible, become active with each other's families. It is one thing to hear someone talk about his or her family. It is quite another to actually see them interact in their family's presence. Make sure your experiences help answer the critical questions:

Pacing both what you share and the depth of your openness protects you from "baring your soul" to someone who doesn't truly care.

> Do you have similar interests?
> Are your energy levels comparable?
> Do you build good memories when you are together?
> How are stresses, frustrations, and obstacles handled?

You can talk about these questions forever. But only when you spend time together will you know more than words could ever tell you.

How Long Does It Take?

You cannot rush intimacy. There is no way to really know someone without spending ample time. Studies have supported this repeatedly. Couples who marry after knowing each other less than two years have close to twice the divorce rate than the couples who date longer than two years. In addition, couples marrying before the age of twenty-two also have a much higher divorce rate than those who marry older. The reason for this is more than just maturity. There is a need to establish autonomy before creating a family. When you exit one family and enter immediately into another, you are likely to transfer unresolved issues from one to the other. Like intimacy, autonomy and maturity require time and experience. In fact, couples who marry for the first time after the age of twenty-eight have the lowest divorce rate. These couples have probably dated the longest and developed a strong sense of personal autonomy.[5]

This is not to say that anyone who marries with less than two years of courtship will have a poor relationship or end up divorced. But I want to stress that your vulnerability is heightened when you do not honor the need for diverse experiences and mutual self-disclosure over time. Without sufficient time, your knowledge of the other person is limited. Although some accurately fill in the gaps for what they did not know, most discover irritating or unacceptable characteristics of the other person, which could have been foreseen and worked on had they just taken more time.

The Three-Month Rule

Whether you are eighteen or eighty, growing to know someone intimately requires certain amounts of time. Some of you have been in a relationship where you shared everything imaginable, trusted this person with your life, became sexually active, and even talked about marriage, only to have a rude awakening around the *third month*. Three months is the "magic number."[6] Not until around three months into a relationship do deepseated patterns start to become evident. By definition, a pattern is a behavior that repeats in a sequence over time. Without time, there is no such thing as a pattern. Therefore, if you are always living in the moment, you are seriously disadvantaged when it comes to understanding a prospective partner. The three-month rule states that "it takes three months for many subtle but serious patterns to begin to surface."

Also, the newness of a relationship is a natural inebriating effect accompanying attraction that typically begins to wear off around the third month. We put our best foot forward until we feel a bit more secure in a new relationship. Then we slack off a bit and let our imperfections surface. This is why it is so difficult to be sure what someone is really like in the first three months. This is also why it is so essential that you keep a grip on your trust, reliance, commitment, and sexual involvement with this person during this period of time.

The future is best predicted by the patterns of the present and the past. Inconsistencies between the situational and relational domains raise questions as to which patterns you should believe. Remember the cynical but lifesaving guideline for interpreting your *relational radar* and synthesizing the different *wavelengths* you are receiving about your prospective partner. Over the past eighteen years of counseling, I have listened to countless clients describe relationships that blasted off only to crash around the three-month mark. Keep all of your bonding dynamics in check for the first three months, and you will significantly increase your safe zone while sharpening your focus on emerging patterns.

Interrogating in Dating

I know what you are thinking. You want to take this book with you on your first date. Before you order your appetizer, you would pull out this book and interrogate your dating partner with all of the questions found in the "Along the Way Find Out About . . ." boxes. You would say something like, "I read this really great book on relationships, and it had some questions that should be discussed in order to really get to know someone. Uh, I kind of thought we could answer some of them while we are waiting for our appetizers. Sooo, how did you know your father loved your mother?"

If only it were that easy. The reality of it is that going out on a date is much more than a job interview—it is more like a step of friendship. Many partners can give you the answers you want in the moment but ultimately not turn out to be the one you would want to end up with. *You just cannot escape the necessity of time.* When you make premature conclusions about a potential partner, those conclusions will usually lead to presumptuous and often erroneous predictions and expectations (not to mention the hurt and disillusionment you often feel). Time reveals patterns, provides the opportunities to observe the person in various situations and relationship contexts, and allows you to safely move deeper in open communication and transparency.

The next several chapters elucidate five crucial areas to explore and understand about your partner. These areas accurately predict what this person would be like in marriage. The areas are discussed in order from the most obvious to the most subtle. Traces of each area can be found throughout the development of a relationship; yet the obvious areas are usually understood earlier, while the more subtle areas are hidden. Although this is not always the case, and I do not presuppose that there is only one way relationships develop, the progression from obvious to subtle can provide a guideline for most dating relationships and help remind you that appearances can be deceiving. You should withhold judgment until after you have explored some of the more subtle areas that usually are more powerful predictors of your partner's marriage potential than the obvious areas.

DON'T FORGET

- Patterns that influence long-term relationships usually are not evident early on.

- Bonds begin to form within the *getting-to-know* phases of a relationship.

- Intimacy equals talk (mutual self-disclosure) plus togetherness (diversified experiences) plus time.

- Avoid extremes such as disclosing too much too soon or sharing too little too late.

- Pay special attention to how a partner acts or treats you in various situations.

- The good doesn't always last, but the bad usually gets worse.

- The four depths of openness are observations and facts, perspectives and opinions, experiences and emotions, and needs and responses.

- You cannot rush intimacy.

- Not until after three months do deep-seated patterns *start* to become evident.

- Time reveals patterns, provides opportunities to observe a person in various situations and contexts, and allows you to safely move deeper into open communication.

5

Find Your Soul Mate

Step One: Getting to Know Your Compatibility Potential

More than two thousand years ago, Plato, one of the most dazzling and influential authors in the history of philosophy, penned the *Symposium*, a series of speeches made by Socrates, Phaedrus, and other philosophical colleagues on the origin and nature of Eros, the god of love.

One of the orators was Aristophanes, a renowned writer of more than forty comedic and ironic plays. He explained the nature of love and the human longing for companionship by weaving together a mythological story of prehistoric humans—creatures who had four arms, four legs, and two faces and two sets of sexual organs. These primeval creatures could not walk upright, being round in shape with their backs and sides forming a circle. However, they moved in a rolling hand-over-hand motion with amazing agility and speed, and they were so powerful that even the gods were intimidated. There were three sexes—male, female, and a combined sex referred to as androgyne.

The creatures, having become intoxicated with their own power, speed, and might, attacked the gods and threatened to scale the heavens to reach them. The council of the gods was just about to send thunderbolts down to earth to destroy them when Zeus stepped forward and in sympathy with these human prototypes, suggested a new plan, "Allow the creatures to continue to live, but humble them and diminish their strength by cutting them in two like an apple is halved."

In most successful relationships, the two partners have a blend of similarities and differences in personalities, backgrounds, and lifestyles.

The plan was enacted, and each being was split into the human form as we now know it—two arms, two legs, and one face—with Apollo healing their wounds. The gods had not foreseen, however, that these new humans would be consumed with feeling incomplete and long to be one with their severed counterparts, neglecting food and drink just to embrace and hold one another. Although the gods devised a plan to lessen this obsession, they could not extinguish the human drive to be reunited with another person, to love and be loved, and to find in another person that which will complete what is missing in oneself.

The search for a soul mate did not begin in the twenty-first century. It perplexed the minds of the greatest thinkers of the fourth century B.C.E., as well as every generation both before and after. But in the past ten years, the quest to find one's soul mate has risen to greater heights than ever before. Internet dating sites, for instance, boast they can provide a means for you to find your perfect match. The largest site at the time of this book's publication, Match.com, was established in 1995 and now has some 15 million members. Add to this dozens of other websites, and at any given time more than 30 million singles are looking for partners on the Internet.

Many of these websites now provide a matchmaking inventory that filters out any incompatible partners and introduces you to only those with whom you would find compatibility. These questionnaires can help identify similarities between you and a prospective partner. However, compatibility is so much more than just having things in common. In an extensive review of forty years of research on the subject of compatibility, researchers from the University of Iowa and the University of Illinois concluded that the evidence does *not* support a clear connection between the similarity of two partners with the outcome of relationship closeness and satisfaction.[1] Basically, research has supported that in some cases, birds of a feather flock together, but in others, opposites attract. In fact, it seems that in most successful relationships, the two partners have a blend of similarities and differences in personalities, backgrounds, and lifestyles. The *balance* of this blend is what makes or breaks the couple.

True compatibility consists of three dimensions: chemistry, complementarity, and comparability. If any of these are missing, true compatibility is compromised. Narrow definitions of compatibility have led to simplistic thinking about relationships (i.e., "I need to find someone just like me") and to mixed and somewhat misleading findings in research (search for the shared magical characteristics that predict relationship bliss). Instead, the soul mate you need is a person with whom you have a rich chemistry, whose differences make you better than you could be on your own, and who shares many of your core values and life goals, as well as some of your personality qualities and lifestyle preferences.

Chemistry: That Intoxicating Attraction

No matter whether you are swept off your feet the first time you lay eyes on your prize, or you are shot with Cupid's arrow long after knowing the goods, one thing is for sure: you *must* have chemistry with your partner. In a study of almost 10,000 married adults from thirty-three countries, mutual attraction and love feelings unanimously are at the top as the essential prerequisites for partner choice.²

Few have not experienced either the presence or absence of chemistry in dating relationships, and yet the majority cannot explain what exactly causes this thing we call chemistry. It has been described as a powerful attraction, a feeling of being turned on, a sense of fitting or clicking with another, an instant connection, a good vibe, and the list goes on. Although much cannot be explained about chemistry, the following warnings have been established.

1. *Chemistry is not always a good judge of character.* We have all known that beautiful, sweet woman who cannot overcome her "thing" for bad boys. Or that super-nice guy who always seems to get together with a controlling and bossy woman. In both cases, the overpowering chemistry saw something in the other person that was contrary to his or her own true character or lifestyle.

2. *Chemistry sees what it wants to see.* Beware of the illusion of chemistry. It can seem so real when you only see certain characteristics of a person, only to vanish when that person's other side is revealed.

3. *Chemistry is not constant even in the best of relationships.* I have watched many partners lose their feelings of chemistry during times of testing (or boredom) only to regain a stronger chemistry after their issues have been addressed.

What does this partner do for me that keeps me holding on, hoping that something more will happen?

A perfect example of the first two warnings is a study that tested the truthfulness of Mickey Gilley's good old country tune, "Don't the Girls All Get Prettier at Closing Time?"³ A team of investigators entered bars at 9:00 P.M., 10:30 P.M., and 12:00 midnight (the bars all closed at 12:30

A.M.) and had volunteers rate the attractiveness of the opposite-sex individuals present at that time. They were also asked to rate the attractiveness of the members of the same sex. The rating scale used was in keeping with Gilley's song (1–10 scale).

The results of this study found that there was a significant increase in the attractiveness of those in the bar as the clock ticked closer to closing time. Of course, alcohol could have played a part. But it is ironic that in three different establishments, the ratings went down between 9:00 P.M. and 10:30 P.M., but seriously increased at the stroke of midnight.

What am I saying? It is "sobering" to admit, but there may be more to the lighting of your fire than just rubbing up against the flame of your life.

It is difficult to explain why we are attracted to one person over another. It is imperative that you address your own issues before you end up depending on a partner to fill that which is missing. This may be the reason you are staying in a relationship with someone with whom you have never developed genuine chemistry. You must ask yourself, why am I staying? What does this partner do for me that keeps me holding on, hoping that something more will happen? In these cases, you are at risk for compromising your ideals and settling. It is worth waiting for that partner who both clicks with you, igniting your feelings of attraction, and treats you in positive ways that do not diminish that attraction.

Chemistry First, Relationship Second

I must confess I was intoxicated by the potion of *love at first sight*. I had just transferred to a small, private college in Philadelphia, and during the weekend orientation I noticed a vivacious, sparkling, attractive freshman whom I knew I had to meet. She seemed to bring an electric energy to every conversation she had, and her smile was captivating and contagious.

It was not until six weeks later that I finally had the opportunity to meet her. I noticed that she was walking about half a block behind me as I made my way toward the other educational building two blocks away. I plotted my encounter. If I was to meet her, there was only one way to accomplish it: I had to walk very, very slowly.

I examined the buildings along the way, looked at interesting trash discarded on the sidewalk, and did a little window-shopping. Just as I was about to open the door, I heard a voice say, "You sure do walk slowly." Mission accomplished!

Now I know that those words have a usual and customary meaning, but that was not what I heard. Most of you would have taken her literally—but not me. I knew what she really meant. You see, beneath her simple observation was an unconscious admission—"I'm in love with you." Yes, you can accuse me of reading between the lines, but she did marry me two years later!

I was no different than anyone else who falls head over heels in love. I couldn't fall asleep that night. I kept thinking about her. I had difficulty concentrating, and when I tried, images of her smile or the sound of her voice interrupted my focus. My romantic appetite couldn't be satisfied—I just couldn't get enough of her. I longed to be with her, and if that was impossible, then I wanted to be talking to her. In this state, there is no sense of reality; you have no orientation to the *big picture* of the relationship. You can't see any horizons, so you don't feel it is necessary to establish boundary lines or stopping points. As a result, it feels like there is no such thing as "going too far"—that is something that applies to others who are not as deeply in love as you are. I write about this part of my life because it is one of two ways couples fall in love: *chemistry first, relationship second*.

One of the most prolific social science researchers on the subjects of personal and romantic relationships is University of Texas professor Dr. Ted Huston.[4] Huston followed more than 168 first-time married newlyweds for fourteen years—from their dating years into their marriages. He identified four different patterns of courtship:

1. *Early exiters*—these couples should have never married. Their courtship was speckled with emotionally draining breakups followed by passionate making up.

2. *Firework romances*—these couples were madly in love and had whirlwind romances but did not create lasting marriages. Their romance was a beautiful burst that lit up the sky but quickly fizzled when confronted with unrealized differences and unrealistic expectations in marriage.

3. *Status quo settlers*—these couples lacked luster in their courtship but set aside their doubts, believing that marriage would breathe new life into their relationships. Most of these couples stayed married but were unhappy. In most cases, the problems that were evident in the dating relationship were experienced at greater levels of intensity with each successive year of marriage.

4. *Stable loving investors*—these couples did not have an overly dramatic courtship. They invested time in trying to build a warm and cooperative relationship. They were almost all happily married some thirteen years after Huston's initial interview with them. These couples had lasting and satisfactory marriages because they both fell in love *and* developed a clear understanding of each other. Huston referred to these couples as the *enduring-dynamics couples* because they had established successful patterns in their relationships in the first two years that changed very little over the next ten years. Falling in love was a core ingredient in the making of a long-term romance, but it also required the building of a strong friendship.

The building of a best-friends relationship between Shirley and me became the foundation for our future. Over the next two years, our in-love feelings were channeled into endless conver-

Along the Way Find Out About . . . Chemistry

- How strong is your attraction?
- How enduring has this attraction been?
- What do you like about your partner's body?
- What attracts you to your partner's personality?
- What are the turnoffs to this partner? Can you live with them?
- How attracted does your partner feel toward you?
- Where is chemistry the strongest, and where is it the weakest?
- Are you attracted to the whole package or just to a part?

sations and experiences that welded a bond of deeply knowing each other. We held back on indulging our passions and concentrated on becoming best friends. I am amazed when I look back at that time in our life that we never had sex. It certainly would have felt natural, but we were committed to first developing the other bonding areas of our relationship. We believed that our sexual relationship should be a part of our marriage relationship, and that this "short" time of courtship was to build a foundation of friendship, trust, and reliance that would be strong enough to withstand the tests encountered over the course of a lifetime together.

Although much more about the sexual relationship will be explored in Chapter 13 (no fair jumping ahead!), it is important to be realistic at this point. Conventional dating practices assume that if you have great chemistry, then there is no reason *not* to have sex. The RAM model warns that going further in the sexual relationship than what you have established in the other areas of commitment, reliance, trust, and knowing your partner will put you at risk for creating a false intimacy, minimizing and overlooking warning signs, and staying in a bad relationship too long. So what is a red-blooded, virile single to do? And what if you have already become sexually active with a new partner—are you supposed to just stop and pretend it never happened?

I was presenting our research findings to U.S. Army soldiers at a conference when a reporter who had spoken to me about the program prior to the conference raised her hand and asked, "Do I understand your program correctly—if I hooked up with an Army stud whom I met and end up having the best sex of my life that night, and then the next day go to a PICK class—would you tell me that I have to stop having sex with him?"

I looked at the other two presenters standing up in front with me, and they laughed and said that this question definitely should be answered by the author of the program. So I responded, "Far be it from me to ever tell anyone to stop having sex. We live in a free country, and you have every right to make your own decision about these personal matters." Then I paused, suggesting nothing more was to be said on this subject.

"However," I slowly continued, "let's say that you and Sergeant Studley continued to see each other every night for a week, and the sex only got better! Let's say that you told your best girlfriend that you think you have finally fallen in love. Let's also say that you were going to go out with him on Friday and that he was going to pick you up at 7:00 P.M., but he showed up at 11:00 P.M., a little drunk and smelling of a perfume you don't wear." At that point the reporter exclaimed, "You're not going to tell me that he was with another woman, are you?"

"Well, let's say you confronted him and after hours of denial, he finally admitted that he was going to be deployed in a month and that he was just trying to make hay while the sun shined. Now, how would you feel about your newfound love?" She readily conceded the point that her risk of being emotionally hurt (among many other ways of being harmed) had been heightened by engaging in sex prior to the development of the other areas of intimacy.

Great chemistry prompts premature sexual involvement. If you find yourself in a relationship where your level of sexual involvement is out of balance with the other areas of the relationship, then you have one of two choices. First, you can choose to continue to stay sexually involved while trying to stay aware of your personal risks and tendency to rationalize surfacing problems because of your strong feelings of connection with the partner. However, this may become damaging to you because you are trying to be emotionally distant from someone with whom you are sexually intimate.

The National Marriage Project conducted a survey of never-been-married singles, ages twenty-one to twenty-nine, from five major metropolitan areas. They found that many women who had a prolonged period of sexual activity in multiple failed relationships and breakups complained of feeling angry, burned, and betrayed.[5] As a result, there was a "cumulative negative impact" on their future relationships, a "global mistrust and antagonism" toward men, and an increased neediness that they brought to the next relationship. Therefore, the first option of continuing in a relationship where the sexual involvement greatly exceeds the other areas of bonding runs the high risk of building up emotional baggage if the relationship does not work out.

The second choice is to back off on the sex until the rest of the relationship develops. "How?" you ask. You would explain to your partner something like this: "I think you and I have something really good going on in our relationship, and I was wondering if you feel the same." If the answer is yes, you would then say, "I am thinking about seeing only you and trying to build a stronger relationship." Again if there is agreement to be exclusive, you would continue, "This may sound strange, but I would like to back off on our sexual relationship and concentrate on our friendship. There is so much to get to know about each other, and I think we could build a better foundation for our relationship if we just slow down, do more together, and deepen our trust and closeness. I know we could possibly do both, but I think we need to have our eyes wide open and sex tends to shut mine."

"No way," you say, "can't be done." Not true. I have known many who have done this, and in every case they feel it was beneficial to both their relationship and to them personally. They almost always are surprised at how enjoyable the "limited" sexual involvement becomes. One couple told me that their feet were rubbing each other while they were watching TV, and it came to a point where they felt like their feet were making love. They had jumped to sex so quickly in the beginning of their relationship that they missed out on the tension that builds when restraint is practiced. Once married, you will need to apply sexual boundaries in all other relationships (no matter how attracted you are to that other person), so don't neglect to develop and test this essential character trait during your time of singlehood. Relationships that begin with chemistry first have to find ways to handle this powerful passion while taking time to build the other aspects of intimacy with minimal risk of being blinded by sex or burned by betrayal.

Relationship First, Chemistry Second

However, this is not the only way people fall in love. There are those who follow the pattern of *relationship first, chemistry second*. A perfect example of this is the love story *When Harry Met Sally*, which portrays the emergence of chemistry from the deepening of a friendship. The movie begins with a tense encounter between Harry, played by Billy Crystal, and Sally, played by Meg Ryan. The initial chemistry is combative and repulsive as Harry shatters Sally's ideals about love and life with his brutal honesty and sarcastic wit.

It is not until their third chance meeting some twelve years later that they start to become friends. The RAM bonding dynamics are woven throughout the movie. The first dynamic of getting to know each other is present with every conversation as they delve deeper into their views on life, sharing more and more intimately about their own experiences. Although Sally is initially skeptical about Harry and his scruples, her opinion of him improves (trust) and their friendship grows as they wind up becoming best friends (reliance).

When Sally discovers that her ex-boyfriend has become engaged, Harry is the first person she calls to come over and console her. He listens to her, comforts her, encourages her, and cheers her up. This tender moment leads to a hug, then another hug, and then a kiss, and that leads to sex.

Complementarity refers to the extent to which differences benefit both partners.

This is where the five bonding dynamics move out of balance with each other. Harry is already dressed when Sally wakes up. She is confused about where he is going in such a rush, and why he seems so cold and impersonal. However, because they have had sex *before* Harry was ready for any kind of real commitment, their intimate moment became confusing and hurtful the morning after.

It is not until the end of the movie that the level of this dynamic (commitment) rises to match the levels of the other four dynamics. Until it does, the relationship is put on hold because of the hurt and pain generated by an imbalance between the intense attachment in certain dynamics (knowing, trusting, and having sex with each other) with a significantly lower attachment in the others (reliance and commitment).

The climactic scene at the end of the movie illustrates the emerging chemistry that followed the development of a lasting friendship. Harry tracks down Sally at a New Year's Eve party and tells her that he loves her. She is unimpressed until he puts into words his relentless passion and feeling of chemistry.

Sally: You can't show up here and tell me that you love me!
Harry: Then how does it work?
Sally: I don't know but not this way.

Harry: Then how about this way: I love that you get cold when it's seventy-one degrees out; I love that it takes you an hour and a half to order a sandwich; I love that you get a little crinkle up above your nose when you're looking at me like you think I'm nuts; I love that after I spend a day with you I can still smell your perfume on my clothes; and I love that you are the last person that I want to talk to before I go to sleep at night. And it's not because I'm lonely, and it's not because it's New Year's Eve. I came here tonight because when you realize that you want to spend the rest of your life with somebody, you want the rest of your life to start as soon as possible.

Harry's description of his chemistry with Sally, now matched by his commitment, softened her anger, and she told him that once again he made it impossible for her to hate him.

Complementarity

The story line of Harry and Sally's rocky romance not only portrays the way that chemistry can follow relationship, but it also illustrates the common saying that *opposites attract*. Significant personality and philosophical differences between Harry and Sally benefited their relationship and actually contributed to the rich chemistry that they shared. *Complementarity* refers to the extent to which differences benefit both partners. Sally was serious; Harry was funny. As a result of their differences, Sally lightened up and Harry grew up.

Shirley and I also found that we were drawn together by our similarities and our differences. We felt like we completely knew each other within the first few encounters, but there was actually much more to learn. Shirley would certainly verify that I spent a long time reflecting on her personality, values, and family background before I made a commitment to marry. She was much more decisive, apparently knowing that I was the one very early on. I know that she must have been frustrated at times by my analytic style, although she did appreciate the qualities that I had that were different from hers. Shirley's strengths came from her practical, insightful decisiveness. Ours was (and still is) a complementary "opposites attract" relationship where we complete each other, becoming something more together than either of us would have been on our own. She amazes me when she takes charge and directs situations and people with straightforwardness and candor. I, on the other hand, have been writing this book for ten years.

When we sit down in a restaurant, Shirley will open the menu, look through the entrées and close the menu before I have moved past examining the subliminal messages in the dessert pictures on the cover. If my weakness is thinking too long before I act, then Shirley's weakness is acting before she thinks. Yet the longer we live together, the more appreciative we are of these opposite qualities and the more alike we have become because of them.

Complementarity was depicted in a scene from another popular romantic comedy, *As Good as It Gets*. Melvin, played by Jack Nicholson, is a rude, reclusive obsessive-compulsive writer who develops a crush on Carol, played by Helen Hunt. On their first date, Melvin crushes Carol with his underhanded criticism of her outfit when he complains that the restaurant required him to wear a jacket and tie, but they didn't say a word about her "house dress." In a desperate attempt to redeem himself and stop Carol from leaving the restaurant, Melvin tells her that he will give her a deeply meaningful compliment. She waits. He explains that since knowing her, he has decided to go to his doctor and try a medicine that may improve his obsessive-compulsive disorder. When Carol doesn't get the compliment, he concisely states, "You make me want to be a better man."

This is a crucial test of complementarity. Do you find that you become a better person by being with your partner than you would have been without your partner? Do your partner's strengths empower you or devour you? Do you feel admired and appreciated for the ways that you are different from your partner? Differences between you and your partner are potential benefits for both of you. Why would anyone want to marry their own reflection? People are attracted to those qualities they lack, and they want to vicariously experience and learn. In many cases, you end up adopting some of your partner's strengths because of your union with that partner.

Earlier, in Chapter 3, we looked at the ways complementarity can sometimes be taken to the extreme, where your relationship ends up compensating for serious deficiencies in your personal development that should be addressed. However, no one personality has it all, and a healthy blend of differing personality styles broadens your perspective, reinforces autonomy in you and your partner's identity, and promotes stimulating discussions and perspectives. Complementarity, then, fulfills the age-old proverb that iron sharpens iron.

One group of scholars attempted to study this blend of similar and different characteristics between couples and found that many of these differing traits were not two separate categories of attributes but were more or less of the same characteristic.[6] For instance, one couple acknowledged that they both were very honest people (similarity), but then one pointed out that his partner sometimes was too honest (difference). The partner agreed, and this led to a discussion of how they have different ranges or comfort zones in this similar area. Another couple stated that they both love music (similarity) but can have a lively two-hour discussion or disagreement about what is important in music (differences). A third couple admitted that one tended to "flip out" under pressure, while the other was more even-keeled. However, they both saw these characteristics as merely differing ranges for the way each coped, and they felt that each partner helped balance out the other's style. The one who overreacted would calm down when listening to the steady-Freddy partner. But then the steady partner would also benefit by taking the situation more seriously and considering

Do you find that you become a better person by being with your partner than you would have been without your partner?

the possible negative aspects. All in all, it was not the similar or different characteristics alone that influenced the success of a couple but how they put them together in a meaningful whole.

So how do you know if some difference will help or hurt your relationship? I doubt there is a foolproof way to know, but there are definite guidelines that you can use to test out the complementarity of your mix.

First, you need to acknowledge the differences between you and your partner. As you know, sometimes differences can be masked or minimized by the strong feelings of attraction and chemistry. In time, though, these differences emerge and should be recognized by both partners. It is vital that this emergence occur during the dating relationship and not wait until marriage. One of the theories of compatibility is referred to as the "disillusionment model." It states that premarital couples often are not tuned in to their differences and may not even be showing their true colors during the dating relationship (who would ever do that?). However, once the honeymoon is over and there is more honesty between them, the difficulties with compatibility become more salient. Identifying your differences during your dating relationship will help establish a basic attitude toward the strengths and weaknesses of these differences.

For instance, Mike and Julie hit it off great. They enjoyed each other's sense of humor, shared similar intellectual interests and recreational activities, and admired each other's styles. Somewhere around the fifth month of their relationship, Mike suggested that they go out dancing that evening. Julie, on the other hand, was more interested in staying at home and just watching a movie. The difference between Mike's and Julie's interests in going out versus staying at home had been noticed before, but it started to become more of a source of conflict after several months into their relationship. Mike accused her of misleading him because she seemed interested in going out more during the beginning of the relationship. Julie, on the other hand, accused Mike of always being restless. She thought that they would settle down and be homebodies more after they had been together for a while.

For many couples, this is not an unusual difference that some discussion and compromise wouldn't settle. But for other couples, this difference in social activity level can be a source of conflict throughout the remainder of their relationships. What determines the outcome is often the *extent* of the difference. You should not assume that all differences can be settled between you and any other person. Some differences are too extreme and will be a continual cause of discontent. The worst thing that Mike and Julie could do would be to minimize this issue and look the other way. Remember, if it bothers you during the dating relationship, it is likely to become magnified in marriage. You should acknowledge differences and be honest about what you want and any compromises you make.

Second, complementarity exists when time ends up refining the blend of differences in mutually beneficial ways. You and your partner will have some conflicts because of your differences. However, if you are moving toward complementarity, these battles should not conclude with one partner dominating the other. Rather, "peace treaties" should be formed that result in mutual gain.

Mike and Julie were willing to compromise and take turns doing what the other partner wanted. What they found, as time went on, is that their blend of differences was actually better than what either of them had been doing on their own. They personified the infamous Gestalt proposition that the "whole is greater than the sum of its parts."

This naturally leads to the third test of true complementarity in a relationship: a deep and mutual appreciation of differences. Mike and Julie grew to depend on the differences that each one brought to the table of their relationship. They frequently would comment about these differences in a positive and appreciative way. Sure, there were times when they collided with these differences, but they had developed a deep belief that "this difference in my partner is for my good." This belief mediated their conflicts and facilitated a mutually agreeable compromise in most situations.

The final test of complementarity is more of an outcome than a guideline. Partners with true complementarity become less different and more alike over time. I am sure that you know some couples who have stuck it out even though they are unhappy and have little to no complementarity. In these cases, they stay distinct from the other, unblended and retaining their own idiosyncrasies without the benefit of internalizing the opposite quirks of their partner. On the other hand, there are couples who have successfully complemented each other with their differences. The longer they are together, the more alike they seem. They

Partners with true complementarity become less different and more alike over time.

Along the Way Find Out About . . . Complementarity

- How are you and your partner different?
- How do your differences benefit you? Your partner?
- Does your partner appreciate these differences?
- Do you like the ways that your partner is different from you?
- Do your differences most often complement or collide?
- What things upset you about this partner?
- How often do you become locked in a power struggle with your partner?
- Do you feel criticized or put down by your partner?
- What do you respect about your partner?
- What do you not respect about your partner?

remind you of a pet and its owner in how they seem to resemble each other over time.

No one has it all, and the differences of your partner can add more to your personality and life than what you could accomplish if you were on your own. This mystical and wonderful experience of complementarity is what Aristophanes was trying to portray with his mythological story of the human search for one's counterpart.

Comparability

If opposites attract, are there any essential similarities? Absolutely. The difficulty is determining which similarities are the important ones. It would be safe to say that the extent of similarity and the specific areas of similarity are quite different for each individual. However, three main areas of similarity between married couples have surfaced in the hundreds of research articles published during the last thirty or more years: personality, values, and lifestyle. At the very least, you should seriously consider the extent of similarity you have with your partner in each of these categories.

I am not suggesting that you and your partner must be similar in every way—quite the opposite. The differences between the two of you make for the opportunity to develop complementarity in your relationship. But these three areas have appeared over and over in the studies on happy and stable marriages. So it is crucial that you find a good fit in each of these areas and that you have thought through the ramifications of that fit for your future with your partner. The following sections describe each area and some of the related topics that make up each area.

Compare Your Personalities
Aspects of this area of personality compatibility will be further explained in Chapter 9 where the subject of the conscience is

examined. Suffice it to say that some characteristics of personality seem to be related to the functioning of the conscience rather than to personality traits. It may just be semantics, but I am going to limit most of this section to personality traits that are clearly distinct from our understanding of the conscience.

The first characteristic of personality you should investigate is your partner's style and patterns of his or her *emotional temperament*. Is your partner extroverted or introverted? Warm or cold? Rigid or flexible? Optimistic or pessimistic? Moody or steady? Loud or quiet? Dramatic or bland? Emotional or emotionless? Expressive or suppressive? Energetic or docile? An active person or a couch potato? These are aspects of the emotional temperament, and you should consider the ways that you and your partner are similar or different. If you are a big talker and your partner is quiet, make sure you won't eventually want something more than just a listening ear.

Many studies have looked at personality traits, and several traits have risen to the top as both preferred and most commonly associated with marital stability and satisfaction.[7] Earlier I referred to the international study of almost 10,000 participants from thirty-three cultures conducted by fifty researchers.[8] They concluded that nearly all cultures placed high importance on the partner qualities of dependability, emotional stability, kindness and understanding, and intelligence. Another investigation of more than 700 men and woman found similar qualities of warmth, expressiveness, intelligence, and humor. You are halfway there if you can honestly say that you are a warm and affectionate person. If you are not, get out of your comfort zone and learn to be more caring, compassionate, and understanding. Then find a partner who shares this essential quality and can match your expressions of warmth.

As mentioned previously, some of these qualities are attributes of a healthy conscience and a mature emotional development and will be expanded more in Chapter 9 when the conscience is discussed. But the findings from both studies are that singles prefer partners who are emotionally healthy. In fact, the first three of these characteristics are the same as those described in numerous other studies on the qualities associated with stable and satisfactory marriages. At least on paper, singles seem to know what they want in a partner that will lead to a stable relationship. So what's the problem? Why are you not getting what you want? The reason appears to be related to the way relationships are built and the criteria used in the decision-making process during the dating years. This is what the RAM is designed to provide—a road map to follow so you can attain your goals in picking a partner. If you are like the majority of singles, you prefer a partner who has these healthy qualities. Are we surprised that mentally and emotionally healthy adults make better marriage partners than those who have emotional problems? It doesn't take a genius to figure out that if you marry a crazy person, you probably will have a crazy marriage!

Check out the patterns of your partner's moods and emotions. Stephanie was thirty-four years old and had never been married, but she had been involved in several serious relationships. She began dating Matt a year prior to making a counseling appointment with me. She had heard some talk about his mood shifts when they first began dating, but she had not seen any evidence. Raised in a supportive and caring family, she had dealt with her mother's angry moods in the past, so she didn't feel threatened by the idea of handling a little conflict.

Matt was energetic, exciting, and upbeat—it was hard to imagine what others saw in him that made them believe that he had emotional swings. The first sign of his true temperament occurred after a situation where he seemed agitated at Stephanie. At first he withdrew, becoming quiet and detached. After a few hours, however, he spiked with an angry and belligerent verbal attack on Stephanie's lack of cleanliness. She was shocked at the extremeness of his reaction and tried later to talk with him about it. He minimized his behavior, claiming that he was just feeling stressed. He appeared perfectly normal afterward and her memory of feeling belittled faded.

Then at the most unexpected times, he would overreact with harsh criticism, reinfecting the wounds that had never fully healed. She encouraged him to meet with his doctor, but nothing

Patterns only surface when there has been sufficient time for the pattern to repeat.

seemed to level out the highs and lows. In the spring, Matt's demeaning treatment had seeped into his routine interactions, and Stephanie came to her first counseling session at my office.

"How can he be so great for weeks and then turn into this?" She wrestled with this question until a fairly simple explanation emerged: patterns only surface when there has been sufficient time for the pattern to repeat. If a pattern repeats in a three-day time frame, then the pattern should be clearly seen after one or two weeks. But what if the pattern doesn't repeat for thirty to forty-five days? Stephanie had drawn her conclusion about Matt's moods after only two months. In actuality, she had only seen a part of the whole, and her initial conclusions were inaccurate and misled.

Make sure you have seen the *pattern* of your partner's emotional temperament. This requires time and patience. In most cases, the three-month rule is sufficient to surface most of the patterns of moodiness. However, some patterns remain hidden for longer periods of time. I was recently discussing the three-month rule (i.e., "It takes three months for many subtle but serious patterns to begin to surface") in an interview when the reporter laughed and commented that most singles practice the three-*date* rule. Although it is true that you may be able to determine the extent of chemistry (this can often be accomplished within the three-*minute* rule) and certain aspects of similarity of interests (the three-date rule), there are definitely some patterns that are revealed only within longer time frames. Fortunately, most of these can be detected by examining the other areas to get to know described in the next few chapters. The challenge you face is to keep limits on the extent of your emotional investment so that you protect your heart. Nothing is wrong with choosing to become involved with or even marry a partner who is hotheaded, dramatic, moody, or temperamental.

However, it is imperative that you know what you are getting into before you become overly involved.

The second area you should look closely at is your partner's thinking style—his or her ability to think, solve problems, reason things through, and mentally put things together. *Ask yourself, "Do I want to spend the rest of my life with a person who thinks like my partner thinks?"* Is your partner a concrete or abstract thinker? What are you? How do you fit together? How do you discuss and solve problems? Do you think that you and your partner are fairly close in your mental abilities? Is your partner significantly smarter than you? Are you smarter than your partner?

Most good marriages continue for many years. That's a long time to be in partnership with someone who doesn't understand your reasoning. You should ask yourself, "Do I want to explain something to my partner over and over again only to receive a blank stare in return?" Can you visualize this scene: "Honey, do you get what I am talking about? No? Well, uh, let me explain it a fourth time." No matter how patient you are, this eventually gets old.

Neither do you want a partner who is so superior to you that you don't quite know what he or she is talking about most of the time. These discrepancies usually break down the communication in your relationship and ultimately suppress the bond of intimacy that should be developing.

Do you and your partner click in discussions? Do you feel intellectually stimulated and challenged by these interactions with your partner? Much of marriage is mental, so make sure that you and your partner have a good meeting of the minds.

The third characteristic of personality that you should consider is your partner's sense of humor—that is, the way your partner makes you laugh. In studies that analyzed couples who were happily married for more than fifteen years, a sense of humor was one of the key elements that united them (along with friendship, commitment, and agreeableness).[9] In fact, researchers Avner Ziv and Orit Gadish found that more than

90 percent of the couples they studied said that humor was a major contributor of positive elements to their satisfaction in marriage. We "laugh together frequently" was among the top ten reasons listed for the success of marriage in another study of 100 couples who had been happily married for forty-five years or more.[10] Humor lowers your defenses and causes you to warm up to a person. It is a highly desirable trait in both friendships and potential mates.

I grew up in a family bonded together by humor, with my father leading the way. He loved puns. I don't recall ever spending time with him when he did not slip in a play on words or an ironic twist on some circumstance happening around us. One of his favorites occurred when he admired a new shirt that I was wearing. He would feel the cloth between his thumb and fore-finger only to grab a hunk of my skin beneath the shirt sleeve—at which point he would exclaim, "Oh, it's *felt*!" Another famous pun would happen whenever I was peeling a banana. He would comment, "My, what an *appealing* banana."

The making of puns was contagious in my family, so everyone took turns naturally chiming in with some pithy observation, while the others would laugh or jeer like the audience at a comedy club. My mother appreciated and understood my father's humor. She was a master of words and could quickly build upon his anecdotes with her own word games. After she passed away when I was in high school, my father married a woman who often did not seem to get his subtle jesting. I remember walking into the kitchen and hearing my father point out to her that she had an appealing banana only to hear her retort, "Not really, it has a bruise right here."

Now you need to understand that I had heard the "appealing banana" comment hundreds of times, to the point where I would find myself avoiding bananas when my father was around. However, my step-mom's clueless responses placed her in the role of the straight man to my dad's puns; she was like a breath of fresh air, because, to me, they were funnier than he had ever been on his own.

Over the course of my own marriage, humor has been central. We laugh together every day. Recently, my wife was diagnosed with breast cancer. It is, by far, the greatest challenge we have ever faced together. Yet not a day goes by when we don't find things to smile and laugh about. She amazes me because the cancer has not diminished her sense of humor.

One day we were reading the notes classmates wrote in her high school yearbook, and it struck us how many of her friends commented on the ways she made them laugh. Choosing to marry a partner who can dish out the humor just as much as she appreciates it has made me feel at home in my marriage. It has enabled us to cope with the little problems, as well as the overwhelming challenges. It has revitalized our routine so that every day is unique.

Check out the personality of your prospective partner. A good rule of thumb is that you should have more similarities than differences when it comes to personality characteristics (as well as values and lifestyle characteristics, which are discussed in the sections that follow). Make sure that you feel accepted, are completely comfortable to be yourself, and have a deep sense of coming home when you are together. These qualities typify the climate of a healthy blend of personalities.

Compare Your Values

The second area of comparability that you need to explore involves the values you and your partner share. Three sets of values—family, religious, and financial—should be considered as your relationship becomes more serious.[11]

First explore the similarity of family values and roles. I have devoted Chapter 8 to understanding family-of-origin influences in the establishment of your own marriage and family. However, you should explore three major questions in determining the similarity of marriage and family values.

The first question is the following: *What are your beliefs about marriage?* What do you believe about the promise "'til death do us part"? What do you believe about the importance

The deep-seated beliefs that your partner has about the permanency and priority of marriage will greatly shape his or her behavior in marriage.

of your marriage in light of your job? Your hobbies? Do you believe marriage is just a secular institution, or do you believe it has a sacred or spiritual element to its structure?

There has been much speculation about the changing beliefs of marriage and the increased number of failed marriages. This borders on the discussion of commitment (Chapter 12), but there is evidence that stronger beliefs about the sacredness of marriage are associated with lower divorce rates.[12] The deep-seated beliefs that your partner has about the permanency and priority of marriage will greatly shape his or her behavior in marriage. It is vital to have an understanding of these views so that your expectations of your partner are accurate.

Have either you or your partner been previously married? This can make a tremendous difference in how a new relationship develops. Previous romantic relationships (including marriages) are detailed in Chapter 7, as are partners with a child.

However, if *you* have one or more children, especially if any of them are under the age of eighteen, then you need to seriously consider a second question: *What are your beliefs on parenting?* Topics such as birth-control methods, family planning, the number of children you would like to have, experiences and enjoyment of being in a parenting role, family-of-origin experiences, and other related subjects are necessary to discuss as your relationship becomes more serious.

If you are already a parent, then you need to consider the impact that your relationship and this partner in particular will have upon your child. There is a delicate balance between your right to romantic happiness and your responsibility to your child. On the one hand, you do not need to abandon the idea of dating and building a relationship because your child "takes up all your time." Think of it this way—if you were married, you would carve out time from your hectic work and parenting schedules to have recreational activities as a couple, romantic dates, and adult time with friends. So why should it be any different just because you are a single parent? Schedule on your calendar the days or evenings you are determined to go out. Find a babysitter (if your child is that young), swap child care with a friend who is also a parent, or talk to some

There is a delicate balance between your right to romantic happiness and your responsibility to your child.

of your single, nonparent friends. Convince these friends that by watching your child they will gain priceless experience for their future children (and you won't even charge them for this). The point is that unless you make dating a priority, it most likely will not happen. Taking charge of your schedule and dating relationships helps anchor you on the slippery slopes of a chaotic life that otherwise would deteriorate your self-esteem and lead to compromises in romance.

On the other hand, you who are parents must give your child an even higher priority when you consider dating. I strongly recommend that you follow the three-month rule for both yourself and your child. Remember this rule? "Significant negative patterns are likely to remain hidden for the first three months of a new relationship." I suggest that you refrain from involving your child with your dating partner during these first three months. Depending upon the child's age, you may introduce him or her but you should not involve the child until you have greater certainty as to what this partner is really like.

I recently was counseling a father who was separated from his wife and facing divorce proceedings. He had his children with him on an out-of-town trip when his attorney called and notified him that the morning newspaper uncovered that his estranged wife's boyfriend was just arrested for his third DUI offense. Needless to say, he was panicked by the thought of his children being driven in a car by someone who had apparently fooled his wife into trusting him. A flurry of questions and mixed feelings flooded my client as he wondered how long his wife had been seeing this man; if this man had, in fact, driven his children anywhere; and what steps should be taken to ensure their safety. One of the greatest gifts you can give your children is to be cautiously selective of the partner with whom they will eventually be entrusted.

Children mirror the trust you place in a partner. If you show trust with a partner, it is common they will trust that person, too. Give sufficient time to test your trust with a partner before you ask your children to do the same. This will ensure security for your children while keeping in perspective the time trust takes to build.

The third question is as follows: *What do you believe about the role of a husband and wife?* Every couple heading toward marriage would greatly benefit from writing out a job description for a husband and wife. Married couples who have differing expectations of these roles experience significantly more conflicts

Along the Way Find Out About . . . Comparability

- How does your partner's personality compare with yours?
- How do your thinking styles and intelligence levels compare?
- How do each of you handle emotions?
- What is your energy level like?
- Do you share a similar sense of humor?
- Do you and your partner share similar spiritual outlooks on life?
- What are your partner's family values?
- How good at nurturing are you?
- How do you handle your money?
- How do you take care of your possessions?
- How many things do you like to do together?
- What are your work habits like?

than those who agree.[13] Dating discussions are not guarantees, but with
regular talks you can clarify your
expectations, negotiate your differences, and affirm your agreements.
Therefore, when you explore family
values, be sure to sort through these
three questions.

*One of the greatest
gifts you can give
your children is
to be cautiously
selective of the
partner with whom
they will eventually
be entrusted.*

The second set of values you need
to compare is the content and extent
of your *spiritual and religious values.*
Dr. David Olson from the University of Minnesota designed a
premarital inventory called PREPARE and a marital inventory
called ENRICH. Olson conducted a study of two groups of
couples from a pool of more than 24,000 couples who had taken
his ENRICH inventory in a two-year period.[14] The first group
included all of the couples who scored lower than 30 percent on
their *agreement* of spiritual and religious beliefs and practices.
The second group was made up of all couples who scored higher
than 70 percent. This eliminated about 11,000 couples who fell in
the middle. The key word here is *agreement*. Numerous studies
have looked at religious beliefs and marital satisfaction, but most
of these studies had a very unclear definition of being religious.
For instance, 80 percent of studies published on this subject
since 1994 used *only one question* to determine whether or not
a person is religious. To add to the confusion, these studies did
not ask about the consensus (or lack of) that existed between the
couple in their faith views.

Olson took the remaining 12,000-plus couples who were
divided between the high and low categories of agreement on
faith issues and compared them on twelve areas. Large discrepancies existed in all twelve areas, especially in *couple closeness*,
communication, and *marriage satisfaction*. Those couples who
were in the category of 70 percent or higher agreement on faith
scored significantly higher in all twelve categories, especially

in the aforementioned three categories. This clearly supported a strong link between a couple's agreement on faith and the quality of their marriage. In the overall evaluation of the 24,000 couples, an amazing 89 percent of those couples who reported that they were "happily married" also stated that they agreed on how their spiritual values and beliefs were expressed.

Although the topic of religion or your personal faith may even come up on your first date, deeper and more meaningful talks will most likely come with time. Conflicts over differences of faith have challenged and strained many marriages. Do not rationalize or overlook your differences. Deal with them directly. Make sure you examine both the content of your faith and beliefs and the *importance* of your faith. I have counseled many frustrated clients who had partners who attended the same place of worship or claimed to hold similar beliefs, but the *magnitude* and *meaningfulness* of their faith had been overlooked. As a result, the differences in their attitudes toward and practices of their faith polarized them after marriage.

The 2002 movie *My Big, Fat Greek Wedding* humorously presented the differences a couple in love might have in their family and spiritual values. Toula, a thirty-year-old Greek woman who is entrenched with her family, meets a classic WASP, Ian, and falls madly in love. In contrast to Toula and her large family, Ian is an only child of parents who have little to no spiritual faith. Toula, on the other hand, is devoutly Greek Orthodox. The story line of the movie follows the exposing of Toula and Ian's secret relationship and the upheaval it causes in Toula's family. If you analyze Toula and Ian (this is why you would not like going to the movies with me), then you would realize that the only reason Toula and Ian's relationship was successful was because Ian adopted both Toula's religion and her family. He was baptized by Toula's priest in order to become an official member of her church, and he embraced her family as the family he never had, including her crazy Aunt Voula. For instance, at the family potluck Aunt Voula became informed that Ian was a vegetarian. "What do you mean he don't eat no meat?" she exclaimed, bringing the entire room to silence in shock. "Oh, that's OK." Voula continues, "I make lamb."

Ian did not try to retain his family values or religious practices. Instead, he became "baptized" into Toula's family and faith, even to the point of living next door to Toula's parents. If you are in a relationship where there are extreme differences, one of the two of you must be willing to make major adjustments so that the basis of similarities is broad enough to handle your differences.

The third set of values that you should consider and talk through is the *management of finances* and your attitudes toward "things." Much can be learned about a prospective partner by recognizing how that person handles his or her money.

Both of my daughters have dated some indescribably cheap guys when they were in high school. My wife and I have made it a practice to always ensure that they had some of their own money when they were being taken out by a date. Of course, there were times where they went Dutch, but there were also times when it was expected that the guy would pay.

I remember listening in disbelief after my youngest daughter in her senior year of high school returned from her Valentine's Day dinner with her boyfriend and recounted the evening to my wife and me. He had told her that he wanted to take her out for this special occasion. So he picked her up and escorted her into the restaurant that he had chosen. She sat across from him at the table, and when the check came, he looked her in the eyes, slid it slowly to her side of the table, and quietly persuaded with a puppy-dog look, "You won't mind getting this one, would you?"

Now let me ask you a question. Do you think that his attitude toward money just might predict how he would handle other things in the relationship? Suffice it to say that when he gave her some massage oil for a gift (which my daughter thought was "weird" especially in light of the fact that they had been going out for only three months), he kindly informed her, "Here, this is for you to use when giving me a back rub."

My wife and I were speechless when she finished telling her tale. We sat around our kitchen table staring at each other dumbfounded. But then, like an eruption of Old Faithful in Yellowstone National Park, we all burst out laughing at the ridiculousness of his clueless self-centeredness. His way of handling money definitely indicated his unconscientious immaturity and self-absorption. The evening ended with my daughter commenting as she headed off to her bedroom, "OK—I guess I need to find another boyfriend!"

Thirty-seven percent of all married couples complain that money management is their number one problem in marriage.[15] It is interesting that a common practice for couples who choose to cohabitate outside of marriage is to keep their monies separate. This separation may cushion the relationship and overshadow some key aspects of cooperation that they should address. Another option that you can follow as your relationship becomes more serious is to work on the budgets and the payment of bills together. Even if you kept your budgets and money separate, it would be both revealing and beneficial for you and a long-standing partner to routinely coordinate your individual finances *together*. Ask yourself, if I entrusted my finances to my partner, how similarly or differently would they be handled? How would my needs and interests be considered? Would I have to worry?

Compare Your Lifestyles

The last area of compatibility that you should consider is the similarities of your lifestyle: work habits, leisure activities, and interests. Enjoyment of the same recreational activities is also highly associated with happy marriages. One study looked at romantic and friendship relationships and found that both were very similar in the importance of quality time together while engaging in mutually enjoyable activities.[16]

Marriage is both a companion relationship and a working partnership. The more couples are comparable in their recreational and leisure activities, the stronger the feelings of love. This is especially true for men. They placed a high preference for choosing a partner who would share their interests and leisure activities. Overall, both husbands and wives felt greater love feelings, security, and satisfaction when these interests and activities were in sync. This makes a lot of sense in light of what we established in Chapter 4—deeply knowing a partner is more than just talking; it requires an ongoing experience of togetherness.

Friends with Marital Benefits

I was invited to interview individuals and couples who were being filmed for an adolescent romantic relationship program. The day was spent asking a series of questions to a range of participants from those who were single and in early adolescence to those who had been married for many years. I decided to have a few questions that I would ask every participant, just to see if the answers would vary according to age and status. By the end of the day, a remarkable discovery occurred. Every participant gave exactly the same answer to one of the questions. The question was, "If you had to identify the most important thing in your marriage (or future marriage, for those who were single), what would it be?"

Every participant stated that the number one quality was a deep, best-friend relationship. I was struck by the image everyone portrayed of great friends spending their lives doing life together—playing house; going shopping; taking walks; attending movies, sporting events, plays, and other recreational activities; and laughing and crying together. No matter what crossed their paths, they would create a lifestyle where they faced it together.

This is what you want to look for in your compatibility with a partner. Yes, you need chemistry. Yes, you cannot manufacture that "in love" feeling. But you need to understand that the process of building a romantic relationship has the same core as building a great friendship. Love and chemistry are magical. But there is nothing magical about building a friendship that will last through the years.

Find a partner with whom you have the three Cs—chemistry, complementarity, and comparability. Your partner needs to be irresistible to you. You and your partner should have key areas that are similar, and your differences should blend together in mutually beneficial ways. These areas of compatibility will enrich your relationship with the feeling of having found a soul mate whom you love, whom you identify with, and by whom you are challenged and complemented.

DON'T FORGET

- Compatibility is more complicated than just similarity.

- True compatibility consists of three dimensions: chemistry, complementarity, and comparability.

- Chemistry is not always a good judge of character, chemistry sees what it wants to see, and chemistry is not constant, even in the best of relationships.

- True complementarity exists when you find that you become a better person by being with your partner, when time refines the blend of differences in mutually beneficial ways, and when partners become more alike over time.

- Three main areas that you should compare with your partner are personality characteristics, values, and lifestyles.

CHAPTER

6

Say What You Mean and Mean What You Say

Step Two: Getting to Know the Skills for Building and Maintaining Relationships

Over many years as a marriage counselor, I have come to see clearly that couples who have poor communication skills lack the necessary tools to build an intimate relationship or resolve conflicts. Although this type of couple may stay married for many years, their relationship is at risk the entire time. They are like a skyscraper built on top of an underground fault that is just waiting for the inevitable geological equation to bring on an earthquake. Once shaken, they can never repair the damages.

Frequently, this type of couple will initiate counseling in the midst of a crisis that has unbalanced their fragile relationship.

They have become comfortable with the missing pieces of their relationship. But after the crisis hits, they lack the skills to work through the conflicts and bring healing to their brokenness.

The more you can establish healthy communication skills before you marry, the more you can enhance your future marriage while also building protection against unforeseen crises and conflicts. The number one complaint couples bring to marriage counselors is a lack of communication.[1] Relationship skills are essential tools in the development and maintenance of a healthy relationship. At the very onset of this chapter, however, I want to clarify a point that is often confused and misunderstood: a dating partner's relationship skills and a dating partner's conscience are not the same—they are distinct!

> *The number one complaint couples bring to marriage counselors is a lack of communication.*

Poor Skill or Ill Will?

This distinction is analogous to the difference between the *abilities* of a worker and the *tools* of the trade. Take, for instance, the differences between the skills of a surgeon and the surgical instruments used for surgery. Imagine an exceptionally skilled surgeon vacationing on some remote island. While the surgeon is dining in a restaurant, a patron collapses with stomach pains. The surgeon quickly determines that an emergency appendectomy is required or the patient's life is at risk. The manager informs the surgeon that the island has no hospital or doctor's office and there is no transportation off the island for at least twenty-four hours. What would you want done if you were the patient?

You can imagine the scene in the kitchen where a pot of boiling water would be used for sterilization and the knife drawer would be the surgeon's tool chest. The surgery most likely would be successful, although the outcome would not have the precision it would have had if the surgeon had worked in an operating room with all of the instruments at his or her fingertips.

Now imagine another scene. You are a patient in need of an appendectomy in a hospital where no medically trained personnel are available (i.e., they all went to the remote island for a weekend trip). All of the surgical equipment, however, is neatly on the operating stand. The coffee-shop worker volunteers to perform the surgery and begins to scrub up. How would you feel? Who would you rather have—a trained surgeon with makeshift instruments or an untrained hacker with needles, scalpels, forceps, and suction tubes?

This is a crude analogy for the difference between the conscience (e.g., the surgeon's ability and training) and relationship skills (e.g., the instruments used by the surgeon). *Relationship skills are the tools the conscience uses.* I have devoted Chapter 9 to the conscience and will review and expand upon this concept that the conscience and relationship skills interact even though they are distinct. However, I wanted to fix this idea in your mind before proceeding with the section on evaluating a prospective partner's two primary relationship skills used in the building and maintenance of any healthy relationship, especially marriage: *communication* skills and *conflict-resolution* skills.

Communication Skills

Communication involves verbal and nonverbal messages, as well as both speaking and listening skills. As with most aspects of getting to know a partner, trying to figure out a partner's degree of skill in these areas is a bit like peeling an onion—just when you think you have stripped it to the core, you realize there yet is another layer. Sometimes the "bad spots" are not in the first few layers but are hiding below the surface. Just as with the proverbial onion, bad spots on the surface are easily detected, but those lodged in the deeper layers require some digging.

When I was first researching and writing the PICK program ten years ago, I happened to be flipping through the television stations and came across an old Steve Martin movie, *The Jerk*. I laughed out loud and figured it was a sign from above; then I picked up my pen and began taking notes.

In this story, Martin plays a character named Navin R. Johnson. If you want an analysis of a jerk, I would suggest you rent the movie. Throughout the movie Navin doesn't manage relationships (or much of anything for that matter) appropriately. He is bad at managing money, he is bad at making decisions, and he is especially bad at communication.

In one scene Navin attempts to tell his girlfriend that he has fallen in love with her. This is how he tries to win her over:

> *I know we have only known each other for four weeks and three days, but to me it seems likes nine weeks and four days. You see, on the first day, it seemed like a week; and on the second day, it seemed like five days; and on the third day, it seemed like a week again; and on the fourth day, that seemed like eight days; and on the fifth day, you went to see your mother and that seemed just like a day; and then you came back and later in the evening it started seeming like two days. So in the evening it seemed like two days spilling over into the next day, and that started seeming like four days of the sixth day on into the seventh day, which seemed like a total of five days. And the sixth day seemed like a week and a half. I have it all written down, and I could show it to you tomorrow.*

How would you like to communicate with someone who is this skilled in the art of confusion? Oh, and I forgot to mention that the entire time she is asleep—not really surprising.

Revealing Yourself

The first area of communication you will encounter is your partner's ability to *self-disclose*. This refers to the way a person "opens up" to you—that is, the extent to which a person reveals his or her various thoughts, feelings, and experiences. Some people are extremely transparent, wearing their feelings on their sleeve. Others are just the opposite—they are closed, hard to read, and private. In most long-term relationships, the ability to put your thoughts and feelings into words is essential.

Marc and Melanie were on the verge of breaking up after four years of dating. Melanie knew that Marc meant well, but his lack of communication had resulted in her buildup of anger and frustration. By the end of the first session, I had listened to Melanie for forty minutes and to Marc for only three. I pointed this out to them, and they agreed to run the next session differently. It became apparent that Marc lacked good communication skills. Melanie was cooperative and kept quiet for a lot of the session. Needless to say, it was one of those sessions where there were many periods of silence.

At one point, Marc attempted to explain something he did in anger that he regretted but could only come up with "I am sorry; you deserve better." When I asked if he had more to say, he said he would like to but he just can't organize his thoughts. I suggested that he write the sentence on the left side of a piece of paper, from top to bottom—first word at the top, last word at the bottom. I instructed him to emphasize only the first word in that six-word statement and then write down next to that word all the thoughts he would derive from that unique meaning. Then he should emphasize the second word and do the same. When Marc had completed this for every word, I wanted him to write out all of these thoughts in paragraph form and then read it to his wife. He worked on this for about ten minutes and then read it to her. She broke down with tears of appreciation as he read his thoughts:

I—I am responsible for what I did, and no one else. *Am*—I still feel badly about what I did. Even though it was days ago, the feeling is still with me. *Sorry*—I feel ashamed that I acted so badly. *You*—You are my one and only love—you are very special to me. *Deserve*—You did not do anything to make me do what I did. I handled my anger poorly. *Better*—I want to handle myself in a way that treats you kindly. In the future, I will calm down before I act so that you are not hurt.

I knew that Marc could not walk around with a pad of paper and write out his thoughts whenever he had to talk. But there would be critical times when he really needed to self-disclose, and this approach could be used to help him express his thoughts with more elaborative sentences.

Needs and relationship responses *refers to the ways you and a partner verbally communicate and respond to personal needs.*

Marc would always be the more quiet partner. Ironically, this is one of the main qualities that had attracted Melanie. She fondly remembered when she first met Marc and appreciated his attentiveness and listening skill. But in time, she felt like she didn't know him, and Marc needed to work at the skill of putting his internal world into words. He was clearly an example of someone who had the conscience and heart to be more expressive but lacked the skill. Over time he developed more confidence and ease with talking and opening up, and Melanie gained greater patience with listening to and waiting for his responses.

If Marc and Melanie were to sit down with you and give you advice, it would not be to avoid the person who wants to be more open but lacks the skill. What they would tell you is to *not wait* until you are married to identify and work on this area. There are many ways to work on communication, especially the skill of self-disclosure. Most people who lack this skill are shy or quiet types who keep a lot inside. You need to make sure that this partner wants to let you know him or her. There are those who *don't* open up because of hidden issues or agendas. In time, most hidden agendas surface, and you should be cautious of quiet partners until their hidden agendas are revealed.

However, Melanie was a talker and initially appreciated Marc's listening ear. She never considered his lack of talking a source of hurt—in the past the men who had hurt her had done so with words not silence. In time she realized that she needed to hear Marc talk—about conflicts they had with other family members or even between themselves, about how he really felt toward her, and about his opinions and outlooks on their lives together.

Consider the balance of openness between you and your partner. Review the levels of self-disclosure that were discussed in Chapter 4, and make sure that both you and your partner are satisfied with the amount of talk you have in each of the four domains of communication (i.e., OPEN): observations and facts, perspectives and opinions, experiences and emotions, and needs and relationship responses.

The first three are fairly common and easy to understand—stories about your day, opinions about your friends, situations you have encountered, views about current events, descriptions of how you felt in various circumstances, and conversations you recount and explain. The first three domains of communication entail the majority of what we share in our talks with a partner. However, the last domain is the one that carries the most meaning for both the *establishment* of a romantic relationship and the *maintenance* of intimacy in a long-term relationship.

Needs and relationship responses refers to the ways you and a partner verbally communicate and respond to personal needs. Putting into words the feelings you have for a partner—your love, appreciation, respect, and admiration—generates and rejuvenates the bonds of intimacy. One study labeled this art of identifying and communicating your emotions as "emotional skillfulness."[2]

John Gottman is a major researcher on the quality of marriage relationships and the founder of the Family Research Laboratory, also fondly called the "Love Lab." This is a scientifically designed laboratory for filming, observing, and studying the interaction patterns of couples. From these studies, Gottman concluded that there is a basic ratio of positive to negative emotions that couples must express to reduce their chances of divorce. (He boasts of being able to use this quotient to predict with 96 percent accuracy which couples will divorce.)[3] Essentially, a couple must have five times as many interactions or verbal exchanges that generate *positive emotions* for every one that results in some negative feelings. The dominance of positive expressiveness creates the atmosphere of warmth and security in a relationship. Ask yourself, how good are you at regularly expressing positive loving feelings in both actions *and* words? This is why those who grow up with expressiveness are at an advantage.

But you also need to pay attention to how your partner makes you feel loved, valued, appreciated, and secure. Does he use words to tell you what he thinks of you? Does she find special ways to express her feelings for you? Has his treatment of you changed for the worse during the first year of your relationship? Does she continue to value you and keep you a priority in her life? Does he build you up or break you down with words? The answers to these questions will indicate the strength of your partner's communication skills, particularly in this area of expressing intimacy.

Few experiences of life create as much self-doubt as trying to decipher an incongruent partner.

We all long to be understood and known. Yet a relationship is strongest when it has achieved *reciprocity*—the exchange between giving and receiving, talking and listening, supporting and being supported, self-disclosing and understanding another, and gaining insight into yourself and insight into your partner. The ability to achieve reciprocity in emotional expressiveness may require that you take some steps of vulnerability with revealing yourself, stepping out of your comfort zone, trying out new behaviors, and maybe even addressing these areas with a partner you have become serious with.

Actions Speak Louder than Words

Communication theorists refer to the comparison of verbal and nonverbal messages as the degree of congruence. High congruence occurs when there are few inconsistencies between these two aspects of communication. Low congruence indicates many inconsistencies between the verbal and nonverbal messages, clouding the meaning of the communication and leading to frequent misunderstandings.

High congruence, open self-disclosure, and an empathetic listening style are essential areas of communication in the development and maintenance of intimacy. The degree of skill in these three areas indicates your potential to share and understand yourself as well as your partner in nonjudgmental ways.

Congruence, therefore, is the consistency between what someone shows outwardly with what he or she thinks and feels on the inside. Have you ever heard the saying, "Your actions speak so loudly, I can't hear what you're saying"? I am certain that the one who penned those words for the first time had become exasperated with a friend or partner who kept contradicting his or her own words with opposing behaviors and choices. When you are in a relationship with someone like this, you will wonder if you are crazy. Few experiences of life create as much self-doubt as trying to decipher an incongruent partner.

Beware of a relationship that has incongruence. These relationships almost always possess the all's-well-that-ends-well pattern. Undoubtedly, you will find yourself in a position of feeling compromised because you accept some wrong when it becomes smoothed over by some right. You would know if you are in a relationship like this, because you never feel secure. Rather, you feel like you never have the *whole* person or that there is always a dagger in the shadows, a feeling of impending doom, and you catch yourself walking on eggshells but not knowing why. It is around this time that you come down with a case of the *self-doubt crazies*.

Imagine taking your partner to a party where he or she completely ignores you and constantly flirts with others who are there. On the way home, you try to talk to your partner about it, but everything somehow becomes turned around on you. You dread the fact that your partner can always outtalk you. It is as if

Along the Way Find Out About . . . Feelings
and Understanding

- Are your feelings congruent with your words?
- How much insight into your own thoughts and motives do
  you have?
- Are you able to put my perspective and feelings into words
  accurately?
- Are you able to put your own feelings into words?
- Do you respect my perspective?
- How do you show me respect?
- How do you handle me when I am emotional?

he or she knows the exact words to say to make you doubt even the most damning evidence. This is where the self-doubt crazies kick in. You begin wondering if you are paranoid: "Am I paranoid or was my partner really flirting?" "Is it all in my head, or is my partner actually a player?"

I have watched clients become consumed by these self-doubt crazies when a partner consistently convinces them that they shouldn't believe what they just saw and that they shouldn't listen to their own intuition. I have experienced this when working with clients in counseling who come to the decision to break up.

Maureen was a perfect example of someone confused by the self-doubt crazies. She had put up with Kevin's passive-aggressiveness for eight months. Anytime she wasn't perfectly in line with his plan or schedule, he would become irate. When Maureen would try to explain herself or put things in perspective, he would deny that he was even upset. But she could bank on the fact that in the next twenty-four hours Kevin would find a way to pay her back for how she offended him.

Maureen became more like an overly self-conscious child with an angry parent when she was with Kevin. He could turn on the charm and make her feel very relaxed. But when she didn't chime in with his agenda, she felt his fury in subtle and manipulative ways. Ultimately, it was his lack of congruence, the lack of outwardly explaining what he was inwardly feeling, that made the conflicts irresolvable.

Incongruence can also occur when someone tries to cover up or smooth over hurtful words with his or her actions. This can be very effective and sweet when the hurtful words happen only infrequently and when some insights and explanations periodically accompany the making-up behaviors. Without these things, the implication is that the *gift says it all*. Yet this is so untrue. A gift or good deed should not be used to smooth over a pattern of hurtful words.

Beth became suspicious of Greg's attentive and affectionate mood when it seemed to consistently follow the day after one of his angry, verbal attacks. She began to see Greg more like a dysfunctional pet owner whose practice was to kick the dog when in a bad mood, but then later pet the dog out of guilt. Greg never fully admitted his assaults; instead, he relied on his actions to appease her upset condition. He would be overly attentive and affectionate the next day, while sidestepping the fact that Beth still felt wounded from the previous day's rant. If Beth asked Greg about the words he spoke to her in anger, he would first act as if he didn't know what she was talking about. If she persisted, he would then fly back into a defensive rage, reprimanding her for dwelling on the negative and being unappreciative of his niceness. This pattern was entrenched in the relationship, never to change. If Beth approached the topic, Greg blew up. If she said nothing and accepted his peace offering of *niceness* following the attack, then Greg felt absolved from guilt. Because he felt he paid his dues, he was never motivated to change his ways.

Words are a window to the heart. The Bible states, "Out of the abundance of your heart does your mouth speak." You can peer into the inner thoughts, feelings, motives, and desires of a person's invisible self through the words he or she speaks. Words give shape and definition to one's inner experience, and they transport the messages of one heart to another. They can cut, and they can heal. They can discourage, and they can inspire. But words without actions are empty. At first they convince, but as time goes on, words lose their value without the backing of matching behaviors. There must be congruence between what is said and what is done. So pay attention to both the spoken *and* the corresponding unspoken messages.

I was different than most boys in that I did not like chocolate or peanut butter. But one thing I did like was honey. When I was two years old, we bought a farm and moved there from our inner-city home. We inherited from the previous owners no less than twenty-one quart jars full of honey lining the shelf in the basement of the farmhouse. I loved to take a big scoop of that partially sugared honey and spread it on toast immediately after it popped up from the toaster. This made sure the honey would melt on contact from the warmth of the toast. It was fortunate for me that no one else in our household really ate much honey. Therefore, my metabolism has been permanently fixed in high gear.

When I was ten years old, I lugged the last jar of honey up the basement stairs. Needless to say, I became frantic. To make matters worse, the beekeeper had retired. It became apparent that if I was to continue to feed my childhood addiction, then I had to take over the hives. So I talked to my parents and purchased on loan the necessary equipment and protective gear from a local beekeeping store, along with the bible of beekeepers—*The ABC and XYZ of Beekeeping*. (Luckily for me, the town in which I grew up was known as the bee capital of the world.)

During that time I learned that bees have an advanced form of nonverbal communication. The explorer bees fly miles to find pollen-rich areas. Then they return to the hive, and, encircled by hundreds of bees, they do a dance that communicates the location of their findings according to the position of the sun and the distance they traveled. They accomplish their complex communication completely without one word.

People, too, have complex "dances" that communicate messages without words. It is crucial to figure out the dance steps of the person you are dating, because before you know it, you are on the dance floor and one of you is taking the lead.

The Balance Between Talking and Listening

Listening entails many nonverbal dance moves. For instance, have you ever had a conversation with someone who kept looking at his or her watch while you were talking? Or couldn't keep his or her eyes off the television? Or became restless and antsy? Did you get the message?

Many times the nonverbal message speaks more loudly than the verbal. This is one reason why you should pay attention to your intuition, hunches, inner feelings, and vibes around a partner. You probably pick up on the message of the nonverbals but just are not aware of it. Make sure you are "reading" the other person correctly so that you don't jump to the wrong conclusions! Your interpretation of his or her nonverbals can become a topic in a future discussion, which will help clarify your understanding of what that person usually means by his or her body language.

So what is a good listener? Listening is more than just passive silence. If you are a good listener, then you must be able to convince the person you are listening to that you have really heard and understood him or her. The more personal and meaningful the shared content, the more important this listening skill is. As a good listener, you are like a writer researching a character to be exact about what this person thinks and feels. You listen to what is said so you can reflect it with such accuracy that the person talking will feel like you are reading his or her mind. You become a connoisseur of that person's thoughts, feelings, perspectives, and beliefs.

This kind of listening is extremely active. You need to temporarily put aside your own opinions so that you are truly looking

Along the Way Find Out About . . . Talking
and Listening

- How much do you like to talk?
- When I tell you my ideas, do I feel validated by you?
- Do you listen to me? How do you listen to me?
- How much do you self-disclose about your day and life?
- How detail-oriented are you?
- How do you show you value my opinion?
- Can we talk like best friends?

through the eyes of the one who is talking. This skill can be learned if it does not come naturally to you or your partner. When I was in graduate school, we had specific classes designed to learn and practice these communication skills. We used an acronym for checking our listening "posture": SOLER. This stood for

Square off—make sure your shoulders are square with
     the person talking.
Open—keep your arms and legs uncrossed so that you
     have an open, nondefensive position.
Lean—lean forward toward the person talking.
Eye contact—keep eye contact with the person talking.
Relax—stay relaxed as you listen.

The point I am trying to make is that most people have to work to develop this skill. Our classes in graduate school extended over a two-year period. If it takes that long for grad students, who are in a counseling program and already have fairly developed communication skills, to master these listening skills, then how much longer will it take those who have bad communication habits to break and no classes to take? If you need to improve in your listening skills, then know that there are books and classes to help you master this, but also know that it takes work and time.[4] Pay attention to how your partner listens to you. Do you feel your partner could accurately represent what you think and feel to a stranger who never met you? If not, then maybe you and your partner should work together to deepen your speaking and listening skills.

Imbalanced proportions of talking and listening in partners can lead to frustration and feelings of isolation over the years of a relationship.

Throughout the course of life, you want a partner who can get into your world and make you feel understood. In national surveys, wives state that the number one desire they have in marriage is to feel understood by their spouse. Without the artful skill of engaged listening, this is unachievable.

Finally, check out the difference between the amount of talking and listening your partner brings to the relationship. An ideal balance exists, and it is expressed in the rule of reciprocity that I mentioned earlier: *there should be similar amounts of listening, talking, disclosing, and initiating between you and the person you are dating.* Imbalanced proportions of talking and listening in partners can lead to frustration and feelings of isolation over the years of a relationship. Try to find someone who shares your interests, values, and perspectives on life, and who can relate them to you with words and actions that are congruent.

Conflict Resolution

Up to this point, what have we covered in this important arena of communicating with your partner? First, your communication should be mutual and reciprocal. Second, there should be

Along the Way Find Out About . . . Resolving Conflicts

- How argumentative or defensive are you?
- Can you put your love into words?
- Do you withdraw very often? When?
- Do you attack or blame very often?
- Are you passive-aggressive?
- What are your weakest skills?
- How often do you say you're sorry?
- Are you good at reconciling and making up?
- Do you initiate conversations? Apologies? Affection?

similar balances in the amounts of self-disclosure, listening, sharing, and initiating that you and your partner generate in your relationship. Third, make sure you clearly read both words and actions, as well as the verbal and nonverbal messages, and clarify the meaning of what was said and done. Look for high degrees of congruence between these two areas of verbal messages and body language. Your partner should be able to identify his or her feelings and put them into words. Finally, you should have a growing feeling of security with your partner, being regularly valued and affirmed by both actions and words.

Communication skills pull a couple together in intimacy, while conflict-resolution skills bring them back together after a disagreement has torn them apart. Without these skills, a couple's intimacy and bond will eventually erode. Teaching partners how to communicate, especially to manage and resolve an argument, is one of the most common activities of therapists. Like all skills, this one can be learned and improved with a little bit of good information and lots of hard work and practice. If you have a partner who lacks the skill of resolving a conflict, then you should seriously consider addressing this issue and making sure a pattern of working through problems or differences has been clearly established in your relationship.

Do You Have the Attitude?

Most couples whom I have counseled and who have had problems resolving their differences have also had negative attitudes that clouded their attempts. Some were overly defensive, while others were overly stubborn; some jumped to conclusions, while others wouldn't even listen. Most of these clients never acknowledged anything good, valuable, right, or even remotely worthwhile in their partner's point.

Five qualities are essential to the smoothing out of rough words or rocky times. A lot is made of the technique of conflict resolution. But form without heart is just an empty shell; so make sure that both you and your partner have the inner qualities for the task. First, it is vital that both of you can speak your minds. You can refer to this as *mutual assertiveness*. You could be the best listener, but if your partner is not willing to let you in on what he or she thinks, then you will spend your days fishing. Have you ever fished in a relationship? Fishing sounds like this: "Is there something wrong? It seems like something is not right—are you feeling OK? I hate to keep asking, but is there something I said or did? I promise I won't overreact if there is, but you need to tell me and not keep it to yourself, if in fact there is something."

The second quality is a *mutual respect* of each other's views. This is the attitude where you say to your partner, "You have a point that I should consider." So many couples whom I have watched argue in a counseling session appear to relate to each other as if their partner doesn't have a thought in his or her head worth listening to. I have found myself asking each partner, "Why did you choose to marry someone so far beneath you?" That usually stops them in their tracks. When they tell me that they did not err in this way, then I ask, "So your partner has a good mind and usually a good point. Then what is it?"

The technique of restating your partner's point must be preceded by believing and respecting that your partner *has* a point worth your time. If both partners develop and maintain this attitude, even though their emotions are ignited, they will much more successfully resolve their differences.

Similar to this quality is a third that is almost always lacking with an argumentative couple: *humility*. It is almost comical to watch someone stop and acknowledge a partner's worthwhile point, but then go on to press his or her own point as if the partner's didn't even exist. Such people look like tightly wound springs waiting to be sprung when they are restating their partner's view. They remind you of the person who seems to be listening to you but the entire time is only thinking about what to say back to you. Humility not only admits when one is wrong, but also admits to not being fully right. I usually find ways to put together a combined view from the points of both partners that is better than either was by itself.

The last two qualities are strongly related to each other: *a willingness to forgive* and *a resiliency to bounce back* after the conflict is resolved. Partners who are quick to let go and can reset their emotions fairly fast don't allow conflicts to pile up.

These five qualities of the heart set the stage for moving through the steps of conflict resolution. They set you in the position of being able to see your partner's perspective without dropping yours; they keep your partner in a positive light so that you want to take turns with your partner explaining your points, rationales, and feelings as well as listening; and they enable you to acknowledge and admit how you "came across" to your partner, thus validating your partner's perspective. These are the most frequently prescribed steps in relationship books on conflict management and resolution. However, without the development of the five essential qualities of the heart, these steps are usually ignored in the heat of a battle.

Make sure that your communication resolution, just as your openness and listening, is mutual. If you are doing all the apologizing, all the fishing, all the listening, all the self-humbling, or all the respecting—then you need to back up and address this major imbalance in your relationship. Communication is the key to opening doors of intimacy and closing doors of misunderstanding and hurt. But it requires joint effort. Even though you may have enough skill, motivation, and know-how to do the work for the two of you, resist your inner promptings and wait to see if your partner reciprocates and matches your efforts. You deserve a partner who has skills similar to yours and whose heart is just as willing to use them.

DON'T FORGET

- Relationship skills are the tools of the conscience.

- The first area of communication you will encounter is your partner's ability to self-disclose.

- High congruence, open self-disclosure, and an empathetic listening style are essential areas of communication.

- Beware of relationships that have incongruence.

- A balanced relationship should involve similar amounts of listening, talking, disclosing, and initiating between you and the person you are dating.

- Good conflict-resolution skills involve mutual assertiveness, mutual respect of views, humility, willingness to forgive, and a resiliency to bounce back after the conflict is resolved.

7

"And My Third Wife Was a . . ."

Step Three: Getting to Know the Patterns from Other Relationships

I was speaking to my good friend Tom about how the patterns from other relationships can predict what a partner will be like in marriage. Tom is my resident expert on single fathers and dating, having raised a teenage daughter as her custodial parent for seven years following an unexpected divorce. A woman once told him on a date that she uses a simple guideline for figuring out how a man will treat his wife in marriage: look at how he treats his mother, dog, and children. We decided there was wisdom in her idea that what you do in one relationship will often repeat in another, but we also realized that her three examples were only the tip of the iceberg.

Retracing Our Steps

Before we delve into this chapter, let's review where we are in the steps of figuring out a partner. As mentioned earlier, I have referred to each of the five areas to explore in a dating relationship as "steps," because they often surface in a progressive fashion with the more obvious characteristics being detected first and the more subtle features staying hidden until later in the relationship. My hope is that these steps provide direction and timing to how you sort through and draw conclusions about the many things you discover in a dating partner over the first few weeks and months of the relationship.

You do not leave one step when you move to the next step, and relationships can develop in many varying ways. Still, the importance of each of these five steps is not altered or minimized by the uniqueness of your relationship. With that in mind, let's retrace our first two steps in order to regain our bearings.

Your dating relationship began with getting to know some of the elements of compatibility between you and this person. This included the chemistry you two have—your attraction, sense of connection and being in sync, and feelings of passion and fascination. You have also become aware of some similarities and differences. The similarities are important because they create a common ground. Differences, on the other hand, need to come together in complementary ways. This concept of complementarity suggests that differences, when respected, can add more to a relationship than even many similarities. In this first step of your relationship, you have been weighing out the blend of your chemistry, comparability, and complementarity.

You also have taken the second step of gaining some understanding into the extent of skillfulness this person possesses in communicating and resolving differences. You have watched the way this dating partner talks to you, matches your openness, handles his or her emotions, and uses body language. When you become upset or your feelings are hurt, you observe the way that your perspective and feelings are considered and how the conflict is ultimately resolved.

The third step, *determining patterns of how a dating partner relates to others*, moves you in a more subtle direction. It is difficult to know which patterns from other relationships are actually seeds planted in your relationship that in time will sprout. For instance, would you worry if your dating partner

- is rude to a waiter?
- is always in conflict with a boss?
- is mean to his or her children?
- has road rage?
- has extremely poor relationships with his or her family?
- is divorced?
- has had many sexual partners?
- lies to friends to avoid conflicts or hurt feelings?
- has never been able to make a serious commitment?
- was accused of being overly controlling in previous dating relationships?
- has cheated in the past?

How do you know if any of these matter? Let's face it, no one is perfect and you can always find dirt somewhere in the past. How do you know if the script from your partner's messed-up relationships is actually being written into *your* relationship—changing only the names? We have all heard the saying, "History repeats itself." Does this have any validity when it comes to relationship histories? The answer is a resounding yes.

Finding the Common Denominator

Each relationship you are in feels distinct from all others. Your relationship with a parent (or some parental figure) may seem to have no connection to your relationship with a dating partner. The way you relate with a coworker may seem to be completely different to the way you relate with your friends (or your children, if you have any). However, remember that the most common element in all of your relationships is *you*! The same "you" relates to the coworker, talks on the phone to your mother, and then goes out on a date with your partner. There are common elements within all of your relationships because you are the same person in every relationship. It is true that some relationships bring the best out of you and some the worst—but when you add them all up, you have a spectrum of the good-to-bad relationship behaviors in you and no one else. Although this may seem obvious, we tend to live in ways that deny or minimize this fact—likely because we hate to admit that we can act in those embarrassing ways that certain people or situations seem to draw out of us.

What you know about a partner's past provides a clue to his or her future.

I refer to this as the theory of relationship continuity. There is continuity (i.e., similarity, connection, overlap) between the ways you and I act in our various relationships. We tend to think that what we do at one time of life will not affect other times of life, how we act in one situation will not affect another, and how we treat someone in one relationship will not influence the way we treat someone else. But in reality, each of your steps follows in line with the previous while moving you in the direction of your next step.

Let me use an analogy of how a river winds back and forth between the banks it previously cut out of the earth, while continually eroding and creating future paths. I grew up on a farm that had a river running through it. It was a boy's playground with banks of gray clay for molding works of art, infinite rocks to throw, and plenty of crawdads to catch. Each day that I ran back to this river, I would find it in the same place. It was predictable and seemingly unchanging, although it was constantly in motion.

Thirty years after we moved from that farm, I went back and walked my old stomping ground. The river was the same but different. It had hewn new paths that resembled the old, yet it had moved deeper or farther to one side or the other. Erosion had relocated the banks, making some corners sharper while others had become more rounded. Yet the river still retained a similar shape to the river I had once known so well.

One part of the river was unrecognizable. It was a section that had been straightened by the county because it ducked under the road and the natural course of the river was eroding the buttresses of the bridge. It amazed me that they had to straighten the river for such a long distance from the bridge to avoid the water cutting its old pathway again.

This made me think about the ways that our relationship patterns or "scripts" are like this river. Sometime in the past, scripts were etched into the landscape of your relationships. The constant flow of new experiences followed within the banks of those scripts, reinforcing their already formed paths. Over time, subtle changes modified the patterns of these scripts by simply exaggerating or diminishing certain features, while still keeping their basic form. Like the river of my youth, major changes in your scripts require extensive reconstruction. Patterns will replicate unless a new course is charted. The ruts of old habits must be systematically filled in while new routes are being reinforced. It is not easy, but it can be done.

Your understanding of this continuity of relationship scripts will help you take the ways that your partner treats others and translate them into predictions of your future with this partner. In other words, what you know about a partner's past provides a clue to his or her future.

Think of it like this. Everyone has a limited number of relationship scripts that they follow. These scripts can be categorized by situations and types of people. For example, when you are angry with a boss, a different script comes to mind than if you are angry at someone in your family. Just because you handle these similar situations differently according to the type of person you are involved with does not mean that you are inconsistent or fake. However, when you leave one job and take another, it is likely that you will bring the same set of relationship scripts to your new boss that you followed with your previous one.

It is also possible that in time these scripts will overlap because your boss may start to feel like family or a family member may remind you of a boss. This can happen even when these scripts greatly differ and stay very distinct for a long time. At first you may act quite differently with one person than you act with another. In time, the roles you and this person maintain become blurred, and scripts from other relationships slip in. If this is true for you, then it is also true for the partner you are considering. Once again, this can be a great advantage for you because you can use the ways that your partner treats others as a forecast of how that partner will treat you as time goes on.

A variety of situations reveals the spectrum of scripts you can expect from a partner.

Kurt Lewin, the universally recognized founder of modern social psychology, was born in 1890 and immigrated from Prussia to the United States in 1933. During his short forty-seven years of life, he proposed and developed numerous theories about people and what he called their life spaces. He neatly packaged in a simple yet ingenious formula the way to understand the differences between how people react in similar situations: $B = f(P \times E)$. Let me explain. Human behavior (B) is the result (f stands for "function") of the interaction between characteristics of a person (P) and his or her environment (E). The way in which someone acts is the result of both the situation and the person. On the one hand, you cannot overlook the uniqueness of the situation when you watch how someone acts. But on the other hand, no situation excuses a person from responsibility for his or her actions.

I would like to revise one part of Lewin's formula to fit my theory about other relationships and how they provide useful information about what a partner will be like in a relationship. The formula would be revised as $S = f(P \times E)$ where my term *scripts* (*S*) replaces his term *behavior*. Therefore, you get to know a person's relationship scripts by understanding the interaction between that person's specific personality characteristics and the unique aspects of his or her situation. However, you cannot conclude what a person is like by how he or she acts in one or two situations, but by how he or she acts in a variety of situations. A variety of situations reveals the spectrum of scripts you can expect from a partner. To go back to my analogy of the river, only after numerous explorations of the lay of the land where the river runs, in every possible weather condition, will you be able to accurately map its course and predict its movements.

When you take all of your partner's differing relationship scripts and put them together, you can then see the spectrum or range of how this partner acts in relationships to others and most likely to you. Some people may have very narrow ranges with little variation between how they act with one person or another; others have broad ranges that, at first, may look like they are one person in one setting and someone different in another. These ranges are impossible to know in the beginning of a relationship. They only become apparent as you see a dating partner interact with others, hear stories of past relationships, and take on different roles in your relationship with that partner. Judging a dating partner by just one script may be very misleading because it does not recognize the other ways this person acts—or the *range* of differences in his or her relationship scripts. Don't be fooled! Some of the scripts your partner practices with others may eventually be directed toward you.

Who Are the "Others"?

You should consider three groupings of others when deciphering the relationship scripts used by a particular dating partner: *peripheral* others, *meaningful* others, and *romantic* others. You can imagine these groupings of relationships in three life spaces represented by concentric circles (see Figure 7.1). The circle closest to you signifies those people to whom you are the closest (romantic partners), and likewise, the circle most distant from you involves those people who are most removed from you.

Some of these scripts will be witnessed firsthand by you, and some you will only hear about. Later in this chapter I outline a model for you to follow as you explore the relationship scripts that are in your dating partner's past, especially any previous romantic relationships.

The Good Samaritan

The first interactions you are likely to encounter with a dating partner will be with those on the periphery—that is, others who are strangers or just acquaintances. "What can I learn from watching how someone treats a stranger?" you wonder.

The question of what you can learn from how someone treats a stranger was the subject of an intriguing research study

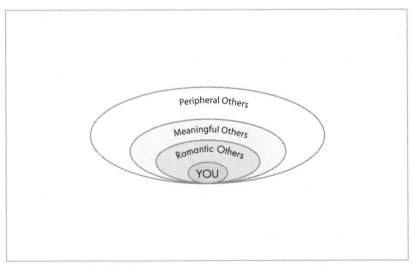

FIGURE 7.1 Circle of Others

conducted at Princeton University in 1973.[1] The study was called the *Good Samaritan* study because it tested the biblical story of the helpful Samaritan. Jewish law stated that you should love your neighbor as yourself. The researchers organized a meeting with sixty-seven seminary students and had them fill out a questionnaire to assess different aspects of their religious faith, values, and personality. They gave the students one of two tasks. The first task was to read the Good Samaritan passage and then give an extemporaneous talk on this story. The second task was to organize and prepare a talk on occupations that seminary students might pursue in addition to ministry-related jobs. All students were given the same map to show them how to get to the room in another building where they would have to give these talks.

The researchers then imposed one of three distinct time conditions on each student. The first condition was a rushed time frame in which the researcher interrupted the explanation of where to go by looking at the clock and telling the student to hurry because the student was already late. The second condition was a moderately urgent time frame where the researcher told the student that he or she needed to go right over because everything was ready. The third condition, a relaxed time frame, acknowledged that there may be a wait, but the student should head on over anyway.

As the students followed the map, little did they know that that a man pretending to be injured had been planted by the researchers in an alley where the students were directed to walk. This man—or a confederate, as he is called in a research project—could not be missed. He was positioned in a doorway, slumped and motionless with his head down and eyes closed, and coughing and groaning as the students walked by.

The results were fascinating. First, this research supported the idea that there are certain behaviors or relationship scripts associated with specific situations for the majority of people. In the case of those who were told they had to "really hurry," 90 percent did not make contact with the stranger. On the other hand, 63 percent of those who were told that they had plenty of time to get to their presentation made an effort to help.

Second, researchers found evidence that the same situation will bring out a range of personal reactions, thus revealing the differences among people. Even though all of those who participated in this study were seminarians, there were some who did not approach the stranger but were distressed by the sight, apparently torn between their own responsibility and his need. There were others who did not even seem to take notice as they rushed by, and then there were those who stepped over the man without showing any concern for his condition. And finally, there were a small number of seminarians who came to be referred to as the "superhelpers" because they insisted on making sure that the confederate (victim) received all the assistance he needed, even if that was more assistance than he stated that he wanted! Therefore, this study supported both ideas that certain situations or contexts prompt common relationship behaviors or scripts in the majority of people, as well as the idea that individual differences will be evident when you see how someone handles a situ-

Along the Way Find Out About . . . Treatment of Strangers

- Do you treat others in any hurtful ways?
- What are the patterns found in your other relationships?
- How do you act toward people you don't know but are angry with?
- How do you treat service people—restaurant servers, cashiers, attendants, and so on?
- What is similar and different between the ways you treat those you don't know and those closest to you?
- How do you show compassion to those who are struggling?

ation compared to others, even those who are very similar to this person (all were seminarians).

You Can Tell a Tree by Its Fruit

What exactly differentiated those who helped (especially the superhelpers) from those who did not was unclear from this study. The only factor that seemed to possibly identify these individuals from the others was a firm set of values and convictions. The superhelpers appeared to have core attitudes that took to heart the morals these individuals espoused.

Since this study was published in 1973, many other researchers have sought to understand what personal qualities really make the difference between how individuals handle others and their needs. Two additional studies help identify these characteristics. Researchers from Columbia University and the University of Colorado combined their efforts to locate and study those Europeans who took daring steps to rescue Jewish Holocaust victims as compared to those who stood by and did nothing.[2] Specific personality traits were found to distinguish the heroes from the bystanders in 93 percent of the cases. Although six total personality characteristics were representative of the rescuers, three traits rose to the top: mature moral reasoning, deeply held moral beliefs about responsibility toward others, and a strong sense of empathy for the pain of others. These three characteristics were evident even in some heroes who were only children. Manya, an eleven-year-old girl, urged a Jewish man to hide in the cellar of an abandoned building near her home. Over a two-year period, she channeled her outrage at the pain of victims into providing her stowaway with clothing supplies and food, even if it required her to give him part or all of her own meals. Another young child, Annie, a ten-year-old girl, helped her parents hide a Jewish butcher and his wife for two and a half years. Annie was one of hundreds of children who assisted their parents' rescue attempts. She would create fictitious stories to explain the strange noises that occasionally echoed from the upstairs bedroom where they were hidden.

This same topic of analyzing the unique characteristics of those who feel deep compassion and responsibility for the plight of those in their peripheral life space was examined from a slightly different angle in the research study conducted on lifelong altruists. Researchers extensively interviewed sixty altruists who had been chosen by a panel of judges and were featured on a national television show as great examples of altruism in the world today. An altruist is one who is concerned and helpful even when no benefits are offered or expected. The first difference between this study and the others on the same topic was that this study expanded the focus of helpfulness to include many diversified acts of kindness (compared to one act, such as rescuing someone in a life-threatening situation). The second difference was that this study chose people who had role-modeled helpfulness throughout their life, not just at one time or in one circumstance. The third difference was that this study examined not just personality characteristics, but also developmental and family experiences.

The findings agreed with other studies on altruism, including the Holocaust rescuers and the Good Samaritans: those who are helpful have a mature moral conscientiousness, a commitment to personal integrity, a sensitive and empathetic nature where it is natural for them to take on the roles of others, and a persistent drive for what they believe in. These qualities appeared to be consistently practiced in all of their relationships, from the peripheral to the most personal. Many of them described their parents as lifelong models from whom they had adopted these values. They remember their parents facing hardships and still reaching out to help others. They used their own difficulties to enable them to identify with the struggles of others, rather than becoming bitter and resentful.

These three studies give credence to the idea that you should pay attention to the ways that your dating partner treats even the stranger on the street. I go back to my original question—"What can I learn from watching how someone treats a stranger?" What we learned from these studies is that the treatment of strangers many times becomes a window to view a partner's depth of empathy, social conscience, and maturity of moral thinking. Watch how your dating partner treats a waiter or waitress, a store clerk, a cashier, a bank teller, or a salesperson and collect the relationship scripts used by your partner. Put them together like a jigsaw puzzle, and you will have a microcosm of the ways your partner is sure to treat you.

How Closeness and Distance Prompt Scripts

Don and Suzanne had been our friends for seven years. Don could be a little pompous at times but was basically friendly and polite. Somewhere around his early forties, Don began to change. His worst traits, previously bearable because they were subtle nuances to his personality, somehow moved front and center. If I go back to my river analogy I would have guessed that something was flooding Don's life. The usual banks that served as boundaries for his emotions and relationship scripts were lost in the massive erosion caused by this flood of a midlife crisis. He changed his job from sales to management and became obsessed with achieving ownership of the company. He bought the proverbial Harley and started wearing leather instead of starch.

One evening my wife and I were riding in the car with them after catching a movie, and Don stopped at a drive-through to buy a cup of coffee. The attendant forgot to give him his requested sugar packets, so after Don received the sugar, he dramatically ripped them open, poured them into his coffee, and proceeded to drop them out his car window and onto the ground as the attendant watched. I knew at that moment that his wife was in for big trouble. If he could be that arrogant and aggressive with a stranger, then what would he do with his closest partner? Sure enough, not long after that we heard that Don was having an affair. He became cold and detached from his wife. She soon knew all too well what the drive-through attendant felt like when her husband's in-your-face attitude came home in greater doses than it had ever been dished out to a stranger. Unfortunately, Don continued to become more and more of a jerk in his marriage, rationalizing his affair and detachment from his wife. You can be sure, though, that the woman he was having the affair with did not see or believe that the scripts he practiced in his marriage would ever be directed toward her. But you know the old saying, "What goes around comes around"—which is especially true with how your partner treats others.

Sooner or later, all relationship scripts emerge in marriage, even those from interactions with strangers. The reason this doesn't happen immediately is because scripts are filed and accessed by categories of closeness. Remember my three concentric circles of closeness: peripheral relationships with the least amount of closeness, significant relationships with moderate to high degrees of closeness, and romantic relationships with the greatest amount of closeness. Specific scripts are most related to each of those categories of closeness, but they all will eventually come out in any long-term relationship. For instance, you have little to no closeness with a stranger, so the ways of relating (scripts) may *seem* to be very different than those used with a dating partner or spouse.

Let's say that you are dating someone who is known to be demanding and hotheaded on the job, yet treats you with complete respect and is willing to do for you whatever you would like. Because you never see the entrance of the employee scripts into your personal relationship, you might wonder why you should worry that they might enter into your marriage with that partner.

The answer is found in the way that your feelings of closeness vary in a long-term relationship. Think about what happens when you and this partner have a fight. Your normal feelings of closeness are temporarily muffled, and instead you feel angry, detached, and distant. The changes in your feelings prompt scripts that are usually not associated with your close and intimate relationship. What scripts are most associated with distant and detached relationships? The peripheral scripts! The result is that you find your partner feeling and acting toward you in ways that had not previously been a part of your relationship. Instead, you get treated more like a stranger or an employee than as a partner. At that point, you realize that feelings vacillate in all relationships, and with the changes in feelings come a spectrum of scripts.

If your partner tells you about getting angry at a coworker and biting that person's head off, then you ought to wonder when that same attitude will be aimed at you. In Don's case, his midlife issues combined with his affair to increase the dominance of his worst traits and decrease his closeness with Suzanne. This triggered scripts that previously were not in the forefront of their marriage relationship but had been lurking behind all along. You should assume that the way your partner treats a stranger or a worst enemy will most likely be the way you will be treated at some point in time.

> *"What goes around comes around"— which is especially true with how your partner treats others.*

Read This Disclaimer

Before we tackle the question of what you can learn from watching how your dating partner handles significant and romantic relationships, one further point falls under the dating disclaimer that we looked at in Chapter 4. If you remember, most people neglect that disclaimer. It explained the way dating behaviors translate into marriage behaviors: "The good doesn't always last, and the bad usually gets worse."

Some people are great in how they treat others while dating. Even after marriage, this person continues to treat everyone like gold—except *you*, the spouse. They do everything for everybody, always going to the neighbors to do some odd job. But when you need something, this person is completely resentful. This is the proverbial shoemaker who has made shoes for the entire town, but his wife and kids are shoeless. This is an example of the good having gone bad.

Most times, people like this are giving only to boost their own ego needs rather than to benefit others. This can be difficult to determine, and often you have to consider the dynamics from their family of origin in order to understand their behavior. The entire next chapter excavates the influences that childhood experiences and family interactions have on relationships. But suffice it to say, your dating partner's treatment of others typically provides you with a crystal ball through which you can see both the moral fiber of that partner, as well as some of the relationship scripts that in time are likely to become woven into your relationship.

The Friends and Family Plan

What is true for the peripheral group of relationships is equally true for the significant and romantic groups. Here's a quick summary of the theory of relationship continuity that we already described.

1. Patterns or scripts that your partner uses in one set of relationships will most likely be introduced into your relationship.
2. Whatever happened in a past relationship has a high chance of occurring again in a future parallel relationship.
3. Relationships can be grouped together by degree of closeness (peripheral, significant, or romantic).
4. Scripts—attitude and behavioral patterns in relationships—are often prompted by the feelings of closeness (or lack thereof).

5. Therefore, scripts are often divided up among the three groups. A script that is associated with the peripheral group can appear unrelated to the romantic group.
6. However, varying experiences of closeness in a long-term relationship can pull scripts from one group over into another.
7. Therefore, look very closely at the ways your partner treats *all* other people. It may be just a matter of time before you are treated the same.

The second grouping of "others" involves those whom you or your partner consider significant—your friends and family (including your children, if you have any). You typically meet your dating partner's friends early in a relationship. Sometimes you know the friends even before you begin dating. For instance, it may have been a friend that introduced you. Often, it is not until later that you meet the family. This may depend upon the proximity of family to where this person lives and works. If your dating partner has children, you probably will meet them sometime within the first three months. Many times you hear about the children before you actually ever interact with them.

What can you learn from this group of significant people in your partner's life? If peripheral relationships crack open a window to peer into the values and character of a partner, then significant relationships bust down the door. It is within this arena of close relationships that you begin to see subtle signs of how your partner handles power and shows respect. Ultimately, marriage is to be a union of best friends. So check out how this partner treats his or her best friends. Does your partner

- return phone calls?
- answer e-mails?
- admit when he or she is wrong?
- apologize?
- arrive on time?
- keep promises?
- always complain?

- act more like a taker or a giver?
- remember special occasions?
- genuinely listen to friends?
- open up to friends?
- pick friends up or pull them down?
- respect friends?
- constantly act angry or hurt?
- initiate activities and involvement?
- address conflicts or problems in positive ways?
- seem overly dependent?

If your partner does not treat friends in ways that you admire, then what makes you think your partner will do this with you? At the very least, listen to what your partner's friends say about him or her. Many times friends are blunt and accurately depicting. You do not need to believe their every word; on the other hand, do not dismiss what they say, because it will possibly eventually surface in your relationship.

It may make you feel in the inner circle when your partner privately talks about his or her friends, coworkers, or family members. However, take note of what your partner says about them. Is it justified? Is it fair? Is it realistic? Is it accurate? Would you want your partner representing you to someone else?

Yes, there are those who treat a friend better than a boyfriend or girlfriend (or spouse), but not many treat a spouse significantly better than they have ever treated any other friend. In other words, the friendship patterns your partner has developed usually provide you with the extent of the potential of what you can have in a romantic relationship with that person, although it is not a guarantee.

Birds of a Feather Flock Together

Margo described herself as having lived two lives: pre-Steve and post-Steve. "I was a different person before we started going

---

Along the Way Find Out About . . . Treatment of Friends

- How do you treat your friends?
- How do your friends treat you?
- Do you like your partner's friends?
- How are you similar and different to your friends?
- How important are your friendships?
- What do you do with friends?

---

out," she lamented as she twisted her hands. Margo was a junior in college and had met Steve in the beginning of her senior year of high school.

"He was definitely in the cool group in high school," she explained. "I was amazed that he even noticed me, and when he asked me out, I was ecstatic."

"What was Steve like?" I inquired.

"He was a bad good-boy." Margo went on to elucidate. "You see, there were the bad boys who clearly were rebels in their dress, lifestyle, and reputation. Then there were the good boys who were nice, respectful, and well-liked. But then there were the bad good-boys who looked like the good boys, but quietly acted like the bad boys. Most of Steve's friends partied and messed around. They were really confident—no, more like cocky. They were extroverted and seemed to always be where the action was happening."

"And what were you like before you met Steve?" I asked.

"I was definitely a good girl. I was maintaining a 4.0 GPA and never drank alcohol or partied. This is a little embarrassing, but I was still a virgin when I met Steve—he was my first."

"So what happened?"

"We started going out and at first, it was always Steve and I getting together. He was really sweet and spent most of his time with me. After a few weeks, though, we started hanging out with his friends, and I felt totally out of place. They would drink, get high, and talk about stuff I wasn't into. But Steve continued to stick with me, and that made me feel better. This slowly changed, and I found myself feeling more at home with his friends and opening up to their lifestyle. By the time I graduated, I was acting just like them."

Margo and Steve continued to stay together after high school. Margo attended a nearby college because Steve was enrolled in a police academy close to their town. She always drove to see him on the weekends, still hanging out with many from the same old high school group. Margo knew Steve sometimes hooked up with other women behind her back, but she felt completely invested in their relationship, as if her identity was so tied with Steve that she could never break up. Anyway, it was not in her nature to give up or admit defeat. She was determined to make this relationship work.

Margo admitted that the handwriting was on the wall when she thought back to the types of friends that Steve had, but she hadn't given it a lot of thought while in high school.

Your partner's friends will mirror qualities that often exist in your partner.

"I knew their reputation, how they treated girlfriends, and what they were into; I just didn't think it would really affect me as I became involved with Steve. I figured Steve would eventually grow out of his lifestyle. I never imagined that I would become just like him."

You can learn many things about a person just by looking at his or her friends. We already established that your partner's interactions with those in the periphery (i.e., strangers, acquaintances, and general social interactions) will reveal some of the scripts your partner uses. But friendships provide another piece to the puzzle of what a partner will be like in marriage, which the treatment of peripheral others does not entail. This piece is found in the "Birds of a feather flock together" principle of human relationships. Basically, we associate with people who are similar to us in values, attitudes, personality, age, status, and lifestyle. Sometimes it is unclear whether you are drawn to the group because you are similar to them, or if your association with them has shaped you into their likeness. In either case, people have friendships with those whom they resemble. Therefore, your partner's friends will mirror qualities that often exist in your partner.

Margo realized that Steve's friends were more than just people Steve associated with—they were reflections of Steve. Margo had never asked herself the question: What do his friends tell me about this guy? Of course, his friends were not his exact replicas. In fact, you may have friends whom you spend more time helping than anything else. But doesn't that tell you something about who you are and the scripts you follow in your friendships? If you provide regular, free counseling for a couple of perpetually troubled friends, then it's very likely an integral part of your personality is being a tolerant, caring helper. Therefore, both the scripts a person practices *and* the types of friends he or she has will provide you with clues as to what this person will be like as a romantic partner.

"Ex" Marks the Spot

In the previous section, you found that the way your partner relates to people in daily life (i.e., peripheral realm) provides an array of relationship scripts that are likely to occur in a long-term relationship. In addition, your partner's friends and patterns of friendships also portray characteristics of your partner that may be hidden in your dating relationship.

We now come to the last set of relationships—previous dating and romantic partners—that are important to scan for clues about how your dating partner acts, feels, and thinks in relationships.

So what are you to make of your dating partner's past relationships? Is there any value to his or her track record? What if there are skeletons in the closet? Certainly, you do not want to be forever judged by your past. Everyone needs a fresh start, a clean slate, a new beginning. "Let go of the past and reach for the future," we are told. So what are we to believe? When you find an X on the map of your partner's dating history, are you to believe that there is a buried treasure of insight or just an empty grave?

The dilemma many of you have found yourself in as you hear about past romantic relationship(s) can be characterized by two opposing sayings: "History always repeats itself" and "There is an exception to every rule." There is a battle for your allegiance when you learn something from your partner's relationship track record. Usually, if it is negative, you apply the first saying. But when you become a bit more emotionally involved with a person, you become easily convinced that *you* are the one true exception.

"I Was Never in Love Like This"

What do you think when you discover that your partner has a sordid past? Do you remember Tonya and Will from Chapter 3? They had a whirlwind romance, moving in together in the morning, then separating by the evening. Will had a long string of broken relationships and one-night stands. But he convinced Tonya that he had never been in love with any of them. Tonya was his first—true love, that is. However, Tonya learned very quickly that true love to Will was quite fleeting, lasting only twelve hours.

Some common "romantic one-liners" can sometimes be "fatal cover-ups."

- "No one has ever made me feel the way you do."
- "I was never in love until I met you."
- "No one ever understood me (or completed me) like you do."
- "I was never ready to settle down until I met you."

These phrases express the essence of falling in love. Romantic story lines capture this mysterious and wonderful experience of finding true love, your one-and-only, your soul mate, and your best friend.

The danger lies in the next phrase: *"and that is why I will never act the way I did in the past."* In other words, "I acted like a jerk in other relationships because I wasn't really *in love*. But now that I have met you (my one true love), I will never act like that again." Sounds promising, but be careful. It may be misleading.

The idea that true love magically changes someone from the patterns of his or her past is hardly ever the case. A number of research studies have shown that the dramatic changes that occur with a new relationship usually revert back to the prerelationship state by the end of the first year of marriage.[3] Yet it is emotionally intoxicating to think that someone loves you so much that his or her life has been completely transformed. Use the test of the four ingredients for effective change to make sure that your partner's true love is a lasting love—insight, new information, and motivated hard work over time (Chapter 3).

Sometimes a person's dating reputation precedes him or her. At other times, you discover your partner's reputation as you grow in your relationship. In both cases, nuggets of insight usually are embedded in the details of his or her other dating relationship(s). It is imperative that you understand the theory of relationship continuity so you do not overlook clues of future difficulties by dismissing past relationship problems. There definitely are parallel patterns between present and past relationships. Hopefully, you will discover scripts from the past that are similar to what you want in a partner.

Playing Detective

It is an art to excavate these nuggets of insight in subtle ways so as not to interrogate a dating partner. I have developed a strategy for uncovering the vital facts from previous relationships

Along the Way Find Out About . . . Treatment of Past Romantic Partners

- What did your previous partners like and dislike about you?
- What did you like or dislike about them?
- What do you wish you had done differently?
- How do you describe your previous partners?
- How did you fight with previous partners?
- How long were your relationships?
- How did your relationship(s) break up?
- What is your relationship now with the previous partner(s)?
- What did you like to do in the previous relationship(s)?
- How were arguments resolved?
- What did you argue about?

without being judgmental or insulting. I refer to my strategy as the Columbo technique.

Columbo was a short, scrappy, cigar-smoking television detective who always appeared confused and incompetent. This image was his greatest asset, because he would lure the suspect into feeling overconfident and eventually tipping him off to some clue that would convict the suspect. His approach had four basic elements.

1. *Postpone conclusions until all is known.* Columbo had a knack of convincing the guilty that no one suspected them. He did not put people on the defensive. In the same way, you should genuinely listen and suspend your reactions *and* your judgment until you have listened thoroughly (maybe more than once) and reflected on the stories of previous relationships. Develop the ability

of asking questions without appearing accusing or mistrusting. "Innocent until proven guilty" is a good motto to practice, even when you know there are some questionable issues in your partner's past.

2. *The more you know the better.* This is important even though some aspects of previous relationships may be very sensitive. We all make mistakes. We all have our regrets: "Even in a good apple you sometimes find a worm." But patterns are detected through repeated behaviors. Therefore, without some amount of detail you will not be able to differentiate between regrettable actions that occurred during unusual circumstances and patterns that are likely to reoccur in future relationships.

3. *Look at the person from the perspectives of others.* Ask what complaints were made by the former partners. Resist the natural urge to dismiss every former partner as *evil.* Assume that the previous partners were not much different from you (remember, *you* are a previous partner to someone). Add up the complaints, and consider why they were made and what you should expect if they turn out accurate and true.

4. *Test your theories.* This can be done in many ways. Listen to the stories of families and friends. Do they confirm or deny your theory? Watch for any signs of the past patterns in your present relationship. Explore the early experiences of previous relationships, and compare them with the later patterns. Columbo never confronted any suspect with his theory until he had tested it several ways and had become convinced of the accuracy of his interpretation.

It needs to be emphasized again that you are looking for *both* the good and the bad. If you only focus on the bad, you will become mistrusting and overreactive. However, if you always use the good to rationalize the bad, you will become naive. You are on fairly safe ground when the patterns of how your partner related in past relationships are similar to how you would like him or her to relate to you. For better or for worse, history usually does repeat itself.

Dating Partners with Children

This last section may not apply to you if you do not have children and are not considering dating anyone who does. But dating partners with young children has become more common than ever before, largely because of the increased divorce rate over the last several generations. It may be something you face at some time in your life.

This topic gets addressed in both Chapter 5 on compatibility, where I talk about some of what is involved with dating while having children, and this chapter on other relationships. To be honest, on its own this area could be a book. For the purposes of this chapter, I will limit this focus on a partner with children to the salient features that pertain to dating, parenting, and the significance of children in your future relationship. Answers to three questions encapsulate the key content that you should consider in this complex matter. If you are serious with a partner who has children, then you should consider getting additional resources that help facilitate a smooth transition into a blended family.

How Long Should I Date Someone Before I Meet Their Child(ren)?

I addressed this question in Chapter 5 for anyone who has children. I suggested that you should apply the three-month rule because it takes three months for many subtle but serious patterns to begin to surface. The same reasoning applies to meeting the children of someone you are dating. You need to first get to know the person you are dating independently from the children, because your relationship must ultimately become the foundation for all the other relationships. There are many stresses with children that strain the best of relationships. Your ability to handle these challenges will depend upon the strength of you and your partner's skills and bond.

Some people are tempted to immediately "court" the dating partner's children. Many dating partners unwittingly prompt this. I recommend that you resist this temptation. There are single parents who feel desperate for a partner to help with the care of the kids. This may be due to discipline problems, but it could also be due to an empathetic wish for their children to have a father or a mother. This is often the case when the children lack closeness with their other parent.

When you bond too soon with your partner's children, you risk deeply wounding the children if your relationship does not last. This is particularly true when the children crave attention and closeness with a distant parent. Even though your intentions are honorable, it is not fair to the children. Better to wait too long to bond with a partner's child than to bond too soon.

How Is the Dating Relationship Different When Children Are Involved?

First and foremost, it takes *more time* to build a relationship strong enough to handle the complications of blending a family. If the time frame for a childless couple to really get to know each other well enough to marry is two years, then it takes even longer to create a good fit between the family members. The greater the number of children involved, the more time and work is required. Think about it. If both you and your partner already have children, then you have to harmonize your already established parenting styles. Your partner's children are used to your partner's parenting style, and they may have a very hard time adjusting to the different style of parenting you bring to the relationship. In fact, your partner may have an equally difficult time with your approach. These conflicts quickly open the door to power struggles and divisions among family members.

Jaime had been divorced for two years when she met Darren. Her four boys were "all boy." Their father loved the outdoors and instilled in his sons a wild spirit. They were a handful for

Jaime, especially since her divorce. She had done her best to provide assistance with school difficulties, although she often felt overwhelmed and unable to consistently maintain the structure of her home. Squabbles were common, and the critical attacks of her ex only inflamed the tensions between her and her boys. It seemed that they took turns in the ring with her—when one stepped out, another stepped in.

She met Darren on an online dating website and immediately felt a strong connection. He was an engineer who had been divorced for five years. He owned a home in the same neighborhood as his ex so that his three daughters could freely come and go as they wished. The girls were organized, structured, and responsible.

You could caricature the blending of their two sets of kids as the princess and the pea meets Lewis and Clark. No doubt, Jaime and Darren loved each other and were drawn together by the different qualities each saw in the other. Jaime had a spontaneous and igniting spirit that lit a fire under Darren, while Darren's steadfastness and consistency brought security to Jaime's hectic and often chaotic world. Together, they felt fulfilled and complete.

After they married, they realized that blending their differences in the parenting process required more than what they had experienced during dating. Each child widened the gap between their parenting styles. As a result, Darren felt angry at Jaime's lack of follow-through, while Jamie felt insecure around Darren's methodical approach. The kids picked up on the tension in the newly formed family and seemed to become worse rather than better.

Jaime and Darren were not ready for such a radical adjustment. They had not imagined that their love could so quickly turn cold. But this can easily happen when you have not taken enough time to address differences in your parenting styles. They continued to work together. Darren tried to be more patient and less critical, and Jaime read some books on parenting and attended a class on becoming more focused and organized.

In time, they were able to once again appreciate the differences that almost drove them apart. If they had to do it all over again, they would have taken more time to get on the same page in their parenting styles before they married. In a sense, they were ready to marry as a couple, but not as a family.

Dating a partner with children requires that you have both couple dates and family dates. As your relationship with the partner becomes increasingly serious, you will build more of a relationship with your partner's children. It is at this time that it is appropriate to court the children. By this I mean that you begin expanding your relationships with the children. You should even find one-on-one time with them in order to establish stronger bonds. You can talk about your relationship with each of the children and listen to the feelings they have for you. These bonds will greatly help the adjustment process, create feelings of cohesion within the mixed group, and reduce potential power struggles. It is always easier to maintain than to create bonds with step-children after marriage.

A final difference between dating a partner with children and one who is childless is the presence (and sometimes complication) of the other parent in the daily schedule. The visitation structures, the type of parenting arrangement, the extent of each parent's involvement, and the degree of cooperativeness between the parents are just some of the sources of conflict that are not present with childless dating couples. It becomes more important to find a balance between structure and spontaneity in the dating routine. If there is a shared visitation, then you will spend some weekends with the kids and others without. On the one hand, this reduces the time alone you have as a couple; but on the other hand, it provides a built-in schedule for doing things together as a family.

What Can I Learn About a Partner from His or Her Child(ren)?

Dating a partner with children has its advantages, especially when it comes to trying to figure out what this partner would be like in a marriage and family. You have a preview of your future with this dating partner in the ways that he or she manages the kids' schedules, organizes their activities, shows affection, disciplines, talks, handles conflicts, deals with stress, and relates with you in the midst of all these experiences. This was something that Darren and Jaime needed to take more seriously when they were dating. It was not hard to see the engineer in Darren's parenting style. If all you knew were his daughters, you could still get a sense of what Darren was like. They were a reflection of him in many ways. Jaime should have known that Darren would have a low tolerance for chaos and most likely become frustrated and critical if it continued.

Jaime did fine on her own with her kids. When Darren stopped by her house during their dating, he learned that she functioned more in the moment with her boys. This was what Jaime was like as a person, not just a parent. Darren should have known that Jaime and her boys were going to change the mood of his docile home to one of feisty and constant motion with a significantly louder volume. If he thought that his style was going to be dominant, then he had not given enough thought to what Jaime was really like and how entrenched the patterns were in her relationships with the boys.

Both the parenting style and the children's dispositions provide tremendous sources of insight into the partner you are considering. Many of the patterns or scripts that are hidden in a dating relationship are those that have their roots in one's family of origin. These scripts become reenacted in the roles and interactions that develop between a parent and his or her children. Knowing how to "read" a partner's exchanges with his or her children will help you decipher what is important to your relationship and future.

DON'T FORGET

- The theory of relationship continuity says that there is similarity, connection, and overlap between the ways you act in your various relationships. History often repeats itself, so pay attention to how you and your partner behaved in past relationships, as well as how others are now treated.

- Your understanding of this continuity of relationship scripts will help you take the ways that your partner treats others and translate them into predictions of your future with this partner.

- When deciphering the relationship scripts used by your partner, make sure to investigate these four relationship types: peripheral others, significant others, past romantic partners, and yourself.

- Sooner or later, all relationship scripts emerge in marriage.

- Pay attention to your partner's friends, because they often mirror qualities that exist in your partner.

- Practice the Columbo technique: postpone conclusions until all is known, realize that the more you know the better, look at your partner from the perspectives of others, and test your theories.

- Dating someone with children involves consideration of more issues than just your relationship with the partner.

You Can't Marry Jethro Without Gettin' the Clampetts

Step Four: Getting to Know the Patterns of a Family Background

The Apple Doesn't Fall Far from the Tree

Childhood experiences are some of the strongest predictors of what your mate will be like as a spouse and parent. I will never forget Elizabeth, a stoic woman in her late sixties. She was intelligent, rational, and staunch. When she first sat in my office for counseling, she presented an unusual concern: she smoked three cigarettes a day and wanted help in quitting.

One of my immediate thoughts was, "Who is willing to spend money to consult with a doctor about smoking only three cigarettes a day?" The answer probably was a person who has a hidden agenda.

We attempted some behavioral strategies to help her kick her habit, but nothing worked. After several sessions I suggested that we take a break from her cigarette issue. I asked her to tell me about her childhood and early family experiences. As she described her memories, she drifted back in time. Her eyes glazed over, and she seemed to regress to the age of her childhood stories.

"I can remember the day I was adopted," she began. "I was five years old and had been moved around between the orphanage and various foster homes. I stepped off the train with the caseworker and came face-to-face with my new adopted mother. I only had one possession in the world—my little, ragged teddy bear. He had been with me since I could remember and was the only thread of continuity in my life."

By now, she had shifted her posture to pull her feet under her body and was seated on my couch much like a small child. She spoke more intensely, "I stood while this woman explained that she would be my new mother and that everything would be new and exciting in my life. She said we would start with replacing the old bear with a brand-new one. At that moment she took my teddy bear from me and tossed him in the garbage."

Childhood experiences are some of the strongest predictors of what your mate will be like as a spouse and parent.

At this point Elizabeth burst into tears and twisted into a fetal position. For twenty minutes she shook and wept. When she returned to the present, we explored the impact of losing her only source of security and continuity. Although her new mother meant well, it was a devastating experience for a five-year-old girl.

Over the next several sessions we discussed ways to comfort, encourage, and relax oneself. After about the fifth session Elizabeth proudly announced that she had not smoked any cigarettes for two weeks. What was even more important was that she was learning to show and receive affection. She started hugging her grandchildren for the first time ever. This was something she had never done with her own children.

I had a strange follow-up to this case. Six years later I happened to meet Elizabeth again, because of a family crisis. I reminded her of that unique experience of regression during her previous therapy and asked her about her old smoking habit. She was still smoke-free, although she did not remember that counseling session. Even so, she had become freed from a cell of insecurity and self-protection that had locked up her affections for more than sixty years.

Elizabeth had been married, raised a family, been widowed, remarried, and was actively involved with grandchildren. But her early childhood feelings of abandonment had influenced her expression of affection in both marriages and with all her children and grandchildren. Her life demonstrated the effect that childhood development has upon the relationships a person creates. But, Elizabeth also exemplified the possibility of change at any age. With her openness, insight, and effort, she moved beyond her walls and expanded the horizons of her relationship patterns.

Remember, although there is little from your family and childhood that will not influence your present, there is also much that can be altered and redeemed with insight, new information, and hard work. However, *relational insight and change are much more easily accomplished before rather than after marriage.* Numerous factors contribute to receptivity to change. The insecurity of the unmarried state, the quest to impress, and the strong feelings of love and infatuation—all of these factors become blended together to produce a willingness to change and improve. In a relatively short time after the exchanging of vows, this receptivity lessens and an increasing inflexibility sets in. Significant experiences from your family of origin should be discussed and deeply explored as a couple before marriage. Patterns that you want to alter should be identified and worked on before you approach the wedding altar (*"alter* before you *altar"*).

First Area of Exploration: The Degree of Closeness in a Family

America has been called the melting pot of the world. There are still many who wave the flag of their national heritage with pride. Most of us know the stereotypes of these different cultures. As I have conducted the "How to Avoid Marrying a Jerk" seminar over the years, I have made it a practice of asking about hypothetical marriage unions between different nationalities. I do this to illustrate the predictability of certain aspects of family backgrounds.

Susan, an outgoing Jewish New Yorker, was dating Carlos, a recent immigrant from the Dominican Republic. While he thought it was perfectly normal to live one floor below his parents in the same apartment building, Susan saw this as a sign of being tied to Momma's apron strings. What was normal for Carlos was abnormal to Susan. Even though she understood that in Latin culture sons are expected to stay within the family circle until they marry, it became increasingly apparent over the course of their relationship that Susan and Carlos viewed their world through the lenses of their family cultures.

Closeness within a family is generated by an environment of openness and involvement.

Susan, the youngest daughter of two independent Eastern European intellectuals who had moved thousands of miles from their own parents, instilled in her the importance of autonomy. She was raised to believe that you should keep ties with your family while creating your own life apart from their presence. Periodic visits were expected and welcomed, but there wasn't daily togetherness. Carlos, on the other hand, regularly slipped upstairs to his parents' abode for the evening meal.

Who was right and who was wrong? The answer: none of the above. The problem was with the clash of family cultures where both were committed to the way they had been raised. Having to adapt to the way that your partner's family practices closeness can be a source of tension when cultural differences have deep roots.

The Circle of Closeness

Closeness within a family is generated by an environment of *openness* and *involvement*. These two gauges tend to set the temperature of the mood of the home, producing feelings of security and acceptance when expressed appropriately. Close families are open with their feelings and experiences.

Ethnic stereotypes often depict some aspect of how openly affection is shown. It is very likely that the person you marry will re-create the mood and atmosphere of the home in which he or she was raised.

When I reflect on my own family I think this is very true. My parents had a good marriage. They were both quite affectionate with each other. I remember seeing them walk hand in hand or sit and snuggle on a couch. My mother was a caregiver and more verbal and affectionate with her children than was my father. His English and Dutch backgrounds contributed to some of his stereotypical dry humor (I refer to him as the original Mr. Bean), hard work, and perfectionism. My mother, with some of her Irish background, was more animated and expressive.

My father bought a pleasure farm with the hopes that it would be an adventurous place to raise a family of five. He had many fond childhood memories of spending summers on a farm owned by friends of his family. Growing up during the Depression, he found it a wonderful escape for him from life in the big city.

When I was twelve years old, my mother was diagnosed with cancer. Her struggle lasted two long years. During that time we watched her slowly go downhill physically, never complaining, but also never talking about death. As obvious as it should have been, I never realized my mother was dying until just a couple of weeks prior to her death. I overheard my brother talking to her in the hospital during a phone call. He said, "Mom, I love you." For some reason it then hit me—Mom was leaving. She died the first day of my sophomore year of high school. With two sisters married, the third in college, and my brother leaving home to begin his college education, an eerie silence blanketed the large farmhouse. For the first time, my dad and I were more like bachelors than family.

When someone you love dies, there is a definite time and process of grieving. Every member of my family experienced it, although most of us never talked about it. My brother struggled in college, my father started dating within months, and I remember becoming more reflective and independent, radically changing my lifestyle and friends.

During the nine months after my mother died, I longed for a deeper connection with my father. I could not remember anytime when he had said, "I love you." Now do not misunderstand me, I knew he loved me. But I just wanted and needed to hear it. Maybe he had always said it when I was younger, and I had forgotten. Nonetheless, it seemed as if I had never heard from him those powerful three words. I could feel the lingering effects from the hugs of other family members and my mother's voice echoing in my mind, yet my dad was now the only one still with me at home.

I decided that I would make the first step. He was sitting in the living room reading the newspaper. I paced back and forth, carefully planning my words. I would tell him that I love him, and then he would say it back. Maybe I had never said it to him. Someone had to start.

After a long deliberation, I peeked my head into the room. "Dad," I interrupted, "I am going to bed now." He looked at me over the top of the newspaper. "So good night," I continued, "and, uh, Dad, I love you." After a pause that seemed to last a lifetime, he awkwardly replied, "Me, too—good night."

I will never forget that night. I went to my bedroom and thought, "Me, too?" What does that mean? I love you and you love yourself, too? Hey, who loves me?

I did not approach him again with those words until my freshman year of college. I had made a strong commitment of faith during my senior year of high school, and this had helped me resolve many of the issues that were in my life at that time. While I was preparing to leave for college, I decided to embrace my dad and say the words, "I love you" each time I left and returned. So I did!

He would reach out his hand to shake mine, and I would grab it, pull him in for a bear hug, look him in the eye, and say, "Dad, I love you." And he would reply, "Me, too."

You can imagine his chagrin when I would announce I was coming home for a visit. No one likes to be taken out of his or her comfort zone. But I continued my "torture," and slowly he began to say, "I love you, too." That eventually evolved into just "I love you." Throughout the last fifteen or twenty years, I don't think I have ever ended a phone conversation with my dad without hearing him say, "John, I love you," to which I humorously replied, "Me, too."

Patterns from childhood often recur in adult relationships unless essential efforts are made to change.

The expression of affection is one of the major determiners of the atmosphere of closeness within a family. I could have either repeated my dad's earlier discomfort with affection or moved through the uncomfortable feelings and changed the pattern. I chose the latter and worked hard to say and show my feelings. In Chapter 3 I described the four important ingredients necessary for personal change: insight, new information, motivated efforts, and time. I was fortunate to gain insight into my own family experiences at a relatively young age and to do the necessary work to get out of my father's comfort zone and establish a more expressive way of showing love.

Patterns from childhood often recur in adult relationships unless essential efforts are made to change. Therefore, look closely at the background of the person you date, his or her family role, and the specific patterns and experience taken from his or her home. I inherited many good things from my upbringing. But I also improved on the way affection was expressed, especially to my own children.

I cannot emphasize this enough: take the time to explore the family experiences of the person you are dating. Weigh the differences between his or her present behavior and the patterns of the past. Do not assume that the past dynamics will *not* recur, unless you can see clear evidence of your partner's insight and effort at changing them. Discuss the impact of family background, and be willing on your own part to take the necessary steps to prevent a reoccurrence of what you did not like in your own home life.

As mentioned earlier, closeness is produced by an atmosphere of openness *and* involvement. The openness of affection needs to be matched with openness in talking. I have counseled many families who never talk or really listen to each other.

Several years after Elizabeth had her last cigarette, she referred her son, Bill, and his family to me. When they arrived for their

Along the Way Find Out About . . . Family Affection and Aggression

- What was the mood or atmosphere in the home?
- How was affection shown?
- What made you feel special in the family?
- Who were you close to in your family?
- How did you know that you were loved by your mother (or female caregiver)? Your father (or male caregiver)?
- How were conflicts handled by your parents (or caregivers)?
- What did you do when you were angry at your mother? At your father? At your sibling(s)?
- How did your mother and father handle their anger?

first session, Bill, his wife, Jean, and their two boys and two girls distributed themselves among the different seats in my office like mice scurrying to their safe holes in the wall. They politely answered my questions about their personal activities, but had very little eye contact with each other. They admitted that they never talked openly or showed much affection with each other. For the most part, each did his or her own thing with very little involvement of other family members. I asked one of the girls to share with her father some of her experiences in gymnastics—a sport he had only attended twice in the last four years of her classes. At first it was awkward. But as he genuinely probed, she warmed up. She even tearfully explained how much she wanted his attention and approval. With a little coaching, he was able to apologize and affirm his love and interest in his daughter.

Two outcomes occurred. First, at the end of the session Bill and his daughter hugged. The rest of the family was visibly moved and closed some of the distance between them. Expressions of affection will usually flow from open, accepting talks. When you share something personal about yourself, you feel connected. Affectionate exchanges are natural and meaningful after your feelings are understood by someone in your family.

Second, Bill wanted to attend more of her activities, including her gymnastics. This led to discussions about each of the children's interests and their desire to have both Mom and Dad attend more of their events. Openness prompted a greater interest for involvement. With the parents attending these events, the family had more common experiences to share together when they talked. This is an example of the "circle of closeness," a model that describes the momentum a relationship gains when there is a reciprocal exchange between involvement and openness (see Figure 8.1 on the next page). As family members support each other in their respective activities, the stage is set for open sharing and affectionate responses.

Over the course of life, families travel across various terrains. Sometimes a major shift in landscape occurs in the form of a crisis. At other times, changes are subtle. In both occurrences,

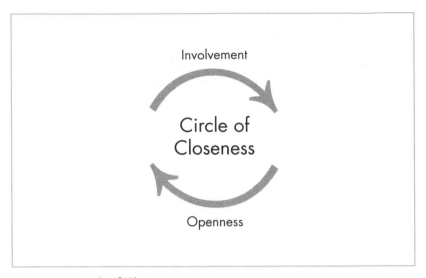

Involvement

Circle of
Closeness

Openness

FIGURE 8.1 Circle of Closeness

the openness and involvement of family members with each other can decrease, interrupting the circle of closeness. When exploring the family background of the person you are dating, look for these types of changes. When these changes happened, insecurity and emotional instability replaced the safe feelings that once dominated the mood of the home.

Andrew was only four when his mother walked out for good. He had two older brothers, John, fifteen, and Bryan, twenty. His mother had crashed into her midlife and had a secret affair with a high school senior whom she had met at her job.

It had been three months since Andrew had heard from or seen his mother. His father brought him to see me because Andrew was experiencing severe separation anxiety. I will never forget the day Andrew walked into my office. He was adorable with his cute suspenders and mini bow tie. His eyes were round like saucers, and his voice gentle and quiet. To become better acquainted, I suggested that he draw a picture of his family. He sat down and went to work for more than thirty minutes. When he was finished, he handed me a complex pencil drawing of lines and circles that practically blackened the white paper. I asked what each "thing" was. He pointed to six circles: "Dad, Bryan,

Bryan's girlfriend, John, me, and Chester—our dog," he replied. A grid of checkered lines covered the entire page.

"What is this?" I inquired.

"A spider's web," he explained. "This is the big spider here in the corner."

"What is it doing?" I asked.

He answered, "It is eating all the stinging ants that are attacking us. We are hiding behind the spider's web to keep safe."

"Your family—they are all hurting? Why?" I wondered.

Tears streamed from his eyes, but he did not move a muscle. "Everyone's hurtin'," he strained, "since Mommy left."

Few adults could have described the mixed mood of this home any better than Andrew. Fear, pain, risk, and the need for protection resulted from the loss of closeness when Mom abandoned the family.

Imagine Andrew in twenty years. We know that this experience deeply affected him when he was four. But how do you think it will impact his perspective on marriage? A wife? A family? His feelings of security and trust toward a wife, the *mother* of his children, will depend on the ways he resolved the deep loss of closeness with his own mother. Gaining an understanding of how Andrew made it through this brutal time in his childhood will provide windows through which you can peer into his future role as a husband and father. Exploring the family background identifies dormant emotional patterns that are likely to bloom in the family you create. Working to change these areas before you marry will prevent repeating them in the family you establish.

Second Area of Exploration: The Structure of a Family

The most important aspect of family structure that is vital to the topic of mate selection is the *formation of roles*. Roles provide a working definition of each member's place in the family. They are like job descriptions. For instance, in one type of family, the role

The most important aspect of family structure that is vital to the topic of mate selection is the formation of roles.

of a father is defined as a powerful, dreaded authoritarian who works for the good of the whole and punishes any member who steps out of line. In another type of family, the father role is defined as a playful, easygoing protector who stabilizes the mood of the home. Think about this. Would the woman who grew up within the first family look at men, husbands, and fathers in the same way as the woman who grew up in the second? Of course not! Similarly, the man who grew up with the authoritarian father role would feel radically different than the man who grew up with the stabilizing father role.

Two crucial relationships influence the formation of these roles: your relationship with your same-sex parent and your relationship with your opposite-sex parent. Before we examine each of these relationships and the things they suggest about what a person brings into a marriage relationship, let's first look at the *way* someone learns.

Connections That Transfer Life Roles

Children learn through connections. Half of what you will know by the end of your life was learned by the time you could talk. Not all learning requires language. Many people learn all about being a spouse and parent without ever engaging in discussion on the topic. So how did they learn? They internalized these things through the connections in their family. Children who do not form connections (attachments) are usually unable to make lasting adult attachments.

John Bowlby, the pioneer of attachment theory in the 1960s, concluded that a child develops a specific pattern of reacting to separation based on the type of attachment the child formed with the caregiver. These types of attachment were later categorized by Mary Ainsworth (one of the most prominent researchers on attachment theory): the secure attachment, the anxious/ambivalent attachment, and the avoidant attachment. Research has tended to support the idea that the style of attachment an infant learns will most likely continue into adulthood. Therefore, this attachment style is like a mental map someone follows each time that person develops a relationship. In other words, the earliest experiences of attachment become the unconscious mold that will be used to cast the script of closeness in future relationships.

Getting to know the attachment style someone had in his or her family of origin often predicts the type of attachments that person will form in the family he or she establishes. Find out who the person was closest to in the family. How did the person feel in that relationship? Did the person experience secure attachments with any members of the family? The connections you made in your first family become the channels of learning and development for the roles you will establish in your next family.

The person you most connected with is often the person you are most like. Usually we think of a connection of closeness, but sometimes it is a connection of conflict that transfers the learning. When a teenager always fights with one of the parents, it usually means the teen is much like that parent. You can be fooled into thinking that the person you are dating is nothing like the parent with whom they always fought. In fact, that person will tell you that he or she *cannot stand* that parent and would never act like that parent. But if you had seen the two of them fight, you would have known that they are cut from the same loaf.

Getting to know the attachment style someone had in his or her family of origin often predicts the type of attachments that person will form in the family he or she establishes.

Connections in the family create the channels for *modeling*. It is natural for children to imitate their parents. In fact, parents often encourage this type of behavior. Dad buys a toy lawn mower for his son, and Mom buys a toy kitchen for her daughter. Gender and role typing are being modeled and encouraged from the first day in the hospital when the baby is given a blue or pink cap.

Occasionally, however, modeling becomes embarrassing. I remember talking to a mother during a counseling session who told me that she had the bad habit of saying "Oh shit!" whenever she would become upset. One day while at church, her four-year-old daughter spilled a cup of juice she was handing to her mother. "Oh shit!" was the exclamation pronounced from those young, innocent lips. A deafening silence fell upon the congregation. With all eyes upon her, the mother said the only thing one could in a situation like this: "Well, you can be sure that I will have a word or two with her father about the language he uses in front of his daughter!"

Modeling is natural for children. You do not have to teach them to imitate their parents—they just do. In spite of the common parental protest, "Do as I say and not as I do," children still do as they are taught by their parents' behavior. Actions are usually more compelling than words.

One of the unsettling aspects of aging is the increasing evidence of parental traits. You will hear yourself say something and think, "That sounded just like my mother." Or you will catch a glimpse of your reflection and for a moment think that you saw your father.

You can be sure that this same progression will happen to the person you marry. Take a good look at his or her parents, and ask yourself what it would be like to be married to their second edition. Although you can never know for sure what has been modeled, you should assume that most things would be imitated unless there was a strong reaction against that specific parental characteristic.

When a child does not like some behavior of a parent, the child sometimes reacts by modifying what is learned. In this case, the child unconsciously vows to never act a certain way. The older the child is, the more likely he or she consciously reasons this promise through. However, subtle aspects of the behavior the child has rejected may still linger because the child encountered and internalized this behavior first. Even though the child reacted negatively and decided to never act in a similar way, another part of the brain was recording and storing away the images of what the child experienced. As a result, most adults have to weed out these "learning experiences" in their adulthood. Childhood vows to never repeat certain negative behaviors experienced in the home are not as powerful or natural as the learning experiences from modeling. Yet you may have developed some of your best traits from *what you did* with the painful experiences that occurred in your family.

What Is Your Role?

Your relationship with your parent of the same sex has the greatest influence on the development of your identity and role definition. What you believe about your masculinity or femininity is largely determined by this relationship. Your understanding of your role as a husband or wife, father or mother is carved out of the relationship you had with your same-sex parent. If you want a preview of what a person will be like as a spouse or parent, study his or her relationship with this parent. This does not necessarily mean that the same-sex parent becomes the mold that automatically casts the child's identity. If this were true, then all brothers or all sisters would be the same. However, the *relationship* with the same-sex parent does reveal much about the development of a person's identity.

> *The* relationship *with the same-sex parent does reveal much about the development of a person's identity.*

Thom's mother, Carol, was an alcoholic, and his father, George, was a classic enabler. Thom took care of his two younger siblings throughout most of the week because his mother was incapacitated, yet on the weekends, everyone had to pretend that Mom had no problems. George helped to clean the house, cook the meals, and manage the three kids while Carol usually socialized with friends and ran errands. To an outsider, George and

Carol had a great relationship. They would often go out with friends or entertain in their home. Everyone knew Carol drank a little too much, but no one really knew what it was like for Thom.

Thom loved his father. He never understood why his dad stayed with his mom, but he emulated his loyal devotion. Thom mastered the role his father modeled and reacted to his mother's neglect by more deeply reinforcing his commitment to always taking care of the family. He did not allow himself to do the things he saw his mother do so flippantly—go out with her friends, pursue her own interests, and act so independently of her family and responsibilities. Thom internalized his father's portrayal of a man in the role of a husband and father as fulfilling that which the wife and mother were lacking. In other words, for Thom to fulfill his role, he would have to have a woman who would neglect hers, because Thom's role meant taking care of whatever the wife and mother neglected. As a result, he looked for his *other half*—the extreme opposite of himself.

There have been many cases where I have "time traveled" with a client who never knew his father until he journeyed back to reconstruct his father's life and tried to fill in the missing pieces of his own role as a husband and father. In these cases, the past cannot be changed. People, however, are dynamic and definitely can change the way they have been *affected* by the past. Thom's transformation occurred when he confronted his father about his mother's alcoholism. George acknowledged his codependency and apologized for neglecting to take charge and deal with the problems head-on. George could see that his helpfulness was steeped in denial and ended up perpetuating the alcoholism rather than compensating for it. This admission empowered Thom, and he worked to change his role in his own marriage.

There is a crisis today in this area of role formation because of the fragmentation of the modern family. How does a boy develop an image of masculinity and learn his role as a husband and father in a family where there is no father? How does a girl form the image of a wife and mother when she lives apart from

Along the Way Find Out About . . . Family Structures and Roles

- Were your parents divorced?
- If so, how old were you? What was the divorce and the postdivorce adjustment like?
- What was your mother (or your female caregiver) like as a wife? Your father (or male caregiver) as a husband?
- What was your relationship like with your mother? Your father?
- Who handled the discipline?
- How were the finances handled in the family?
- Were there any addictions in the family?
- What responsibilities did you have in the family?
- How were things shared among family members?

her mother and spends little to no significant time with her? Although this used to be the exception, it is rapidly becoming the norm. I recently counseled a boy who was brought to his appointment by his ex-stepfather, picked up by his biological father, and taken home to his mother and her live-in boyfriend. Initially, you would think he had three male role models—more than plenty. The reality of this situation was that he had three uninvolved male parents. In many ways, this was worse than having just one negligent father. Figuring out these relationships and their impact on his identity was like unraveling a tangled mess. Yet it was there somewhere inside his head and will certainly surface when he steps into the roles of husband and father.

Just because you were not close to your same-sex parent, do not be fooled into thinking that this parent had no effect on the development of your identity or the definition of your marital role. Absence and distance may have removed some of the influences of the same-sex parent, but identity and role development do not occur in a vacuum. You were influenced by someone, and you may have been affected by your same-sex parent more than you think.

You may need to step into your own time machine and take a look at your relationship (or lack of) with your same-sex parent. Regardless, it is particularly important for you to investigate this area when you are considering someone as a partner. Sometimes you can journey together into the past and talk through the strengths and weaknesses of these relationships. You may need to directly address some issues with a parent or family member before moving on to form your own marriage. Opening these doors of understanding will help you clarify and fulfill the roles you and your partner *want* to have in your marriage and family.

What Is Your Partner's Role?

The relationship you have with your parent of the opposite sex largely contributes to the attitudes and expectations you will project onto your spouse. This relationship forms the lens that colors your view of the person you will marry. There is a natural continuity between your experiences with your opposite-sex parent and the perspective you will have of your spouse, so issues that occurred in the primary relationship will continue to affect the secondary. If you admired this parent, this sets the stage for respecting your spouse. If you felt comfortable with and close to this parent, then the mold is set for a secure relationship with your spouse. However, a girl who disliked certain habits of her father is likely to have some sensitivity toward similar habits of her husband. Likewise, a boy who felt badgered by his mother tends to be intolerant of his wife acting in any related ways.

To better help you envision these concepts, let me trace the development of these roles from the family backgrounds of a couple who came to me for marriage counseling. Duane and Carla sat in my office and described their frustrations with each other and the inequalities that existed within their relationship. Duane felt that Carla had become overextended with activities for others and was not pulling her weight in their marriage. He wanted her to consider doing more in the house or getting a job. He also complained that she was cold and unaffectionate, frequently calling her "Elizabeth," which was her mother's name.

Carla, on the other hand, felt unappreciated for all she would do in the maintenance of their home and the care of the children, and she definitely did not want to take on a job. In fact, she wanted Duane to help out more around the house. They both argued that they put out more than the other and that the balance of responsibilities needed to change. Duane was always complaining that Carla did too much for the children, and Carla complained that she was tired of being the enforcer. Carla felt dumped on by the whole family and was hardly ever in a sexual mood; Duane was never *not* in the mood.

The relationship you have with your parent of the opposite sex . . . forms the lens that colors your view of the person you will marry.

Power struggles usually result from role conflicts and center around one of four areas—sex, children, money, and responsibilities. Duane and Carla mastered all four. In an attempt to equalize the workload, they had designed a makeshift time chart that listed the work they accomplished throughout the day. It had taken them weeks to define what constituted a legitimate work task, but once this was done, Duane "punched the clock" when he went to the office, and Carla did the same when she did the housework. To make matters worse, they posted this job chart in their bedroom, which must have done wonders for their sex life!

To understand the vast heritage of Duane and Carla's power struggles, I looked at their family histories. Duane's grandparents emigrated from Poland before they had children. His grandfather was a harsh man who believed that husbands and fathers had only one role in the family—to provide a living. The chore of raising the children fell upon the wife, who was never employed outside of the home. He suffered through prejudice and mistreatment as he became established in a brave, new world, and he instilled in his boys the ethic of hard work.

Everything changed with the stock market crash of 1929, just one year before Duane's father was born. The steel mill where his grandfather worked, like many industries in the United States at that time, was losing business and became primed for huge layoffs. Shortly after the crash, Duane's grandfather lost everything: his job, his home, and even the furniture he had bought on consignment. He sank into a sullen, angry depression that he tried to numb with excessive drinking.

When Duane's father was born, there were no cheers of excitement. Instead, there were worries about how to feed another mouth with so little food. Duane's father couldn't remember a time when he wasn't working. Everything he and his siblings earned was given to their parents. Duane's grandfather was seldom around, but when he was, he usually was in a drunken rage.

Duane was born in 1954, the era of prosperity. It seemed his father was always at work in the Ford plant, never refusing overtime. Duane's father continued his own father's anger and bitterness, although the circumstances of his life no longer warranted such feelings. When he wasn't working, he could usually be found watching television or tinkering in the garage.

Sometimes in the dating relationship nothing resembles the family patterns from which both came.

Duane was the third generation of angry, authoritarian husbands who delegated all child rearing and housework to the wife. However, the struggle for survival that dominated the life of Duane's grandfather was replaced with a cushy affluence and indulgence in Duane's childhood. His father became increasingly passive while Duane's mother waited on everyone. Because Duane was never close to his father and seemed to show quiet contempt for his father's macho bravado, Carla assumed he would not act in the same way. However, Carla was always bothered by the apparent helplessness of the boys in the family as they took advantage of their mother whenever she was available.

Carla's family also had a legacy of rigid marital roles that extended back several generations. Carla and her brother, Bill, grew up in a matriarchal family. Her father emulated the classic Peter Pan syndrome of the boy who never grew up. He was warm, friendly, and exceptionally outgoing—quite the contrast from her hardworking, stoic mother. The irony was that Carla's father was not truly close with anyone, especially not to Carla or Bill. Because she never experienced this closeness with her father, she felt uncomfortable with intimacy—like it was an invasion of her space. She also had developed a deep-seated contempt for her father's lack of involvement around the home. As the oldest, she became the director and conscience of the family, much like her mother. However, in her relationship with Duane, she was paralyzed by the way she had internalized her father's role as a husband and father. When she looked at Duane through this lens, she resented his neglect and was unable to warm up to him because of her lack of any real closeness to her father.

Sometimes in the dating relationship, as with Duane and Carla, nothing resembles the family patterns from which both came. They were attentive, carefree, romantic, and relaxed. It was only after they were married that the ghosts of their past family structures appeared.

Duane looked at Carla through the lens of his mother and expected her to take on the responsibilities of the home. He reacted to his father's role and tried to modify rather than model his father's example. In many ways, Duane was a much better partner than his father had been—he was more involved with the children, more communicative and relational, and even playful at times. As a result, Duane did not internalize all of his father's authoritarianism, but he *did* retain some passive resistance to female power and passive dependency on the wife and mother in the family.

Carla, on the other hand, had a deep sensitivity to male passivity. She identified with her mother's role of managing the home, but she also projected her father's passivity onto Duane. She perceived Duane as a child who was looking for an omni-present mother. Her lack of connection with her father made the pursuit of closeness with a husband extremely uncomfortable. She had to work at allowing Duane to hold her and show her affection. Both Duane and Carla were primed to have power struggles because of the unaddressed aspects of their own role definitions and the expectations and resentments they had toward their partner's role.

Dormant Seeds Eventually Grow

Carla and Duane characterized the complexity of interacting roles that become evident *only after* the marriage is founded. The seeds of these marital roles usually remain dormant until a couple plants their relationship in the garden of marriage. Prior to the wedding, a couple usually can look at each other outside of the husband and wife roles. Each thinks of the other as a lover, a best friend, a one and only—everything *but* a husband, a wife, and a potential father or mother. Once these labels apply, the roles they learned from their family development are graphed into their relationship, altering their feelings and thoughts toward each other.

"Not fair!" you exclaim. "How can I really know what someone will be like in marriage if these roles stay hidden?" The answer is that you *can* discover them through honest and open communication *if* you know what to look for. Cultivate many conversations about the experiences and effects of your family backgrounds. Define the roles you would like to have in your marriage and then compare how these roles are similar or different to what was practiced in your families. Look at the key relationships between your same-sex parent and your opposite-sex parent. Also, examine the roles that each parent took in their own marriage. Ask yourself, what kind of wife was my mother to my father? What kind of husband was my father to my mother? What would I want to replicate, and what would I want to change? How have I changed the areas I do not want to repeat? What kind of family background or role development do I need to look for in a potential partner to match my expectations? These questions will unearth many of the seeds that have not yet sprouted in your relationship, and they will empower you to more accurately see and direct your future.

DON'T FORGET

- Take the time to explore the family experiences of the person you are dating, especially how closeness, affection, and angry feelings were expressed.

- Pay close attention to the formation of roles in your partner's family structure, especially your partner's relationship with his or her same-sex parent and the relationship with his or her opposite-sex parent.

9

Find Your Mate's Soul

*Step Five: Getting to Know
the Patterns of the Conscience*

This chapter puts it all together. Up to this point, I have been expanding upon only one bonding dynamic of the RAM: getting to know a partner. Four of the five crucial areas to get to know have been identified, explained, amplified, and illustrated.

First, in your dating relationship, you should initially check out the ways that you and your partner are compatible. You should have a strong attraction to each other; feel a good chemistry together; share many of the same values, interests, and activities; and blend your differences in respectful and complementary ways.

Second, you should look at your partner's communication skills. Hopefully, you talk together well, with mutual amounts of openness and listening. You have worked through some conflicts and misunderstandings, and you both can apologize and make the other person feel better.

The third area to get to know entails the way your partner relates to his or her friends and family. You have noted any differences between the way your partner relates to you and to his or her friends, family, coworkers, and even strangers. In addition, you have spent time talking about previous romantic relationships and "investigating" potential problems that might recur in your relationship.

The fourth area that explains a lot about your partner is his or her family upbringing. The two of you should have talked about the families in which you grew up—the overall mood, closeness and involvement of the family, and the ways that emotions were handled and expressed. You have met and spent some time with any available family members and conversed with them about the experiences of growing up together. You have looked intently at the way your partner learned his or her role as a spouse and parent, as well as at the dynamics that dominated those relationships within the family.

The third and fourth areas to get to know provided sources for discovering patterns of relating, which I have referred to as relationship scripts. The fifth and final area to explore with a dating partner, the patterns of the conscience, also provides a crucial source for discovering future and hidden relationship scripts.

Together, these sources of relationship patterns or scripts about your partner are like lenses that sharpen your focus on the true core of the person you are dating. Consistency among the patterns found in each of these three circles provides you with what I call the *Trilogy of Consistency*. At the end of this chapter, I explain how to build your confidence in your partner by examining the consistency among each of these sources of patterns. By the time you have explored these five areas, you should be fairly certain of what your partner is made of. Your search for a soul mate culminates in an understanding of your potential mate's soul.

Brain Mapping

I remember attending a class during graduate school where I silently asked myself, When am I ever going to use this? To my surprise, here I am making reference to that class. The professor discussed an extensive experimental study on the age-old question of nature versus nurture. The experimenters wondered if the songs that birds sing are due to environmental learning or to some imprinted map in their brains. They decided to pit environment against heredity by surrounding an incubating egg with birds from another classification. No birds from the class of the unhatched chick were anywhere present. The question under investigation was whether a songbird would know its own song instinctively, even though it was raised with birds from another classification who sing a completely different song.

The newly hatched chick stayed silent long past the normal developmental period. Just when the experimenters thought they had clear evidence that a bird had to learn its own song from the environment, the young bird made a peep. Sophisticated visual and auditory recording devices honed in on the bird each time it peeped. Further investigation revealed that the young bird only joined in with the others when they would sing a note that matched the song *of its own classification*. As time continued, the young bird appeared to be engaging in a trial-and-error search for just the right note or sound to express its desired song. It appeared awkward as it struggled to rearrange the notes in various rhythms and sequences. Eventually, it succeeded in using the sounds made by the other birds to construct the song that was genetically imprinted in its brain.

This experiment and others like it influenced scientists in the nature-versus-nurture debate and gave rise to a concept known as brain mapping. Brain mapping postulated that every species has different neurological blueprints so that their brains have unique formations of wiring that predetermine global behavior patterns. Language, for instance, is believed to be mapped in the human brain so that it is natural for us to speak, which is a handy excuse you can use the next time someone wants you to be quiet: "I wish I could, but I can't—it's just the way my brain is mapped!"

I believe that the conscience is one of the designs in the mapping of the human brain. Your mind is designed to have the ability to observe yourself and make judgments about what you are thinking, saying, doing, and feeling. Psychology, neurology, religion, and morality have referred to this mental process by different names: the executive function of the brain, the internal self-monitoring system, the super-ego, the observing ego, and the conscience. Common vernacular knows the conscience as the angel on your shoulder, the little voice in your head, the voice of reason, or Jiminy Cricket.

Let Your Conscience Be Your Guide

Few aspects of personality are as overlooked as the conscience is in the choice of a marriage partner. I have frequently asked audiences what qualities or characteristics they look for in a prospective partner. Hardly ever does anyone mention the word *conscience* or *conscientious*. To understand the importance of a good conscience, let's compare it with the highly emphasized area of relationship skills. We all know the importance of good communication, conflict-resolution, and problem-solving skills. If you had to choose, which person would you rather marry: someone with great relationship skills but a weak conscience or someone with a great functioning conscience but weak relationship skills? Without a healthy conscience, skills become manipulative and self-serving. We have stereotyped certain professionals as having exceptional skills but with poor consciences—politicians, lawyers, and used-car salesmen, for starters. The point is that relationship skills are only part of what you need to make a relationship successful. There is more to love than just practicing good skills!

In clinical terminology, a person who has a poor conscience is usually referred to as a sociopath (or a person with some other form of personality disorder). Yet the easily identified clinical condition is often overshadowed by a convincing shroud of charm and highly developed skills. Granted, these skills are indispensable in a healthy relationship, and countless books and programs are designed to improve these skill areas. However, a relationship is much more dynamic than just the mechanical use of skills.

In a classic study conducted more than twenty-five years ago, researchers evaluated the use of relationship skills by a group of married couples who were instructed to discuss a specific area of conflict.[1] The couples were then separated and paired off with a different partner of the opposite sex. This new pair had to discuss a similar area of conflict. When their relationship skills were observed, it was found that those from distressed marriages scored significantly higher with a stranger than when they were with their own marriage partner. The researchers concluded that the *use* of relationship skills was greatly affected by the dynamics of the relationship. In other words, you may be a great communicator at work but inept with your partner, or a patient listener with a friend but intolerant and defensive with the one you love the most.

What makes the difference? It is the dynamics of the relationship—roles, family background, conscience, trust, previous patterns of relating, and other dynamics—that mediate a person's use of skills. Therefore, an exceptionally skilled person may not use those skills with his or her spouse.

In fact, another study found that highly developed communication skills enhanced good relationships but agitated distressed ones. For instance, wives who had a keen ability to predict the impact of their words on their husbands were viewed differently by the husbands in happy marriages in contrast with those in unhappy marriages. Men in satisfying marriages appreciated this quality in their spouses, while men in distressed marriages perceived their wives as using this ability as a weapon. What this adds up to is that the sharper the skill, the deeper the cut. If your partner can talk you out of a bad mood or weave multiple ideas together to make a point, then know that this same skill can be used against you if an equally developed conscience isn't sitting at the controls.

Highly polished skills in the hands of someone with a poor conscience make for a manipulative and self-serving partner.

Remember my fictitious example in Chapter 6 of the surgeon who had to perform an emergency appendectomy without any tools and the coffee-shop worker who also had to perform this same surgery with all of the precision instruments of an operation room at his disposal? I told this story to help you understand that some dating partners possess the right tools but lack the ability to use them properly. For instance, a partner can have a vast repertoire of communication tools without a mature and consistent conscience to navigate their use. Highly polished skills in the hands of someone with a poor conscience make for a manipulative and self-serving partner.

Polished Skills + No Conscience = Disaster

My first counseling session with Marta was prompted by the sudden death of her husband from a heart attack. Marta and Rich had been married for twenty-seven years, raised three children, and were just starting to enjoy their empty nest when fate stepped in with a vengeance. She had lived a fairly protected life and was naive when it came to dating and selecting a partner. We worked through her loss, the challenges of single-parenting her adult children, and her initiation into the world of dating.

Several years after we had concluded our counseling relationship, Marta called for an emergency session. The story she told was almost beyond belief. She had met Mark at a high school reunion. Although they had not dated in high school nor conversed for more than thirty years, she felt an immediate connection due to their shared history. Finding someone who linked to her adolescence made her feel young and carefree.

After six months of dating Mark, who still lived in another state, she accepted his proposal for marriage. Everything seemed like a perfect fit even down to their jobs—Marta was a nurse and Mark was a physician who had retired from practice in order to pursue research as an instructor at a training hospital. He was still reeling from an ugly divorce that, although legally completed, still tied up the majority of his investments and left his credit-card debts in a holding pattern.

Mark and Marta planned a wonderful wedding that took place right around the one-year anniversary of their first date. Mark accepted a position in a teaching hospital close to where Marta lived, and he moved into her home. He was in a financial bind because his house had not sold, and he needed to pay off some credit-card debt that he had incurred during this transitional period. Marta offered to transfer funds sufficient to clear his debts, and she said he could then repay her after the house sold. He reluctantly agreed.

The first year of their marriage was quiet, romantic, and peaceful. Mark would leave for the teaching hospital about an hour before Marta left for the doctor's office where she worked. The only difficulty they had that year was the stress of Mark's lack of finances because of his former home not selling. Almost his entire paycheck went to pay these bills. He had taken a significant cut in pay when he retired from a private practice to take a teaching position, and because his bills were incurred during the time he was in practice, they were hardly manageable with his present pay.

Shortly after they celebrated their first anniversary, Mark left for a medical conference at Las Vegas. Marta talked with him daily on his cell phone, but she never let on that she had plans to surprise him at the hotel over the weekend. Her suspicions were raised when she asked the hotel about the Saturday workshop agenda for the conference and was told that no medical conference was being held at the hotel. Without raising any suspicions, she double-checked with Mark that the conference was actually being held in the hotel where he was staying. She slumped to the floor immediately after ending the call. Her heart sank and her strength drained.

She eventually gathered herself together, having told no one about the unexplained circumstances. Something inside her wanted to go where Mark was staying and prove there was a rational explanation for the apparent lie. But when she arrived at the hotel, Mark was nowhere to be found. She explained her surprise plan to the manager and was let into Mark's room where she determined to wait until he returned.

She admitted to me that she snooped, hoping to find something that would justify his stay at the hotel. However, she found nothing except some puzzling prescriptions for narcotic medications. She did not think that Mark was taking any meds, so the presence of the pill bottles was confusing.

Marta awoke fully dressed and lying on the bed in the morning. Mark had still not arrived back at the room. She inquired with the concierge and manager when she couldn't reach Mark on his cell phone. It was not until late afternoon that she received a call from Mark on her cell phone. He thought she was still in their home state.

She disclosed that she was in Las Vegas and wanted to know where he was and exactly what was happening. He broke down and told her that he had been arrested because of intoxication and would soon be released. Marta took a cab to the police station and was shocked to find out that he actually was up on charges of writing illegal prescriptions.

In the next several weeks, Marta seemed to discover a new secret about Mark every day. First it was that he had a prior warrant for his arrest for writing illegal prescriptions. Then it became evident that he had developed an addiction to these medications, in addition to an addiction to gambling. She learned that he had lost his medical license before she even met him at the reunion, which was the reason that he had left his practice and went into teaching. Then it surfaced that he actually never had been hired by the teaching hospital where he was supposedly going every day. She felt like she was in the scene of *The Shining* where the wife looked through her husband's months of work on writing a book only to find that every sentence was the same: "All work and no play makes Jack a dull boy."

Mark would leave home and then return shortly after Marta left for her job. He stayed at home the entire time—not only reading, watching television, and sleeping, but mostly gambling on the Internet. Mark never admitted any of these twisted facts. Even when Marta had irrefutable evidence, he still denied her accusations. She talked with some of his family members whom she had never known very well and learned that Mark had a long history of indiscretions that preceded her marriage to him. Needless to say, she realized that she didn't know the man she had married.

Marta asked Mark one crucial question: "How could you deceive me like this?" He never could really answer this question. What did become evident was that his conscience did not produce a consistent feeling of guilt. He seemed to feel guilty only when caught, and even then it was erratic. What was lacking in his character and conscience that allowed him to live a double life, spending the day deceiving his wife and then making love with her in the evening, whispering words of passion, devotion, and true love?

Defining the Conscience

How is it that some have an overactive conscience while others seem to have none? How can someone like Mark be so relationally skilled yet so character deficient? What does the conscience predict about the success of your relationship and future marriage? What exactly is the conscience?

The conscience is one of those familiar terms that are frequently used but rarely defined. It comes to mind when you hear a story like Mark and Marta's, or even one less extreme, and you ask yourself that perplexing question: "How can so-and-so sleep at night after what he (or she) did?" You figure that person must feel guilt somewhere inside and is just suppressing it, or that after that person has had a chance to calm down, his or her conscience would kick in and guide the person's thoughts to consider the other side of the argument.

Simply stated, the conscience is your mind looking in the mirror. It examines who you are and what you are doing. It facilitates self-reflection.

The better you understand the conscience, the better you will be able to read your partner's conscience. The conscience performs two basic jobs that amplify this definition. I will briefly explain each of them and then develop these two jobs in more detail.

First, the conscience *monitors* your thoughts, words, and actions according to an internal code of values and beliefs. Like an internal coach, it comments on your performance and provides a constant check-and-balance between your output and your inner values and goals.

The second job of your conscience is to *transport* you out of your own perspective into the perspective of someone else. In other words, a well-functioning conscience helps you understand another's viewpoint, see things from another's vantage point, and empathize with that person's feelings.

Your Partner's Internal Parent

This first job of the conscience is referred to as the self-monitoring system because it involves both a code of conduct and an observer or enforcer. This closely parallels the parenting process. A parent monitors a child according to a moral code or standard. When the child challenges the standard, the parent reinforces the standard. But to do this, the parent must be watching or observing the child. Most parents will concur that consistency is the key.

Keep a close eye on the child, and consistently enforce the standards or rules of the home.

Your internal parent, or conscience, functions the same way as a parent of a child. Your conscience should be watching you and consistently prompting you to adhere to the standards or morals you hold. The healthiness of your conscience is measured by the consistency of the enforcer. You may have clear and even strict beliefs about right and wrong, but if the enforcing function of your conscience is weak, then you will often contradict your own standards.

When it comes to figuring out your partner, be sure to not confuse these two functions. You may like what your partner says (morals and standards of his or her personal code), but the degree to which your partner consistently applies these standards depends upon the enforcing function of his or her conscience. Just like parents, there are good consciences and there are poor ones. Some have really high standards, while others seem to have very loose standards. Some watch closely, but others seem to always be looking the other way.

The shaping of the conscience begins early in life and seems to have lasting significance, as you will see from two major studies I will review. Years ago, when my daughter was three, I was at a drive-up window of the bank and the teller asked if she would like a lollipop. How can a parent say no when the teller announces over her loudspeaker to all minor passengers in the car that she wants to provide free lollipops if the driver would just agree.

The conscience is your mind looking in the mirror.

I looked across at my daughter, whose eyes were like saucers, staring intensely at me. I thankfully accepted the flavor chosen by my daughter, but I told her that she would have to wait until after lunch to eat her sucker.

As we drove away from the bank she asked, "Can I hold it?" I reluctantly complied. I then noticed that she had separated the wrapper covering the lollipop, creating a small portal through

Along the Way Find Out About . . . the
Monitoring Conscience

- How consistent are your attitudes and behaviors with what you say you believe?
- What rights and wrongs do you feel strongly about?
- How do you handle it when you are wrong?
- How defensive are you?
- What common defenses do you use?
- What makes you feel guilty at times?
- What do you do when you feel guilty?
- Do you tend to repeat the behaviors, attitudes, and reactions that you previously felt guilty about?
- Who do you feel accountable to?
- How do you react to authority figures?

which she could examine the succulent temptation, and she was holding it next to her nose.

"What are you doing?" I inquired.

"Smelling it," she replied.

A few minutes later I caught her sticking her tongue between the split in the wrapper and licking the lollipop. "I thought I told you *not* to eat the lollipop before lunch!" I scolded. At this point, I attempted to activate her developing conscience. "Tell me, what do you think of what you are doing?"

She looked at her treat and then at me, and she defiantly explained her behavior: "I am not eating the lollipop. I'm just *tasting* it."

You need to get to know your partner's self-monitoring system. This means that you need to know what your partner believes (i.e., code of conduct) *and* the consistency by which your partner follows his or her own standards (i.e., enforcer of code). A weak enforcer was considered to be a "Swiss cheese conscience" according to Freud. Defensiveness, denial, rationalizations, and lack of guilt can create holes in the conscience so that sometimes things strike, but other times they pass through without even making a dent.

The conscience guides a person's behavior; therefore, the degree of trust you have in a partner primarily will be related to what you believe are the maturity and consistency of that person's conscience. This does not mean that you think your partner will never make a mistake, but it does provide you with a measure of confidence in his or her integrity when you are not around.

Slippage, on the other hand, occurs when your conscience lets you get away with contradicting your code. The less slippage you have, the stronger your conscience. A partner's personal code is made up of his or her standards of conduct and relationship morals. Some examples of these are:

- I should keep my partner my first priority.
- I should always tell the truth (i.e., honesty is the best policy).
- When I am wrong, I should admit it and apologize.
- I should work hard.
- I should respect your opinion, even if I disagree.
- I should stay faithful to my partner.
- I should express my emotions respectfully.

Early on, most dating partners directly or indirectly disclose their personal code (this doesn't mean that you have to completely believe them). Even on first dates you sometimes hear a partner say things like, "Hey, when I am wrong, I admit it," "Cheating is the lowest form of betrayal," or "I've been known to be a workaholic." Each of these statements reveals a value or moral that this partner holds in his or her personal code. There is more to getting to know a partner's conscience, however, than just understanding their code.

You also need to become familiar with the strength and consistency of the code enforcer in your partner's conscience—this takes time and transparency. Watch closely how your partner handles feelings of guilt. What you want to see is a partner who quickly admits to wrong because the feelings of guilt register without much defensiveness or denial. Long arguments where you have to convince your partner that he or she was wrong or should feel guilty are a definite reason to worry.

There is a direct link between the enforcing function of the conscience and impulse control. Anyone who is impulsive also likely lacks a healthy enforcer. In other words, the self-monitoring system filters your impulses before you act on them. If your partner is impulsive, then he or she lacks a strong filtering system.

A landmark study on the conscience was conducted back in the 1960s by Walter Mischel at the Bing Preschool on the campus of Stanford University.[2] He gave four-year-olds the choice of eating one marshmallow right away or holding off until he came back into the room a few minutes later and then getting a second marshmallow. The focus of this study was to measure a child's delay of gratification and the ability to control his or her impulses.

Some of the children who chose to wait stared at the marshmallow with their chin in their hands. Others laid their head down next to the marshmallow and never took their eyes off of it. Then there were those who couldn't get enough of sniffing the marshmallow. In contrast, some of the children lacked impulse control and had the marshmallow in their mouths before the instructions were even completed.

The most fascinating results came from the follow-up studies on these same children (which are still continuing to this day and even include their marriages and children). Fifteen, twenty, and even thirty years later, those who exercised self-control consistently scored higher on just about every test administered than those who immediately ate the marshmallow. The ones who waited were more assertive, competent, hardworking, cooperative, and successful at coping than those who were impulsive. The instant gratifiers tended to achieve poorer grades and turned out to be more stubborn, indecisive, and stressed-out.

A key component in the self-monitoring system of the conscience was the ability to delay gratification in order to achieve a goal. More than you ever would have thought so, learning about your partner's attention span and impulse control during childhood may be a very strong predictor of what that partner will be like in a long-term relationship with you.

On the flip side, some partners have *excessive* guilt. This can interrupt and disturb relationships. This is a partner who worries incessantly; feels responsible, guilty, or both over many things beyond his or her control; and often seems mentally tortured. The Five-Factor Model (FFM) of personality is one of the most widely researched and accepted representations of the groupings of personality traits.[3] One of the five categories is conscientiousness (i.e., dependable, responsible, productive, able to delay gratification, and ethical) and another is neuroticism (i.e., thin-skinned, anxious, worried, concerned with adequacy, fluctuating moods, and brittle ego defenses).[4]

Which personality trait do you think is most highly associated with stability in marriage, and which is most often linked with instability? The number one preference in a partner was conscientiousness, and those who were married to a conscientious partner reported feeling the most content.[5] Conscientious partners had the best chances for not divorcing, whereas low scores on conscientiousness and high scores on neuroticism were associated with those who would divorce.

You can think of these two traits joined together on one scale (see Figure 9.1 on the next page). What the FFM calls high conscientiousness is really just a healthy and active conscience. Low conscientiousness is actually an underactive or nonfunctioning conscience. Mark, Marta's husband, was an extreme example of someone who had a nonfunctioning conscience. There are other partners who have underactive consciences. They may not have secrets like Mark, but they lack feelings of guilt when they are in the wrong. You might think that this dating partner deep inside feels guilty under the layers of his or her defenses, but in many cases the person does not. As mentioned before, a Swiss cheese conscience produces guilt inconsistently. You never know who you will be with when you and your partner get together. One evening your partner is thoughtful, attentive, and quick to apologize. The next day your partner is angry, blaming, and attacking. A healthy conscience regulates your moods. Without a healthy conscience, moods are expressed unchecked.

Neuroticism, on the other hand, is basically an overactive conscience that drives a person into guilt, anxiety, and insecurity. If a partner with an underactive conscience appears too uncaring and detached, then a person with an overactive, neurotic conscience cares too much. Men, in particular, describe themselves as unhappy in a marriage with neurotic-type partners.[6] Neurotics often are rigid, are controlling, and lack spontaneity. They have a high need to be in control of their own world, yet they usually want their partners to take care of them. They are oversensitive and overreact to feeling slighted or controlled. As a result, when you date a neurotic, you will feel in a bind—the proverbial "damned if I do, damned if I don't." In time, you realize that the irony of their overactive conscience is that it actually makes them very self-centered.

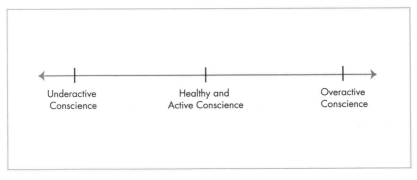

FIGURE 9.1 Conscience Continuum

Do Only the Good Die Young?

Put conscientiousness at the top of your list of qualities you want in a partner. A consistent and healthy self-monitoring conscience has been identified with stable and lasting marriages over and over! A growing body of evidence shows that partners who have emotionally healthy consciences live years longer and have more successful marriages than the average.[7] A group of multidisciplinary researchers from the University of California, Brandeis University, and the State University of New York at Stony Brook teamed together to conduct a series of studies on the famous Terman database to determine if there were any childhood predictors of longevity and marital happiness. What they found was shocking.

Without a healthy conscience, moods are expressed unchecked.

Before I explain their studies, let me briefly describe this extremely unique database of personal and family information. Lewis M. Terman and Catherine Cox were awarded a grant of $20 million by the Heritage Foundation in 1921 to conduct a lifelong study of 1,528 gifted elementary-school children.[8] Follow-up surveys and studies were administered approximately every five years. In addition, files of newspaper clippings, legal documents and certificates, and interviews with parents, spouses, and study members were compiled on each of the participants.

One of the childhood characteristics that Lewis Terman evaluated was conscientiousness. He defined it in a way very similar to the description of conscientiousness that came to be used in the FFM in the early 1990s. Terman compiled profiles of each child (around eleven years old) on his or her truthfulness, lack of egotism or vanity, and prudence (i.e., good impulse control). Putting these areas together provided him a picture of each child's conscientiousness. The original intent of this project was to study human intelligence, but the results went far beyond this.

Changes in the leadership of this project over the span of eight decades brought fresh ideas and heightened attention to new issues. Their years of data collection produced rich and extensive findings on marriages, careers, educational achievements, child rearing, family practices, aging, retirement, and causes of death for more than 1,500 individuals over the course of their lifetimes. The project continues to this day.

The team of researchers that used this Terman data was interested in the widely held belief that marriage has a protective effect on health. Numerous studies have established that married individuals live healthier and longer (i.e., four to seven years longer) than those who are single.[9] This is supposedly due to lifestyle changes that come with marriage. For instance, the presence of a partner seems to lower risky behaviors while heightening the awareness of healthy activities such as exercise, proper eating habits, and regular medical care. Marriage also seems to increase financial resources so there are more opportunities for the pursuit of these healthy activities. Finally, it is believed that marriage enhances psychological well-being (although some of you who have been previously married to a jerk would strongly argue to the contrary).

Conscientiousness in childhood consistently predicted those who lived longer and never divorced!

The team of multidisciplinary researchers questioned this long-standing belief that marriage *alone* adds years to one's life. They wondered if perhaps the same personal qualities that lead to happier marriages could also be responsible for the greater longevity.[10]

Because those who participated in the Terman database were evaluated in the area of conscientiousness when they were children, the researchers could trace those who were highly conscientious as children into their marriages and even determine for many of them their age at death. What the researchers found was that only one personality quality was linked with longevity and happy marriages. Conscientiousness in childhood consistently predicted those who lived longer and never divorced! In fact, conscientiousness was as powerful a predictor of life span as were the biological risks of blood pressure and cholesterol.[11] It was also the childhood personality quality that stood out as the strongest predictor of a marriage that would last a lifetime.

Are You Your Partner's Conscience?

Before moving to the second major job of the conscience, let me briefly review what we have already covered and maybe mention one word of warning. We learned that the potential for a conscience is genetically imprinted in the brain and that it is natural for someone to observe and monitor him- or herself. We also established that the first major job of the conscience is to monitor a person's thoughts, feelings, and choices. This means that your partner should be monitoring him- or herself with standards, values, and a personal code of conduct. However, just because your partner has the capacity for a conscience does not automatically mean that he or she possesses a healthy or well-developed conscience.

Two areas determine the health and functioning of a partner's self-monitoring system: his or her personal code and the enforcer of that code. Do not assume that the standards a partner holds are the same as yours; they could be very different than the ones that you practice. But once you feel that you understand these standards, be sure to check out your partner's ability to consistently apply them. These two areas provide you with an accurate picture of how your partner will act and think both when you are present and when you are absent.

The last thing you need is a partner who is one person with you and another when you are out of sight. This happens when a person lacks in this first area of self-monitoring. If you are not careful, you can find yourself slipping into the role of the conscience with your partner. In other words, you fill in where your partner's conscience is deficient. This is my brief word of warning. Becoming your partner's conscience may go unnoticed by you for a while, but it becomes exasperating in time.

A little bit of this is normal. For instance, when I was young, I remember my older sister prepping her husband to refrain from some of his more base habits when coming over to a meal at my parents' home. Sure enough, he would lean back after the feast had been devoured and let out a long belch, announcing that the longer and more resonating the sound, the more meaningful the compliment. Although his gesture of gratitude completely disregarded his wife's conscientious prompting, it was fairly innocent. But you know that the next time my sister prompted him to behave himself, she probably became a bit more convincing.

If the offenses are more serious, an accumulation of nagging, mistrust, and disrespect occur in a relationship. You realize that your partner's conscience doesn't get the job done, so you step in to fill the vacancy. Before you know it, you have become your partner's "conscience enhancer." Resist the temptation to apply for this job. Let your partner live by his or her own conscience and decide if you like what you see.

Measuring a Conscience's Skillfulness

The second major job of the conscience, the transporting system, enables you to see yourself from outside perspectives. The conscience works like a Star Trek transporter to propel you out of your perspective and into another person's viewpoint. You see how your thoughts, attitudes, and actions affect your partner. You feel what your partner is experiencing. You know what you look like through his or her eyes.

Several additional names have been given to this same (or very similar) basic personality attribute of the conscience: emotional intelligence,[12] emotional competence or skillfulness,[13] and affective social competence.[14] All of these terms are used to describe concepts very similar to this transporting function of the conscience.

Basically, a partner who has a well-functioning transporter will anticipate your needs. This is not to say that your partner must be psychic. But you want a partner who will be a connoisseur of your interests and desires. Much of what makes a relationship work are the reciprocal acts of thoughtfulness and support that flow from the conscience's transporter.

Getting to know a dating partner's conscience transporter is not that difficult when you know what to watch for. Usually it is the little things that eventually add up to a pattern that, when magnified a bit, forecasts the future.

This was never more evident than during the years of raising two daughters and watching them date. Several of my firstborn's boyfriends earned nicknames that described their conscience transporters. For instance, Sam came to the door to pick Morgan up for their first date while she was in high school. He had been in our home once before when a group of friends were over playing basketball. Morgan was not yet downstairs, so Sam and I chatted in my office (I was administering a battery of psychological tests, of course!). I excused myself to go check on the progress upstairs, and when I returned to my office Sam was gone. I started walking around my house looking for him. When I stepped into the kitchen, I noticed that the refrigerator door was open. Sam's head popped up over the door, and he cheerfully explained, "I am just getting myself something to drink." At that point I knew his middle name—Space Invader. Sam the space invader. Just what I want to date my *innocent* daughter—a space invader.

Becoming your partner's conscience may go unnoticed by you for a while, but it becomes exasperating in time.

He didn't last long, but another suitor, the mole, did. Drew was the quiet type who always looked guilty of something—like he had something to hide. It was a common occurrence that

Along the Way Find Out About . . . the Transporting Conscience

- Do you understand my perspective?
- Do you validate my perspective when I explain myself to you?
- Can you understand and even anticipate how I feel sometimes?
- How do you respond to my explanation of my view and my feelings?
- What special things do you do for me?
- How often do you initiate activities or conversations that are about me or are something that I like?
- How often do you put yourself second and me first?
- How controlling are you?
- How much attention do you give to my spoken needs? Requests? Unspoken ones?
- What are your moods like? How stable or unstable are they?

Drew would come over to see Morgan. Our family would be hanging out in the kitchen, laughing and talking. Next thing you know, Drew has moved into our rec room in the basement. This happened several times before I finally looked at my daughter and said, "Why does Drew always go down into the basement? Why doesn't he hang out with us and talk? What is it about the basement? Is it because it is dark? Underground? Does he come from a family who lives underground? Is he from the mole family? Is he a mole?"

That clinched it. From then on, Drew was known as the mole. He has gone down in the annals of our family history as the quintessence of unconscientiousness. Every day there was something—he forgot to call; he forgot to come; he forgot his money when they went out to eat; he didn't inquire about his girlfriend's activities, sports, or involvements; he overlooked a birthday, anniversary, or romantic holiday. Every day brought some small (and sometimes not so small) unconscientious act. It was the cumulative effect that revealed the exasperating pattern.

I'll never forget how Morgan told us that she and Drew were finished. She looked at us with a tear in her eye and a smirk on her face and said, "I sent the mole back underground today—six feet under."

Morgan learned that a partner's conscience can be understood by the major patterns that are revealed by the accumulation of repeating minor incidents. Although it is good to give a partner the benefit of the doubt, she also learned to trust her judgment more when the same type of attitude or behavior has repeated three or four times. This requires that you group attitudes and actions into similar categories so you can gain some sense of what are the norms for your partner and what are the exceptions.

A good example of how this is done is found in one of the subtests on several standardized IQ tests. The task is to find the common denominator in two different items. For instance, how are a window and a door alike? Clearly you could say that they both allow some kind of entry, or that they both open and shut. But if you thought about the larger category that they are a part of, then you would say that they both are architectural features of a house or a building. Therefore, the task requires that you try to find the overarching category where these two items fit together best. In the same way, you need to accurately label your partner's treatment of you and place it in the correct category so you can gain an accurate idea of what your partner's habits of conscience are really like.

Some of you may be thinking—"Hey, that's keeping score." In a way, it is. But you are also keeping score of the good in your partner. The goal is that you fully know what your partner is like and that you draw accurate conclusions from the time you spend together. Minor incidents that repeat over time reveal major patterns. Basically, you want to give credit where credit is due and detect problems where problems exist.

The Trilogy of Consistency

To be fair, some of the most blatant offenses can be exceptions, and some of the most subtle offenses can be patterns. Everyone will err at one time or another. It will be much easier to reconcile an offense when it seems to contradict the usual conscientious pattern in the relationship. But if it keeps surfacing in spite of repeated discussions, then you need to seriously wonder if the "exception" is not in fact the "norm."

Learn to decipher what your partner will be like as a spouse by considering the consistency between the three major sources of patterns, or relationship scripts. I refer to this as the Trilogy of Consistency. This brings us right back to where we started at the beginning of this chapter. The three major areas that should be compared for consistency are (1) the patterns of your partner's conscience in your relationship, (2) the patterns in your partner's family background, and (3) the patterns of your partner's relationships to others, especially previous romantic partners (see Figure 9.2).

Red flags always wave over any inconsistencies between these three areas. The first area to start with is how your partner treats you. Add up the big and little acts of your partner's conscience. Research points to a warm, kind, gentle, and understanding conscientiousness that is most often linked with marital stability and enjoyment.[15] Does your partner consistently practice this way of relating to you? What are the norms of his or her conscience, and what are the exceptions? Consider the amount of time you have known this partner so you avoid drawing conclusions prematurely. What you see is most likely the best-case scenario of what your partner's conscience is really like.

Next compare the attitudes and behavior of your partner with what you have learned about the dynamics of his or her family experiences. Do they look similar or different? Differences between the present and the past should always raise a red flag of concern. It is not imperative that your partner have no "blemishes" in his or her past family relationships. But it is important to know the impact this family had on your partner and what your partner internalized from those experiences. In other words, the ways the family shaped your partner and what he or she did with those experiences are vital to the way this partner will act in his or her own marriage and family.

Minor incidents that repeat over time reveal major patterns.

However, the seeds that were planted in a person's family background may not germinate during the dating relationship. Therefore, you should look for the inconsistencies between the dating behaviors and the family patterns. If they are similar, then you can feel a bit more confident that the way your partner treats you will last into the marriage. If there are areas of concern from

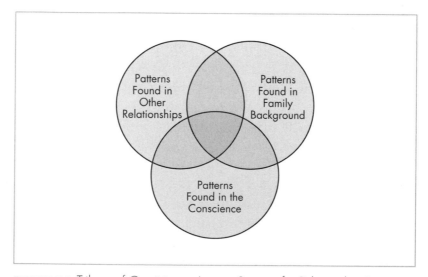

FIGURE 9.2 Trilogy of Consistency Among Sources for Relationship Scripts

the family relationships, then you need to know what steps, if any, your partner ever took to improve those issues.

For instance, just because your partner does not think the severe conflicts he had with his mother will ever affect his relationship with women or a spouse does not mean he is immune from being infected by those family experiences. Just because your partner does not believe that her controlling mother will not shape the way she thinks and feels as a woman and particularly as a wife and mother does not preclude her from being shaped by those early interactions. What your partner believes now may not be what he or she will believe years later when the impact of the past becomes evident. However, you want to know the likelihood of these seeds germinating in marriage so you and your partner can work together to dig up these potential sources of conflict and root them out before you marry.

The final set of patterns that you should consider in this Trilogy of Consistency is the way your partner relates to others. This includes past romantic partners. Again, if the ways that your partner treats you are similar to the patterns from his or her family background, and if they also agree with the patterns from other relationships, then you have three major sources of consistent endorsement of your partner's character and future marriage behavior. However, if there are inconsistencies within this trilogy of patterns, then you have some work cut out for you and your partner in this relationship.

There is a Turkish proverb that I heard years ago: "Measure a thousand times, but cut once." The better you understand the five areas you need to get to know and the clearer your comprehension of the Trilogy of Consistency, the more secure you are with pacing the development of your closeness and intimacy (which we will cover in detail in Part III), then the more you can relax and feel confident in your choice of a partner. The starting point is to look in the mirror and make sure that your own internal monitor and transporter are working properly. Then find a partner who "thinks like you"; two partners who share this quality have the greatest chances of success in marriage.

DON'T FORGET

- Without a healthy conscience, relationship skills can become manipulative and self-serving.

- The conscience monitors a person's thoughts, words, and actions according to an internal code of values and beliefs.

- You get clues by watching how your partner handles feelings of guilt and admits to being wrong.

- Impulsivity may be a sign of a weak enforcing system.

- An active conscience is beneficial, but an overactive conscience can result in neuroticism, which is a lack of spontaneity, rigidity, hypersensitivity, and a tendency to overreact to feeling controlled.

- Resist the temptation to *become your partner's conscience*; instead, let your partner live by his or her own conscience and then decide if you like what you see.

- The conscience also transports you into your partner's perspective, prompting understanding and empathy.

- Minor incidents of unconscientiousness can add up to a major pattern.

- Determine your level of confidence in *knowing* your partner by looking at the consistency among patterns from the conscience, patterns from the family, and patterns from other relationships.

PART III

. . . While Following Your Heart

This last section transitions from the *thinking* side of choosing a partner to the *feelings* of the heart. Relationships are very complex. Most books that attempt to address this subject tend to fall into one of two categories. The first is the academic and theoretical. These books are written for the classroom, not the living room. The second, the books geared toward the average single person, often water down or simply sidestep many of the more complex aspects of falling in love. As a result, you get some pithy wisdom or a laundry list of do's and don'ts.

So I will try to describe clearly and understandably the intricate and involved journey of falling in love, by tapping into the universal bonding features (referred to as dynamics) that comprise each and every one of your romantic relationships. I propose that these five dynamics interact with each other to produce the overall feeling of love and connection you have with a partner, beginning with the initial encounter and continuing until the final hour of your relationship. Understanding the order and logic of these five dynamics empowers you to make safe and insightful choices. Defy their natural balance and you increase your risks for emotional harm.

10

Sketching the Date-Mate Profile

RAM Dynamic 2: Should I Trust You?

At 7:55 P.M. on December 2, 1956, a bomb blasted apart the Paramount Movie Theatre in Brooklyn, New York. Six patrons were injured, three seriously. It was a miracle that no one was killed. In fact, it was a miracle that for sixteen years these random and dreaded attacks on innocent citizens had never led to a death. By the time the terrorist, who had become known as the Mad Bomber, was finished, more than thirty bombs had paralyzed New York City, holding both the public and the police hostage in fear and perplexity.

The carefulness and competence of the attacker had stumped the police and detectives for those past sixteen years when Inspector Howard Finney took an unorthodox, bold step and approached a criminal psychiatrist, Dr. James Brussel. Criminal profiling had been informally conducted by two physicians,

George Phillips and Thomas Bond, in search of answers to the clues about the serial murderer Jack the Ripper. But never had an official investigation hired a professional in the field of psychiatry to examine case files and attempt to assemble the pieces together in an accurate portrayal of an assailant. Although initially unsure of his ability to contribute to the identification and apprehension of the Mad Bomber, Dr. Brussel became increasingly confident as he defended his description of the invisible attacker. Let me summarize his conclusions.

The bomber was male, around the age of fifty. He had been both employed and injured by the first company he bombed, Consolidated Edison. He had a psychological condition known as narcissistic paranoid disorder and classic to the symptoms of paranoia was oversensitivity to criticism. He spent most of his time with foreign people and was of Slavic nationality himself. He lived in Connecticut, had a high school education but had not attended college, and was Roman Catholic. His mother died when he was young, and he lived with a single female relative. He was meticulous and neat and would wear formal clothing. Because of this, Dr. Brussel predicted that he would be wearing a three-piece suit with the vest buttoned when the police arrested him.

Anyone who contemplates marriage is a profiler in the dating process.

These deductions sounded preposterous to the investigating detectives, although Dr. Brussel explained and defended his portrait based upon psychological theory. For instance, because paranoia peaks around age thirty-five and the attacks had started sixteen years prior, Dr. Brussel estimated the attacker's age to be fifty-something. He generalized the neat and perfectionist qualities of the lettering on the notes, the construction and planning of the bombs, and other aspects of the evidence to conclude that the bomber would both dress neatly and have a more perfectionist lifestyle. He analyzed the lettering and wording on the notes to determine education level and nationality. He even suggested that the police publicize everything they knew, because narcissistic paranoids crave attention and would be more likely to come forward and be found out. When this was questioned because it was so contrary to normal police proceedings, Dr. Brussel explained that if anything publicized was untrue, the Bomber would want to clarify it to the public. If everything that was printed was accurate, then the Bomber would be prompted to reveal something more in order to stump the investigators and prove his superior intelligence. Finney, unable to argue with Dr. Brussel's logic, followed these suggestions. Just as predicted, the Mad Bomber stepped up his attacks and wrote more revealing letters. He even called Dr. Brussel with a threatening phone call.

The search for priorly injured workers in the Consolidated Edison Company and its subsidiaries led to the investigation of George Metesky, a Slavic resident of Waterbury, Connecticut, and a perfectionist. He lived with his two unmarried sisters and attended St. Patrick's Catholic Church regularly. His neighbors found him standoffish, but after the flurry of articles about the Mad Bomber, he appeared friendlier and more outgoing. When the police came to his house and arrested him, he pleasantly and politely admitted to being the bomber. He was still in his bathrobe. The police asked him to dress before they escorted him downtown, and when he walked out of his bedroom he was wearing a three-piece suit, with the vest completely buttoned!

Don't you wish you had the profiling skills that Dr. Brussel possessed? In many ways, you and anyone who contemplates marriage is a profiler in the dating process. Although you are not looking for a mad bomber (or a jerk, for that matter), you are constructing a mental profile of the person you are dating. As you explore each of the five predictive areas—compatibility, relationship skills, and the patterns from the person's family background, other relationships, and conscience—you place what you learn in a mental file. Each piece is examined and compared and contrasted with the others to construct an image of the person you are dating. I refer to this mental portrait as your *trust-profile*, or profile for short. It is your profile of a partner and not the partner him- or herself that generates your feelings of trust or mistrust.

It is not just during the dating process that you profile others. Profiling is the natural way the mind works to evaluate the degree of trust you should place in another person. Although this happens automatically, it is to your advantage to actively engage in the process of placing your trust. The better you understand the way that your mind compiles a profile of a person whom you are getting to know, the more active you can be in determining the amount of trust you should invest.

Constructing a Trust Profile

Trust is a word frequently used in relationships but also one that often escapes practical definition. *Webster's Dictionary* defines trust as the "firm belief or confidence in the honesty, integrity, reliability, and justice of another person or thing." But

- How does this confident feeling of trust develop?
- How can you tell when you should trust a partner?
- How can you avoid becoming too trusting?
- Doesn't trust just happen naturally?
- How can you trust again after your trust has been betrayed?
- Why can you sometimes have mixed feelings of trust at the same time toward the same partner?
- Why can you sometimes feel a deep trust at one point in time but then feel an overwhelming mistrust at another toward the same partner?

These questions highlight some of the perils and pitfalls of determining the measure of trust you should place in a partner. Trusting a partner goes far beyond just believing your partner will be faithful and true. There is more to being a trustworthy partner than just the promise of fidelity. Trust encompasses every aspect of a partner—from something as simple as trusting that your partner will call you at the promised time, to trusting your partner to support you through your most difficult nightmare. Take away trust, and you lose the core of intimacy; live without trust, and you will be consumed with insecurity, anger, and paranoia. Regain trust with one who is trustworthy, and you will experience the healing power of this bonding relationship dynamic. Trust is the ground from which all your expectations grow.

Trust: Willingness to Be Vulnerable

Trust creates vulnerability because it is so intensely bonding. It is as though you place a piece of your heart into the care of your partner each time you take another step of trust. With every step of trust, you draw closer to that partner. In fact, if you think of the friend you have trusted the most, this friend usually will be the one you also are the closest to.

So how does trust develop? Let me first explain it with the RAM as a visual aid. During the process of getting to know a person (the first bonding dynamic of the RAM), you gather new pieces of information about your dating partner. The RAM represents this relationship process of gaining new information about your partner by raising the Know slider. It is important to remember that getting to know someone, just as with each of the five relationship dynamics, is bonding. This deepening knowledge leads to the second relationship dynamic of building trust, where you arrange these pieces into an internal, mental profile of your partner.

As the profile of your partner becomes more developed, you should be in a better position to determine the degree of trust this partner deserves. Like the other four relationship dynamics, trust also is extremely bonding. You lose objectivity when you trust someone. Trust leads you to interpret your partner's actions and motives in the best light; trust prompts you to rationalize any warning signs of a partner's behavior in order to not jeopardize the security you feel in your bond with that partner. Trust then becomes a lens that positively alters your view of a partner, blocking out the shortcomings while highlighting the strengths.

When Trust Puts You at Risk

Although the bond of trust is an important ingredient in forgiving your partner when you have been hurt, you need to be cautious that you do not compromise your emotional safety and mental judgment just to maintain the security of having someone love you. This is represented on the RAM by the Trust slider being placed significantly higher than the Know slider. This bind held Melissa in her relationship with Joe.

Melissa and Joe sat down in my office and talked about how their long-standing marriage relationship had deteriorated over the last several years. As they described their problems, nothing really added up to explain Melissa's emphatic need to get help. Joe was pleasant, controlled, and cooperative in the sessions.

When I walked out to the waiting room for their fourth appointment, Melissa sat alone. She explained that Joe refused to come back because he did not feel there was any need for the counseling. Melissa said she needed to talk with someone, even though he did not see any reason to join her.

At the end of the session, Melissa stopped before walking out the door and disclosed a secret she had never told.

"Joe goes into rages," she quietly confessed. "Sometimes, he gets physical with me," she concluded.

The next session she described the pattern of Joe's emotional and physical abuse.

"I never know when he will flip out. The last time, he was working in the yard with me. All of a sudden he started complaining that there was too much work and that it should have been done by the kids. Before I knew what was happening, he had me pinned up against the outside garage wall."

She slipped off her jacket and revealed the back of her arm that was severely scraped and bruised. After explaining more details of her husband's explosion, I asked her how often this had happened in the past.

Trust then becomes a lens that positively alters your view of a partner, blocking out the shortcomings while highlighting the strengths.

"Sometimes five or six months passed between rants, and other times it was a matter of only one or two weeks."

We discussed her options. She strongly insisted that she would not report this. She had never reported any of his attacks in the past and was not going to start now. Her reasoning was that she knew that Joe was better than what he looked like during one of his rages. She believed that at some point Joe would face this aggressive behavior and change.

When I asked if she had ever been able to talk with him about his abusiveness, she reluctantly told me that he never would admit he had done anything hurtful to her and that he denied any emotional problems. There had been times when she was so hurt and angry that she would show him her bruises and attempt to convince him to talk to someone, maybe even his doctor, to see if there would be a medicine that might help. Even though Melissa stayed calm, Joe always became angry and threatening during these conversations. Eventually, Melissa's hurt and anger would subside and she would go on as if these incidences had never happened.

She potentially had a strong support network of friends and family who would have helped her confront him with the physical evidence of his assaults if she had only revealed her secret to them. Why did she keep these attacks to herself? How did she block out his violence and interact in normal ways with him over the past twelve years?

Basically, Melissa had a trust-picture of Joe that never had incorporated his abusive spells. Even though she had to deal with the pieces of her experience with him that frightened and perhaps even traumatized her, she did so by keeping them distinct from her trust-picture. In this way these incidences were just an exception to her trust-picture and not indicative of what Joe was really like. She maintained an overidealized trust-picture that kept rationalizing and denying her repeated experiences of abuse.

It was an enormous step for Melissa to sit in a counselor's office and admit that these violent episodes were real. Last year, he had broken her arm; although again, no one had a clue that she had been abused. Her openness in counseling seemed to naturally lead her to begin disclosing these abusive occurrences with some of her closest friends and family. The more she talked, the more the contradictory pieces of her experiences with Joe came together in a single, somewhat disturbing picture. Joe had a nice side to him, but he also had what was referred to in the last chapter as the "Swiss cheese conscience." He could block out his raging behaviors and not even think about what he had said or done, let alone the harm he had done to his wife. Melissa's *lack* of an integrated trust-picture kept her level of trust much higher than what she really knew about Joe. This immobilized her when she did try to confront Joe, leaving her only able to approach him when her emotion reached an inescapable level. However, once the transient emotion passed, her unrealistically positive trust-picture kicked back in and pushed Joe's abusive pattern back into the shadows of her mind.

The Trust slider on the RAM moves up to represent the increases in your level of trust (see Figure 10.1). Always try to keep it lower than what you know about your partner. In other words, *stay in the safe zone*. In order to do this, you must avoid trusting a partner more than you really know him or her (see Figure 10.2). This is why it is critical that you understand the way you are putting together the pieces of what you unquestionably know about a partner (profiling) as you construct your trust-picture of that person. Whenever your trust exceeds what you know about your partner, your risk goes up.

Your developing profile of a partner generates the degree of your overall confidence or trust in that partner. All of your beliefs and expectations about how your partner will treat you, meet your needs, talk to you, and behave in various settings are produced by this internal, mental trust-profile. When you are disappointed, then your profile is altered in negative ways and your trust is diminished (you would move the Trust slider

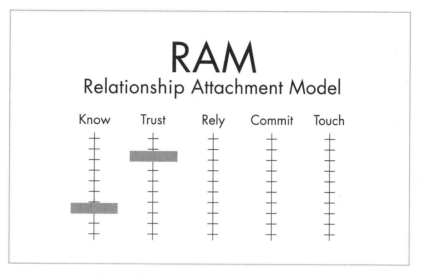

FIGURE 10.1 High-Risk Relationship: Overtrusting and Naive

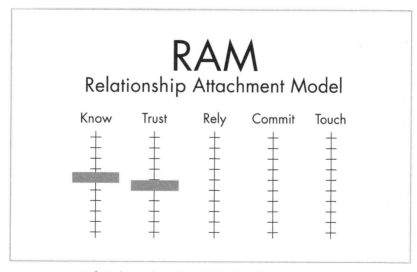

FIGURE 10.2 Safe Relationship: Trust Who You Know

down on the RAM). But if you are treated in ways that meet your expectations and needs, then your profile of your partner is altered in a positive manner and your trust grows. This is why your confidence in a partner varies from time to time.

Dr. Jekyll and Mr. Hyde Partners

Have you ever felt like you were dating a partner like Joe who could be the most wonderful partner you ever knew at one time and a total jerk another? Why do you sometimes feel like you are involved with two totally different people? Let me further explain how this happens.

On one occasion, your partner looks like the compilation of your worst dating nightmare. Then the next day something happens, and you have a 180-degree change of opinion. Now you view your partner as one who can do no wrong.

Basically, you have rearranged the pieces of your trust-profile and moved the most positive pieces to the forefront and pushed the disconcerting ones into the shadows. These variations in the mental profile of your partner and their corresponding shifts of trust create major changes in your feelings of closeness, safety, and security. This is exactly what was happening in Melissa's mental profile (i.e., trust-picture) of Joe. This explains why her feelings of closeness returned immediately after her initial anger subsided; she filtered out the negative pieces of her relationship with Joe and maintained a positive portrait in her mind.

If you are living just to feel secure, like I think Melissa was, you will keep altering your trust-profile in ways that override what you are growing to know about your partner. Those negative pieces threaten your image of security and love. You end up living with a partner who is more in your mind than in reality.

The most sobering part of these shifts of perspective is that they can happen so fast that you don't even realize they occurred. At first, you clearly see the pieces that hurt and anger you, and you conclude that they are a persistent pattern in this partner. However, you erase them from your profile as soon as your partner pulls the right strings and tells you what you want to hear. For instance, this may happen when your partner apologizes with excessive contrition, makes you feel guilty, threatens something drastic, withdraws and emotionally abandons you, becomes enraged and attacks you, or argues for so long that you can't remember what originally upset you.

The arrangement of the pieces of what you know about a partner then determines your level of trust in that partner and the feelings of security and closeness that come from that level. When your profile mutates from positive to negative, your feelings of closeness diminish. This can make you insecure and long for that feeling of being loved by your partner. If you are not careful, you will end up constructing a profile that is grossly inaccurate from the real person you have a relationship with—and only will provide a fleeting feeling of security at best.

Initial Impressions

No one enters a new relationship with a mental blank slate. Everyone brings previous profiles and tidbits of information from other partners and relationships to each new partner. You can think of these preexisting profiles as databases. The three primary databases that comprise your collection of previous partner experiences, images, feelings, trigger-points, and fantasies are

1. *your stereotypes*—ways that a partner is similar to your fixed and conventional opinions
2. *your associations*—ways that a partner reminds you of someone else
3. *your ideals*—ways that a partner fits your ideal hopes and standards

These existing databases set you up either to be an excellent judge of character or to be too trusting or too suspicious. If your databases are filled with disappointments, hurts, and broken trusts, you will become biased in one direction or the other. In order to protect yourself and pace your growing trust in a relationship, you must recognize how your mind is constructing a profile of the person you are getting to know from what you are learning about him or her *and* from what you are bringing to this relationship from your databases of stereotypes, associations, and ideals.

These mental databases are the starting points for your initial feelings of trust toward a dating partner. You want to accurately alter your profile with each piece you gain from your ongoing experiences as a couple, the emerging patterns, and the new things you discover about this partner. However, the *meaning* of how a partner acts and treats you is determined by your unconscious comparison of his or her actions to ways others have treated you in the past.

When drawing conclusions from initial impressions, your mind determines the trustworthiness of another person very similar to how the profession of profiling works. A profiler approaches a crime scene with an established set of standards to compare the evidence of the present criminal with previously documented crime patterns. For instance, in 1974, the U.S. Federal Bureau of Investigation (FBI) formed the Behavioral Science Unit to investigate serial rape and homicide cases. They gathered extensive facts about these crimes from interviews with thirty-six criminals. Next, they compared each piece of information to create different categories of similar traits and unique identifiers of the offenders.

These categories of criminal patterns were brought to the evaluation of each new crime. Investigators would sift through the evidence from a crime scene and compare each piece of information to these categories to determine a match, referred to as a "hit" (no pun intended). When the profile was completed, the total hits were tallied for a comparison between the unsolved crime and the corresponding categories of past crime patterns to make further implications about the traits and habits of the specific criminal.

In the same way, you compare each of the new pieces of experience and information you have gained in your present relationship to your prior dating and relationship experiences. Every time there is a hit between what you are learning about your partner and some stereotype, association, or ideal, you would naturally assume that the other characteristics from that database should also apply to this partner.

If you are thinking to yourself, "This is too much work. There's no way I can do all this!" Then you need to realize that you already do all this. You just are not aware how active your mind is when you are getting to know a new dating partner (or anyone for that matter).

Recently I was interviewed for an article on the PICK program, and the reporter told me she was going to include a rebuttal to my program from her own experiences with dating. I asked what she was going to write and if I could respond to her remarks. She agreed.

She stated that she liked to just relax and have fun when she entered into a new relationship. She did not want to have to analyze everything and worry about figuring out all this "stuff" from a guy's family, other relationships, and so on. It took away from the innocence and spontaneity of romantic love.

I thought for a minute about her rebuttal and then let her know that I totally agreed with her. In fact, everything she said was exactly what I would like to help singles accomplish by learning this RAM for dating. However, I also told her that I think everyone who dates analyzes the other person whether they like to admit it or not. At that point she burst out, "I always overanalyze everyone and everything—that is why I try so hard to *not* analyze a new dating partner. On the first date I am wondering about ridiculous things like what this guy will look like when we are old and gray!"

I reassured her that this is somewhat normal and that she will be better able to relax and just enjoy the moment if she knows where she is going and how she plans to get there. It is like driving a car on a trip and feeling lost because you are unsure of where you are. You can't enjoy the ride, because all you can think about is looking for the signs that will tell you exactly where you are. But when you have a road map, know where you are going, and see that you are right on track to getting there, then you can relax and enjoy the scenery.

In the beginning of a relationship, you may feel enraptured with this seemingly perfect new dating partner. If you know that you are making lots of assumptions and that you won't let that infatuated feeling raise your trust too high, then you can keep your boundaries and totally enjoy the thrill of the ride. If everything goes south somewhere in the second month, then you have not entrusted your deepest secrets, planned out the rest of your life with this person, and set yourself up for deep hurt and rejection.

Early in a relationship, your profile of a partner will be more influenced by what you fill in than by what your partner contributes.

The reporter then admitted that her taste of fun definitely soured when she let herself become overly involved with a guy who she later discovered was a jerk. We concluded that understanding how trust is built and following a plan for constructing that trust breeds confidence and a feeling of control in new and uncharted relationships.

When you stop and think about it, you are always comparing a new relationship with your previous experiences. You use preexisting mental molds to initially determine the trust value of someone you have just met. So each new experience is automatically compared to these three already-existing databases: your stereotypes, ideals, and associations. From these comparisons, you determine the meaning and value of each bit of new information.

Filling in the Gaps

At first, the pieces of your experience of a new partner are disjointed. This is why, starting with your first impression, you fill in the gaps of what you know about a partner with information you have in your existing mental databases. This information from your stereotypes, associations, and ideals interacts with your first impressions of a dating partner to prompt your opinions and expectations (see Figure 10.3). Based on your opinions and expectations, you rely on a partner to meet those expectations. What actually happens (i.e., *experiences that test out reliance*) then alters your developing trust-picture, confirming or denying the files you used to fill in the gaps. We all make assumptions when we form an opinion of someone after only one encounter. However, you should reserve your conclusions (good or bad) until enough experiences have accumulated to reveal patterns. Initial impressions will often change as a result of new ongoing experiences.

Early in a relationship, your profile of a partner will be more influenced by what you fill in than by what your partner

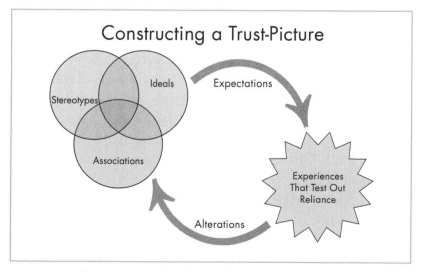

FIGURE 10.3 Constructing a Trust-Picture of a Partner

contributes. This is why, during the first few months of a relationship, you are in the most danger of investing an overabundance of trust with an underdeveloped trust-profile. Because trust is so bonding, your feeling of connection and attachment to your partner can rise high above the matured accuracy of your mental picture. You should exercise boundaries on your trust during this time so that you protect yourself from drawing premature conclusions, or filling in the gaps with an overidealistic approach.

These three databases are illustrated by Sharon when she first met her blind date. She walked into the restaurant lobby anxiously looking around for another loser. This was her stereotype of guys she met online—losers. They never looked like their picture, so she focused her sights on the dorkiest looking thing sitting by himself, bopping his head to the background elevator music. Just when she was about to bite the bullet with an introduction, she heard a voice from behind her inquiring, "Excuse me, would you happen to be Sharon?"

She turned to come face-to-face with Brad Pitt's twin. At that moment it did not really matter which Sharon he was looking for, he found her. In her initial act of profiling, she drew an immediate mental sketch from her *association* database (he looks just like . . .) and it registered a positive hit from her *ideal* database (what I always wanted was a guy who looked just like . . .).

However, things took a turn for the worse as they were eating dinner. Brad's look-alike told her that he was "between jobs" and "living with his mother." Uh-oh! She pulled the "loser" file back up from her *stereotype* database and compared it with his situation—another positive hit but with a negative implication.

The rest of the evening was uneventful. Although Sharon wanted to believe her motives were of a higher order, she had to admit to herself that her decision to go out again was simply because of his awesome looks. She reassured herself that she needed more time to reveal patterns and it would only be fair to meet with him several more times to get a thorough "look," even if he was not her type. She thought about the three-month rule and decided that she would have to simply suffer through it.

Sharon filled in the gaps with contents from her three databases until the details of his life and personality became more apparent. She avoided the dangers of premature conclusions, although she was cautious and determined not to let his good looks sweep her off her feet.

On their third date, he invited her to his place for dinner and a movie (he'd do the cooking). She arrived at an attractive home that turned out to belong to him. After a few more *subtle* questions, she learned that he had a consulting business and was "between jobs." Also, she discovered that he had promised to help his mother get back on her feet after his father's untimely death. He had a small area of his home set apart for her residence.

Sharon realized that rather than being a loser, he was actually quite thoughtful, giving, and empathetic. These new facts greatly changed her initial interpretation of the information that pulled up the loser folder and made her take a second look at her negative stereotypes.

Over time, with self-restraint, open-mindedness, and diverse experiences, you can construct an accurate mental profile of a partner that correspondingly leads you to take safe steps of trust. You may have to look past some of your stereotypes or differentiate between this partner and your associations, but you can gain an accurate profile if you take the needed time and explore the right areas.

Sharon could have easily overreacted to either her initial positive association or her initial negative stereotype. Instead, she resisted her primal urges to act on the moment and invested the necessary time to build an accurate and well-rounded trust-profile.

Cleaning Out Your Files

What are you to do if your database has several corrupt files in it? What if you had so many bad experiences that you can't see a present partner apart from the ghosts of your past? What if you don't trust?

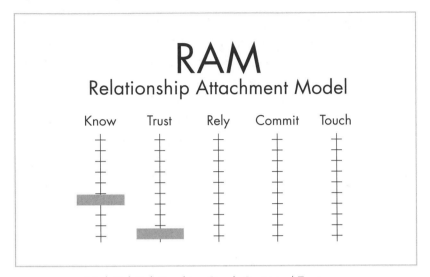

FIGURE 10.4 High-Risk Relationship: Overly Restricted Trust

Using the RAM to picture this relationship pattern, you would place the Know slider fairly high, but the Trust slider would remain low, even though you have strong evidence in your relationship to increase your trust in this partner (see Figure 10.4). It is smart to hold back on trusting a partner when it is not merited; however, this particular pattern emerges when there is sufficient reason to move ahead with trust, but you feel a persistent reluctance. This pattern occurs with people who struggle to develop trust.

It is as though there is a ceiling to your trust. Your dating partner can do something right one hundred times, but as soon as you find one slipup, you say to yourself, "I knew it! It was just a matter of time before the true colors would be revealed. Those one hundred good times were just exceptions!"

This pattern is the same as what happened to Melissa after Joe divorced her. The irony of her marriage was that she realized that Joe was much more messed up than she had ever let herself realize throughout their twelve-year marriage. Joe announced that he was going to leave her. Strangely, he reassured her that it had nothing to do with her—it was all his issues. Later, it came out that he had been seeing someone behind her back.

After he left and Melissa was alone, it was as if someone pulled back the curtains and opened her eyes to all of the abuse she had been looking past. The trust-picture of Joe became much more integrated with his good qualities no longer standing independent of his lack of conscience and abusive behaviors. She was shocked that she could have overlooked so much for so long.

I think Melissa's awakening *to* her nightmare left an indelible mark on her stereotype of a partner. As a result, her negative stereotypes and associations of how a partner can be two-faced began to dominate as she dated. Her developing trust-picture was skewed because she could never fully integrate her positive experiences with these negative files in her databases. Therefore, her profiles of new dating partners were always overshadowed by her memories of Joe. If she could have cleaned out those files from her mental databases, then her trust-picture would have been altered in positive ways when a partner consistently treated her positively, and one slipup would have been seen in context with the one hundred affirmations.

Typecasting Partners

If you have experienced a profound betrayal of trust, then all three of your databases are likely to have corrupt files. You probably have some stereotypes that cast all partners as cheaters, takers, or abusers—it is just a matter of time. I remember one single rationalizing her reluctance to date with the belief that there were no good available partners because all the good men were married. (I think some married women also have this same stereotype but with one twist—the good guys are just married to someone else.)

Stereotypes, at best, are overgeneralizations, and these specific stereotypes are based largely on an inaccurate portrayal of facts. They may be accurate to your previous dating or marriage experiences; however, they are not true of all potential partners. You may have endured childhood abuse, neglect, or mistreatment that shaped your stereotypes and associations in extremely negative ways. Or perhaps your harsh realities of relationship pain came in adult relationships that eroded your optimism and hopefulness, leaving you cynical and untrusting.

After several years of learning, soul-searching, and attending the PICK program (twice, actually), Melissa went out with a man she had met on an Internet dating website. She knew that anyone on a dating website can falsify his profile and look much better than he really is, but she also felt confident in her newly developed ability to pace a growing trust. She had turned her pain into a gain, figuring that she clearly understood the signs of an inconsistent conscience. She also knew that she had taken enough time to work out her initial emotional neediness that engulfed her during her divorce process and over the course of the following year, and she had achieved a peace with her aloneness.

Matthew had a good balance of being a straight shooter and knowing how to nurture. He was not one of those guys who overpowered Melissa with attention and love talk. Instead, he expressed genuine interest in her while respecting her need to go slow. He seemed to be able to enjoy the present without pressuring her for the next step.

There was one time in the third month that Matthew had a conflict at work and was fuming about it when he arrived at Melissa's home. She immediately sensed his angry feelings and became quiet and withdrawn. Matthew assured her that he was just upset with work, but she seemed reluctant to believe him. He suggested that she listen to him rehash the work situation, talk with him about his options, and see that he is not going to become explosive or violent. "You will never build trust in a man again unless you first take a step of trust," Matthew explained supportively.

She agreed, and by the end of the evening she was feeling secure again. He also felt better having talked out his work conflict and having gained Melissa's perspective and ideas. Something happened that Melissa had never really experienced with Joe—anger actually brought her and Matthew closer.

Melissa's healing process in her ability to trust culminated with a situation where Matthew again became angry, but this time with her. Melissa had borrowed Matthew's cell phone when she traveled to a conference because her phone had broken. Matthew was happy to lend his phone to her but asked that she be sure to write down any messages from calls that she answered because he used that number for work. She omitted telling Matthew about two messages, one that resulted in a severe reprimand from his boss.

When she saw Matthew angry, she immediately retreated to a withdrawn and defensive stance. He became even angrier because it seemed like she was denying him the right to even be appropriately angry. Matthew knew that they could begin to reenact the old patterns between her and Joe, so he went to Melissa's home and asked if they could sit down at the dining room table and have a business meeting. He smiled reassuringly that it would be beneficial for them in their relationship.

They talked about the situation, and she apologized for neglecting to relay his messages to him. He accepted her apology and then pointed out that it was not a big deal. But even if it was, he was not going to treat her in the ways that Joe had. They discussed the ways she had been brainwashed to react to any sign of her partner being angry with the same degree of fear and panic that she had when Joe was angry.

Melissa became more trusting, which allowed Matthew to be less filtering with his feelings. He watched her grow to trust that he could be angry without threatening her in any way. Matthew knew that if she had not healed in her trust, then their relationship would have been handicapped. He believed that she could come out of her past and let go of the pain. However, he also knew in his heart that if she didn't, then he would not be able to continue in a relationship with her. He could help her heal, but he could not keep walking her through the steps of differentiating between Joe and himself. If she stayed stuck, he knew that he would never be given the trust that he deserved.

Trustworthy Partners

Matthew exemplified many of the characteristics of a trustworthy partner. Of course, many qualities make a partner
worthy to be trusted. Eight personal traits in particular rise to
the top in several research studies that examined personal attributes strongly associated with stable and fulfilling marriages.[1]

Mature	evidenced by the ability to delay grati-fication and put someone else's interest before one's own
Adaptable	flexibility with changes
Responsible	indicated by a track record of following through on various promises and responsi-bilities
Relational	a need for companionship, interaction, and interpersonal activities
Insightful	an ability and openness to see and understand oneself from other perspectives
Assertive	a determination to express what is in one's mind in appropriate ways
Giving	an enjoyment with making another happy
Emotionally stable	normal ranges of emotion (i.e., few to no extreme moods or mood shifts) and a receptivity to the emotions of others

Forgive, but Don't Trust

A final word on this whole subject is that there is a difference
between forgiveness and trust. The origin of the English word

forgiveness meant "letting go." Years ago you would have heard someone say, "Forgive the ropes," when they wanted you to let go of the ropes. Forgiveness is the act of facing the pain and anger that someone has brought into your life and letting go of any need or desire to pay that person back.

Trust, on the other hand, is a confidence in the integrity of a person to act in a particular way. Forgiveness is past oriented; trust is present and future focused. Forgiveness is about letting go; trust is about holding on. Forgiveness is something undeserved; trust is something earned.

I have used a lighthearted and fictitious illustration of trust versus forgiveness in sessions with clients. I explain to them, "Let's say that at the end of our session we stand up to leave the room, and you open the door for me and politely offer, 'After you, Doc.' But just as I walk through the door, wham—you slam it on the back of my heel. As I double over in pain, you profusely apologize, explaining that I had said something in the session that upset you and you lost all impulse control as I walked out the door.

Healthy relationships are sustained by forgiving spirits.

"I reassure you that I will forgive you, and we set our next appointment. Once again, after the appointment, you hold the door for me. I walk through but then, wham—you slam my heel in the door just like the first time. I pick myself up off the floor to hear you begging my forgiveness again, explaining that once more I had angered you and you were unable to contain your fury.

"Now," I explain to the client, "I would certainly forgive you that second time. However, I would never trust you to hold the door open for me again."

Healthy relationships are sustained by forgiving spirits. No one survives twenty, thirty, forty-plus years of holding it together without ample times of letting it go. Find out how your dating partner forgives you. Find out what your partner is like when he or she is angry at you. Find out how your dating partner handles your anger, especially when it is directed at him or her.

At the same time, know that repeated times of forgiving the same offense may indicate a reason to rethink your trust. It may not be an issue of forgiveness; instead, it may be a warning sign of untrustworthy patterns. This can be confusing at times. You may wonder if you were being unfair or allowing your own stereotypes or associations to color your trust-picture of your partner. Fill in the worksheet (Figure 10.5) to sort through your data files and gain better clarity on the ways your partner fits the MARRIAGE qualities. Over time and with careful thought, you will become confident in the accuracy of your mental trust-picture of your partner.

DON'T FORGET

- It is your trust-profile of your partner and not the partner him- or herself that generates your feelings of trust or mistrust.

- Do your best to stay in the safe zone. Avoid trusting your partner more than you really know him or her.

- Three databases comprise your collection of previous partner experiences: stereotypes, associations, and ideals.

- Beware of *filling in the gaps* with an over-idealistic approach.

Qualities of a Partner	Stereotypes of a Partner	Associations with a Partner	Ideals for a Partner	Partner Traits
Mature				
Adaptable				
Responsible				
Relational				
Insightful				
Assertive				
Giving				
Emotionally Stable				

FIGURE 10.5 Worksheet for Sorting Through Your Data Files

Directions: In the first column, Stereotypes of a Partner, list all of the positive and negative stereotypes you have with each of the eight MARRIAGE qualities. Then think of specific people whom you associate with each of these traits. These people often become lenses that color your view of a dating partner. Write down the names of these people in the Associations column. In the Ideals column, write out ways that you would want to see each of the MARRIAGE qualities practiced by a partner. Finally, compare these columns with the actual traits your partner possesses.

11

If I Scratch Your Back, Will You Scratch Mine?

RAM Dynamic 3: Will You Meet My Needs?

⊂⊃

In order to have a smooth transition from your dating relationship into marriage, you need to master the important area of embracing your partner's needs. Equally important, you must be sure that your partner will also embrace your needs; this mutual embracing of needs leads to a deeply satisfying relationship.

- What are the characteristics of a partner that will meet my needs?
- How do I know my partner will care about meeting my needs?
- If my partner and I are compatible, will we automatically meet each other's needs?

- What if my partner and I have different needs?
- How fast should I grow to depend on my partner?
- How do I know if my partner is overly dependent?
- How do I know if I am overly dependent?
- How do I know that my partner will give to me like I give to him or her?

Brian and Sandra had a great thing going while they were dating, because their lives were simple and their needs were few. They had not anticipated the changes they would face with the additional roles and responsibilities marriage would bring. It is possible to unearth a gem during dating who turns into a jerk in marriage.

Her Needs

"If I had known that Brian was going to act like this, then I would have never married him. When we were dating, he was wonderful. We both were working on our graduate degrees and spent most of our time talking, studying together, and escaping from the academic grind with some fun, mindless outing. We were best friends.

"I never thought I could meet a man who was so nice, so good-looking, and so intellectually stimulating. We would sit for hours surrounded by a sea of books and papers, pizza boxes, and coffee cups while discussing art (my major) and psychology (his major) and every other topic imaginable. I had visions of spending my life on this island of intimacy.

"We married by the end of our first year together and moved into a small apartment that was part of the married housing for graduate students. We named it our honeymoon tree house, because it was a third-floor apartment that overlooked a huge oak tree. Nothing could have made that year sweeter. I had never felt happier.

"Even though that was only three years ago, it seems like another lifetime. We graduated together and bought a small fixer-upper in a suburb outside of the city. I took a teaching position in a community college in our town, and Brian accepted an internship in a downtown clinic while pursuing his doctorate. I became pregnant—we called her our housewarming gift—but as guilty as I feel saying this, that seemed to be the start of our downhill spiral.

"To be blunt, Brian does nothing to help out, not even the typical stuff a guy would do, like taking out the trash or trimming the hedges. I take care of all of the shopping, meals, housework, chauffeuring, day-care arrangements, and even our social calendar. On top of that, I also mow the lawn, clean the gutters, and have learned how to do basic plumbing and drywall repair.

"Brian and I have not been out alone since Amber was born, and I know that if we ever do go out, it will only be because I plan it and make it happen. He doesn't take the initiative for anything. The house is a wreck; he has not completed one project in the two years we have lived there. He's become such a jerk!

"He walks in the door, tries to avoid me and Amber, and sneaks off to his study the first chance he gets. I have tried to talk to him about what is most important—our relationship, our family, our home—and he seems to listen, but nothing ever changes.

"Frankly, if things don't get better, I am seriously thinking of separating. I do everything anyway."

His Needs

"Well, that's her story—but she hasn't told you all of the facts— like the stress I am under with my doctoral program and working full-time at my internship, or that I travel an hour every day to get to my job at the clinic and usually go right from the clinic to my classes. Four days a week I don't get home until 9:30 P.M., and then I have homework to finish before I go to bed.

"I feel terrible about spending so little time with Amber, but I don't have a choice. Sandra used to understand the pressure of tests and papers, but now she seems to think that I can just blow off my assignments and relax. She is always mad at me.

"You wonder why I avoid her when I walk in the door? It is because she bombards me with a list of things to do and reasons to feel guilty. I know it sounds weak to hide from my wife, but Sandra makes me feel so inadequate. Her dad had a nine-to-five job, and when he arrived home, he sat down to a hot meal and an evening with the family. Maybe we will have that schedule some day, but we both knew that we would have to make sacrifices over the next few years in order to achieve it. At least I am doing better than my own father who was always drunk and ranting.

"Buying this house has been a big mistake. We should have rented an apartment like what we had in grad school. At that time, we just called maintenance with any problem we encountered and they took care of it. But with our house, it is always something—leaky faucets, cracks in the ceiling plaster, electrical outlets that stopped working, and a washer that keeps breaking down. I never have time to work on anything, and Sandra hates me for it.

"I don't really want a divorce. But every time I try to talk with Sandra, she becomes vicious, attacking and blaming me for everything. She is the one who is acting like a jerk. She never supports or helps me with any of my responsibilities. Somewhere along the way, I think she stopped loving me. So what am I to do?"

Mutual Need Fulfillment

"Why can't you *both* get what you want?" I prodded. When they fudged and talked around the question, I asked it again—this time more forcibly than the first time.

"You have come to me for counseling, and it is clear that you both have above-average communication skills and intelligence and that you bring to this situation a history of getting along—so figure out some way for both of you to get what you want."

Sandra and Brian were speechless. They looked at me, then at each other, and then back at me. Obviously they had become convinced that there was no way for both of them to be happy. They had become polarized.

"Listen," I continued, "having a baby will change your life, and buying a house at the same time doubles the stress. You were used to a simple lifestyle with lots of togetherness and little responsibility. But you both have become stuck in a *me-first* attitude toward marriage."

At this point, Brian and Sandra joined forces to convince me that their relationship was, in fact, hopeless. This is usually a good sign in relationship counseling, because the couple is mobilizing rather than staying paralyzed in their polarization. I took advantage of this by putting a twist on their perspective and sending them back to the glory days of their dating.

"I have an assignment for you. It is essential that you put serious thought and time into it. Brian, I know that you will say that you already have too many incomplete assignments, but I want you to put this one at the top of your pile this week. What good is your degree if you lose your marriage in the pursuit?"

"Sandra, I realize your time is also stretched thin, but remember how your parents always made time for each other. This is your chance to squeeze time out of your hectic routine to ultimately improve the quality and perhaps the destiny of your marriage."

When they both nodded in agreement, I then asked them, "How much time can you commit to this assignment during the next seven days?"

Brian thought an hour or two, but I retorted, "You must commit at least five hours over the course of the next seven days. Think about it, you both were arguing with me that your relationship has deteriorated to the point of separating, but when I want you to make a concerted attempt to change specific areas, you act as if it can be accomplished with minimal effort."

To be honest, I think I guilted them into agreeing to set aside an hour a day for the next seven days. If the truth were known, when relationship counseling is unsuccessful, it most often is because one or both of the clients do not put forth enough effort to accomplish the needed changes. So to seal their deal, I even asked them to sign a contract that they would fulfill this agreement. Then I told them what their assignment was.

"I want you to pretend that you are back in grad school during that first year of your relationship when you were dating and madly in love. Every day for one hour, I want you to think about that time and, knowing what you now know, write a plan for how you would meet the changing and emerging needs of your partner from that time until now. However, you are not allowed to change any of the facts or events of your life—the timing of your pregnancy, the demands of your doctoral program, or the purchase of your home. Nothing can be altered except the way you made your partner feel loved, fulfilled, supported, and affirmed.

"You must come up with at least ten significant needs that your partner now has and how those needs are different than when you were dating. Your plan must address how those needs came about and what you are going to do to respect and fulfill them."

Both Brian and Sandra scrambled to write down this assignment. It was becoming apparent to them that they would have to work harder at changing this marriage than they had anticipated. In fact, they wondered if the seven hours a week would realistically be enough time.

Before I tell you how Brian and Sandra handled their homework, let me explain the logic behind my assignment. First, the primary problem of Brian and Sandra's relationship was rooted in their dating period. Their marital conflicts were not proof that they did not belong together, that they never were really in love, that they should never have taken the step of marriage, or that they should have lived together first in order to test out their relationship. Rather, they had been naive and shortsighted while dating. They should have discussed their family backgrounds more as well as what they expected in their future roles as both spouses and parents. Brian was reenacting his role from childhood where he dealt with the conflicts of his family by hiding. His father would drink and rage. So Brian had learned to blend in with the furniture, be invisible, and always read the mood of the home as he walked through the front door.

Sandra, on the other hand, was feeling more and more alone in the home. She resented Brian's busy schedule and became increasing critical about his lack of involvement in the routine maintenance and the care of Amber. However, the more emphatic she became, the further he withdrew. She expected Brian to take care of the household projects just like her father had done, even though she knew Brian lacked those skills.

I am not suggesting that you and your dating partner need to anticipate every problem you might encounter in marriage in order to have a plan for dealing with it. That would be unrealistic and overly controlling. However, some changes are clearly foreseeable and should be discussed and prepared for. This is especially true when your relationship is in an "incubator setting." A relationship incubator setting is an environment or context in which your relationship becomes established but that *limits* the degree you and your partner could know each other. This is because you can't know a partner without taking time for mutual disclosure and *diverse experiences* together. Incubators minimize the influences of the past and distort expectations for the future. Thus in incubator settings, it is imperative for you to talk more about the family dynamics and roles that occurred during your upbringing. Many of the influences from those relationships may be dormant in the incubator setting but will flourish once you move out of the incubator into an environment that prompts parallel patterns of relating (e.g., you have a child together and now are in the role of a parent, which brings to the surface your own childhood experiences of being parented).

Incubator settings also distort the expectations of the future. Unrealistic expectations of marriage will set you up to be disappointed with the developments of married life that otherwise could have been viewed as positive. Brian and Sandra could have enjoyed the struggles of their early marital years had they known that many couples fondly look back on those times of becoming established. Although it tends to be the norm today to get established first and then marry, it was just a generation or two ago when the norm was reversed—to get married first and then together become established. Many couples of that era reflect affectionately upon those first years when they were poor and in love. It is similar to Grandpa reminiscing about walking five miles to school barefoot in the snow and uphill both ways. "Ahhh," he sighs, "those were the good ol' days."

Sandra and Brian were squandering their "good ol' days" by not working together because they had become polarized. Polarization is the most common form of power struggle in a relationship. It occurs when each partner can only see his or her own point in direct opposition to the partner's point. In counseling it usually looks like one partner talking while the other continually shakes his or her head "No." When it is the turn of partner number two, the first thing that is said is some version of "Absolutely not." You will never hear a polarized partner summarize or validate the point (or even a portion of the point) that was emphasized by the opposing side.

Try to See It My Way

Polarization was the primary problem with Sandra and Brian's relationship, with the seeds of this power struggle having been planted in the incubator of their dating relationship. When a couple becomes polarized, it is because each has come to believe that his or her needs and perspectives are positioned on an opposite and completely unrelated side to the partner's. Polarization cripples a couple's ability to meet each other's needs. It produces a tunnel vision that focuses only on what one needs and not on what the partner needs. It is based on the unspoken belief that the partner's needs are unrealistic and demanding, and that it is impossible to meet those needs without compromising self-respect and self-fulfillment. Therefore, each person becomes an advocate for self to the exclusion of the other.

In contrast, research has found that satisfying relationships are characterized by a simple formula: *two people mutually meeting each other's needs*. This formula, when activated in a relationship, generates cooperation, support, and feelings of deep fulfillment. In other words, relying on your partner and having your partner rely on you is another colossal source of bonding and connection. Just as with knowing and trusting, relying on someone intertwines vulnerability with security, giving with receiving, sacrifice with needs, and the understanding of a partner with the assertion of self.

Polarization cripples a couple's ability to meet each other's needs.

The hallmark of a mutual or reciprocal reliance is the belief that meeting the partner's needs meets a need within oneself. It is based on an old theory called dialectics. In Chinese philosophy it is referred to as the yin and the yang. Simply stated, dialectical thinking proposed the idea that opposite poles are actually connected on a continuum and that the two points being argued actually belong together under a larger, encompassing umbrella point. To the dialectical partner, the question is never "Who is right?" Rather, the question is "How do our views fit together?" Nothing stands independent of its opposite; rather, the two positions have common elements that allow harmonizing and blending.

Intimate relationships and especially marriage achieve high levels of mutual satisfaction only when both partners are focused on putting the other person's needs and wants first. Brian's and Sandra's attitudes had deteriorated to the point of only thinking about their resentments toward each other for not helping or being fair. They needed to recognize that a focus on the other person, rather than focusing solely on oneself, would have led to a greater sense of self-fulfillment. In other words, Sandra's needs were Brian's prescription for his growth and success, and Brian's needs were Sandra's prescription for her growth and success. This depicts the interconnectedness of opposing needs and views with a dialectical framework: find your life (by centering on yourself) and you will lose it; lose your life (by centering on your partner) and you will find it.[1]

A study conducted in 1984 confirmed this essential bonding core of two partners putting each other first and striving to meet the other's needs over one's own needs. Researchers interviewed newlyweds individually to gauge the degree of equity or fairness in their relationships. The newlyweds were asked a series of questions about how their partner related to four areas of personal well-being: personal concerns, emotional concerns, day-to-day concerns, and the attitudes toward opportunities gained or lost.

> *love feelings need to be protected during challenging times.*

These researchers found that the individuals participating in inequitable relationships were distressed. In fact, the more inequitable the relationship, the more distressed these individuals felt. On the other hand, those who were most comfortable in their relationship felt they were receiving exactly what they deserved from their partner—no more and certainly no less. "The best kind of love relationship," the researchers concluded, "seems to be the one in which everyone feels that he or she is getting what they deserve."[2]

Brian and Sandra's Discovery

So what happened to Brian and Sandra? I am pleased to tell you that they came back to the next session having done their homework and feeling quite enlightened. First, they revamped their views of their dating relationship. They acknowledged that if they had done even a little of this type of work during that year, then they probably would have handled the changes and stresses much better. They were embarrassed to admit that they never even talked about how they would support each other when foreseeable changes impacted their relationship, like Brian's work and school schedules, their unexpected pregnancy, or even the purchase of a fixer-upper. They assumed their love would guide and protect them through those challenges. Now they see that it was just the opposite. Love feelings need to be protected during challenging times.

Sandra thought about ways she could step in and help Brian with his research. She offered to use her break at school to go to the college library and find sources on his paper topics. When she proposed this to him in the session, he lit up with excitement. I had to gently bring them back on track because they became engrossed in brainstorming about his most recent topic and angles they could take to approach this topic. Sandra spontaneously erupted with a surge of energy, commenting that she felt just like she used to feel when they were in grad school together. I pointed out that her focus on meeting Brian's need actually met a need in her.

The session became still when Brian quietly took Sandra's hand and apologized for withdrawing into his academic cocoon over the last year. He knew that she needed more of him, but he had fallen into an old rut from childhood. So he promised to walk in the door and give Sandra and Amber the first hour. He also suggested that they set out a money jar that could be used to hire professionals to finish some of the projects that he didn't feel he could do. He thought he could start packing his own lunch and dinner and then put that savings into the jar.

I asked Brian how he felt with carving time out of his hectic schedule to address some of the needs and wants that Sandra was struggling with. He thought about it for a minute, and then said confidently, "Adequate!"

Both Brian and Sandra continued to unfold their plans for making the other person feel supported and fulfilled. At the end of that session, Sandra exclaimed that she felt like they had just celebrated Christmas. I suggested that a good motto for their relationship would be to try to outdo each other with acts of love.

By the end of their counseling, they had a completely different outlook on their marriage. I reminded them that they had both accused the other of being a jerk. They admitted that they had, in fact, both become jerks in how they became self-absorbed, focusing on their own needs and neglecting the other's.

A Good Partner Turned Jerk

Brian and Sandra exemplify a central way that good partners can become jerks. Partners who become self-absorbed for any reason, even because of emotional pain, will require more than they can give. Brian and Sandra indulged in the ecstasy of their newfound love for the first year of their relationship. However, they did not learn to love in the deeper and more substantive ways. Not until love requires sacrifice does it earn the right to be called love. I have never heard a client complain, "My partner is such a jerk because he or she is always making sacrifices to make me happy."

So how does someone become a jerk? I think there are basically two paths. First, there are the hard-core jerks who have had major character deficiencies all of their lives. These people seem to be unable to help themselves—acting like a jerk is as natural to them as breathing. They don't even have to think about how to be a jerk. It just flows. Maybe a horrible childhood or young adult experience resulted in their jerklike ways, but that injury is now out of reach, having become covered with calloused defenses and twisted thinking. If they can get better, it will only be with an equally hard-core effort. This type of jerk can take a potentially good relationship and turn it bad.

The second path begins with a potentially good partner who has become "jerkified" by forces either outside or inside the relationship. Affairs, work stresses, financial problems, and other demands are examples of the outside forces that can turn a good partner into a jerk. Communication and conflict ruts, bitterness, apathy, and neglect are examples of the inside forces that can often mutate the best qualities of a partner into the worst. In my optimistic thinking about the mental health of eligible partners, I would like to believe that at least half of those who have been dubbed "a royal jerk" are not seriously impaired in their character (the first path) but rather suffer from a temporary state of "jerkiness" (the second).

Partners who were good for an extended period fit the adage, "One partner's trash is another partner's treasure." Although they are usually salvageable if the negative forces acting upon them are altered, they often become discarded as unfit. But it is common that they then revert back to being relatively decent marriage material because their circumstances change or the stuck patterns of the old relationships are broken.

Not until love requires sacrifice does it earn the right to be called love.

This was the case with Brian and Sandra. They both had the makings of good marriage material but slid down that slippery slope of self-centeredness in their relationship. If you think your partner is a jerk, but you have had more than a four- or five-month history together of positive, loving, and equitable treatment, then you should reconsider your conclusion. Anyone can become a jerk under the right circumstances. You need to decide whether the jerk you sometimes see in your partner is the exception to the real person or simply *is* the real person.

Brian and Sandra's focus on each other in their first year slowly eroded as Brian became more entrenched in his bad habit of withdrawal and Sandra increased her demanding tactics. At first they brought the best out of each other. With the major life changes, they ended up sliding into a rut of bringing out the worst. This culminated in a breakdown of their closeness and ultimately, their commitment. When they finally were willing to step out of their self-absorbed bubble and look at what each other needed, they rediscovered that good potential the other had for closeness and love. A fulfilling relationship requires that the two partners be more concerned about giving than about receiving.

Addicted to a Newfound Love

Some people think that focusing one's attention on making the partner happy can be a recipe for personal disaster. This is true when there are serious imbalances between your levels of trust and dependency. You are in an unsafe relationship when you depend on a partner who has not earned your trust or who has consistently broken your trust.

This is portrayed by the RAM when the Rely slider is significantly higher than the Trust slider (see Figure 11.1). Try to keep your reliance on a partner as close to the level of trust you have in that partner as possible (see Figure 11.2). This ensures a feeling of safety, because you have matched your reliance with your measure of trust. In a similar way, make sure you do not try to meet a partner's needs beyond your level of trust in him or her. You are at risk not only when you depend on a partner beyond your trust, but equally so when you have a partner depend on you for needs much greater than the developed trust you have in him or her.

No one enters a new relationship with a clean slate.

Determining when you should take each step toward a greater reliance on your partner for meeting your emotional and physical needs is a delicate and dangerous course. No one enters a new relationship with a clean slate. Rather, you approach each

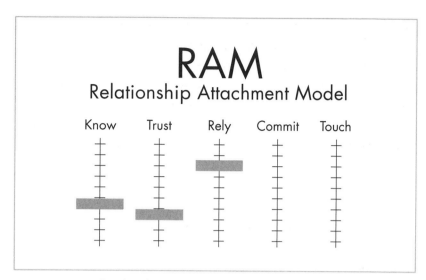

FIGURE 11.1 High-Risk Relationship: Overly Dependent

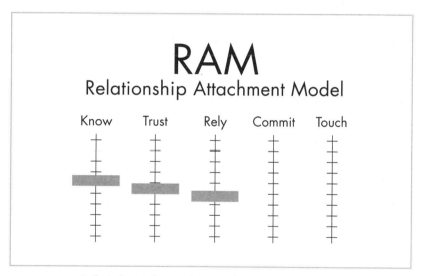

FIGURE 11.2 Safe Relationship: Rely on Whom You Trust

relationship with a specific set of needs and wants. Some may long for a partner to depend on. If you are the sole head of a household, for instance, then you have been solo with more responsibilities than any one person was meant to carry. You have probably expended all of your energy working and trying to further your career with additional jobs, evening classes, or attending seminars and workshops; and you have been taking care of your children, chauffeuring them to all of their activities, and trying to find time to do something fun but feeling that all you do is yell. You fantasize but then become cynical about finding a partner who will step in and help out to relieve you of the pressure and strain of being alone. Do you think you approach a relationship in the same way as the confident and carefree single whose greatest pressure is deciding what to do on a Friday night?

Some may feel needy without any specific reason or present circumstance. It may be your personality or because of something in your background. In Chapter 3 we covered three major contributing experiences of life that cause a person to feel emotionally depleted and set that person up to become overly dependent on a partner. However, there may be no clear explanation why you feel lonely and vulnerable to forming too strong of a dependency.

It is imperative that you understand your own personality and emotional state at the time you enter into a new relationship. Make sure you have not been primed to become immediately overly dependent because of some unique or temporary influence on your emotional shape. Various conditions besides just the rebound effect create vulnerability toward losing yourself in another partner: insecurity, loneliness, impulsivity, unresolved childhood issues, and others.

Addicted to Loving

It is equally dangerous to have an exaggerated need to be needed. In this case, your partner's reliance on you ends up disproportionate to your reliance on him or her. You spend all your time and energy taking care of your partner. In some unhealthy manner, this act of selflessness does not lead to a reciprocated attention to you, but rather to the ultimate loss of your self.

Years ago I was teaching singles the PICK program and played a small segment of the 1968 Columbia Pictures musical version of Charles Dickens' *Oliver Twist*. It was a scene in Fagan's hideout where the villainous and cruel Bill Sikes demanded that his girlfriend, Nancy, kidnap young Oliver from the secure family where he had been placed and bring him back to the inner-city gang. When Nancy refused, Bill first grabbed her around the neck and then backhanded her, knocking her to the ground. It is such a disturbing scene that every time I have shown it to a group of people, you can hear a pin drop.

As Bill walks out the door, Nancy slowly pulls herself up from the floor, surrounded by the speechless boys who helplessly watched their only mother figure be physically assaulted by a bully. Nancy moved toward the door while the background music introduced a song that explained why she would stay with an abuser who was her exact opposite—"As Long as He Needs Me." In this beautiful and moving song, she explains that regardless of what others may see in Bill, she knows that he needs her. In fact, *he knows* that she will always love him as long as he needs her.

Nancy's unhealthy need to be needed led to a horrifying and violent end when Bill beat her to death with his cane. If we plotted her levels of trust and reliance on the RAM, then it would look like the unsafe imbalance portrayed in Figure 11.1. She knew he was not to be trusted. She had a realistic mental profile of Bill as an angry and controlling man who only "loved" her for what he could take from her. Yet Nancy was addicted to taking care of him. Her dependency overrode her lack of trust and clarity of judgment.

Nancy typifies how emotionally and physically unsafe a relationship becomes when there are extreme imbalances between the extent of reliance and the amount of trust that either partner has. She also exemplifies the ways that an addiction to loving compromises logic (in the Trust scale) to maintain the intensity of feeling needed (in the Reliance scale). Be sure to search your own soul to make certain that you are not bringing to your relationships a bent toward neediness that will lead to a relationship pattern like Bill and Nancy's.

Emotionally Constricted Partners

There are partners who seem to never emotionally bond because they lack a normal capacity to give intimately to the needs of their partners or to allow their partners to give to them (or both). In other words, they resent partners who depend on them, they won't let their guard down and take vulnerable steps to need their partners, or they have some combination of these two limitations.

This type of person is often known initially as a pillar of strength. If your partner is this type of person, however, in time you feel like you are in a relationship with a pillar of stone. When it comes to interacting in personal or intimate ways, these types appear more mechanical than human. In the language of the RAM, their reliance level is significantly lower than their

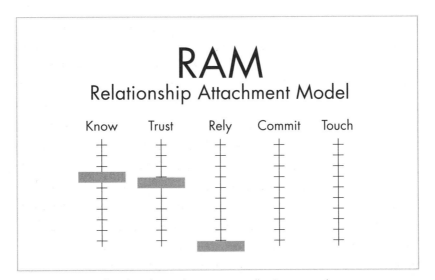

FIGURE 11.3 High-Risk Relationship: Emotionally Constricted

trust level. It is as though there is a ceiling to their ability to depend or be depended upon by a partner who has earned their trust (see Figure 11.3).

This inability to form a healthy mutual dependency in a relationship can be traced back to childhood in many instances. Those who have accumulated emotional baggage from previous adult relationships may be *reluctant* to rely on you or let you depend on them, but they usually do not lack the ability to form this kind of bond. Typically, you will find that those who lack the ability have a history of avoiding mutually dependent relationships.

The emotionally constricted personality often had a parent or caregiver who modeled this same emotional coldness. Usually, one parent had a marked deficiency of emotional bonding that set the mood of the marriage and the home. The other parent struggled to cope with the spouse who could not bond. This spilled over to the children. Some children would follow in the footsteps of the emotionally closed parent, some children ended up neglected, and others became emotionally enmeshed with the parent who was deprived from having any needs met by his or her partner. In all three cases, a disruption results in the development of the ability to emotionally give and receive that is at the heart of the bond of reliance.

There is a difference between partners who cannot develop a normal reliance in a relationship and partners who have quiet personalities and low emotional expression. These latter partners can be very giving and can form strong bonds of looking to a partner to meet their needs. However, both types of partners may look similar for a while. Unfortunately, signs of an emotionally constricted partner may not show up for months. If you are concerned about the ways your partner pays attention to what you want and need in the relationship, or the ways that your partner lets you know and give to his or her needs, then you should keep track of the balance between you and your partner's emotional investments. I refer to this as your IRA account.

Maintaining the IRA Account in Your Relationship

I have been independently employed for most of my life. For a short time, however, I worked for a practice where they would match the amount I chose to invest in my 401K. I didn't have any difficulty adjusting to this generous act of reciprocity. Whatever I put in, they put in the same amount.

The process of testing a healthy reliance involves a similar balance between the investments you and your partner make in the relationship. The acronym *IRA* represents three exchanges that you and your partner repeatedly engage in that deepen the bond of mutual reliance and can also help protect you from getting out of balance in that reliance.

The first exchange involves making an initial *investment* of trust a little beyond what you already know about the person. For example, you may open up about something a bit more personal than what you had previously shared. If your step of faith is honored, then your trust-picture is altered in positive ways and your reliance grows (see Figure 11.2 on page 255).

The second exchange involves watching to see if your partner reciprocates your gesture. This act of *reciprocity* creates a balance between what you and your partner each are investing in the relationship. For instance, if you consistently go out of your way to show interest in your partner's activities, you would expect your partner to do the same for you. A warning flag goes up with an imbalance between your investments in your partner and the ways your partner invests in you.

The final exchange that generates a stronger dependability in your relationship is the *accumulation* of consistent experiences of meeting each other's needs. This accumulation effect grows as the first two exchanges are repeated over time. You learn more about each other and slowly develop a deeper security that your partner will be there for you when needed. This accumulation of the back-and-forth exchanges cultivates a stronger and more secure confidence in your partner, while shaping the trust-picture in more positive ways.

Hand in Glove

Keeping track of your IRA account will help you pace the development of your trust and reliance. Time is essential to the building of a healthy and safe relationship. What you ultimately want in your relationship is the feeling that what your partner needs is what you like to give and that what you need in the relationship is what your partner likes to give. This *good fit* is similar to what we called complementarity in Chapter 5. In that chapter we found that the similarities between you and your partner should produce a strong bond of identification, while your differences should stretch you to become more than what you would have been on your own. This only happens when both you and your partner are committed to mutually meeting each other's needs.

Pacing your relationship with the exchanges found in the IRA means that you hold back on trying to meet needs in your partner that go beyond the level of your trust. It also means that you look to your partner to first meet your less personal and meaningful needs before moving on to deeper levels. Only after there has been an accumulation of experiences where your partner has consistently earned your trust should you then let your reliance grow. Pacing requires time, but without this essential component, your risk of forming a premature emotional dependency on someone who you later realize is not to be trusted will greatly heighten.

DON'T FORGET

- As your dating relationship becomes more serious, talk through ways you and your partner want to meet each other's needs in light of foreseeable changes.

- Polarization occurs when you believe that your needs and perspectives are positioned on an opposite and completely unrelated side to your partner's.

- Satisfying relationships have a simple formula: two people mutually meeting each other's needs.

- Changes result in new needs and often require new ways of meeting those needs.

- A good partner can turn into a *jerk* when forces either outside or inside the relationship make him or her self-absorbed.

- Developing a reliance on your partner beyond your proven trust in that partner runs high risks.

- Some partners seem emotionally strong but end up really being unable to emotionally bond.

- Maintain a healthy pace in developing your trust and reliance by keeping track of your IRA account.

12

My Word Is My Bond—Maybe

RAM Dynamic 4: Can You Keep a Commitment?

The 1987 movie *The Princess Bride* initiated both of my daughters into the dreamy world of romance, as they repeatedly engrossed themselves in it. In this classic tale of the enduring commitment of true love set in the days of castles and princesses, Westley and Buttercup fell deeply in love. Westley was a lowly servant whose famous line, "As you wish," became the hallmark of his love for Buttercup. He informed Buttercup of his intentions to leave, only to return after becoming financially capable of taking care of her.

In a tragic turn of events, Buttercup was led to believe that Westley had been slain by the dreaded Pirate Roberts. In her grief, she chose to compromise her heart and marry the prince.

Before the marriage was consummated, however, Westley (incognito, of course) kidnapped Buttercup with the hopes of learning why she did not live up to her commitment. While standing on the edge of a ravine, he lashed out at her apparent betrayal, recounting the supposed death of her beloved.

"Faithfulness he talked of, madam—your enduring faithfulness. Now tell me truly. When you found out he was gone, did you get engaged to your prince that same hour, or did you wait a whole week out of respect for the dead?"

At that moment Westley's attention was diverted, and she pushed him down the steep hill, yelling, "You mocked me once, never do it again. . . . I died that day! And you can die too for all I care!"

Westley violently tumbled down the ravine. When he was about halfway down the hill, three words faintly drifted up to Buttercup's ears, "As . . . you . . . wish."

With a sudden realization of who her kidnapper truly was, Buttercup flung herself down the hill in pursuit of Westley. At the bottom, after helping each other up, Westley implored, "I told you, 'I would always come for you.' Why didn't you wait for me?"

"Well," Buttercup hesitated, "you were dead."

To which Westley replied, "Death cannot stop true love. All it can do is delay it for a while."

The Heart of Commitment

Commitment is a persevering, unwavering devotion that even death itself cannot sway, a loyal determination to fulfill what one has promised, an ever-present "we-ness" that sustains a union through the years. Commitment is both the pledge and the proof of true love. It is what the 94 percent of surveyed never-been-married singles most likely were imagining when they stated, "When I marry, I want my spouse to be my soul mate, first and foremost."[1]

I believe that the heart of commitment is an abiding spirit of belonging to each other. It is the feeling that, no matter where you are, you are at home with this partner. "I belong to you and you belong to me" is the pulse of true devotion in any couple's relationship.

Commitment is inherent in love, and love is at the core of commitment. Beverly Fehr at the University of British Columbia conducted a study on the overlapping definitions of love and commitment. She found that the participants in her study generated sixty-eight attributes of love and forty attributes of commitment, with both love and commitment sharing twenty-one attributes. This meant that one-third of the attributes of love were terms also used for commitment, and more than one-half of the terms used to describe commitment were also used to describe love.

Commitment has this ideal thread of someone driven by desire and devotion. But if we are realistic, the fiber of commitment is not only woven from the strand of "I want to," but also has the intertwining strand of "I have to." Obligation, responsibility, and dedication demand perseverance when a commitment has been made. Regardless of your obstacles, genuine commitment presses on.

Just think of a few of your most recent task commitments. It could have been a paper you had to do, a project around your home, a volunteer position, or a favor for a friend. In many cases they started with a want-to but became more involved than you had ever imagined. Just when you decided to throw in the towel, the have-to set in. So what did you do? You bit the bullet and fulfilled your commitment. If I asked you which mind-set was the true commitment, the want-to or the have-to, you would have to conclude that both are essential components of this bonding force.

The Strands of Commitment

"I have been going out with Olivia for eleven years, since I was sixteen years old," Ethan explained as he looked intently at me from the couch. "We were best friends in high school and stuck together even though we went to different colleges. Yeah, we had our times of questioning, but we would come back together more sure. All of our friends were bugging us to marry, but we wanted to make sure we had everything in place before we tied the knot.

"Something happened about six months ago. She withdrew emotionally and sexually from me, complaining about things in our past that had never been an issue until now. It made no sense, until I found an e-mail from a guy at her workplace whom she told me was just a friend. Now I know he is much more. I have made my share of mistakes, but we always had a great relationship up to this last year.

"When she talks about us, it sounds like some other couple. I think she revised our entire past to make the good look bad and the bad look worse than it ever was, just so she would feel justified in what she is doing. I want to leave her, but I can't. She is the only real relationship I have ever had, and I don't want to lose her. I definitely don't want to start over. My family loves her, and we had planned out our entire future together. I will do anything to get her back; I just don't know how."

Ethan's commitment to Olivia was made up of a mixture of love and desire, memories and connections, fears and anxieties, and feelings of betrayal, rights, and responsibilities. Making sense of commitment is enormously challenging as your relationship becomes more complex.

When you look at Ethan's confusion, you can actually untangle the two basic strands that I previously mentioned, the want-to and the have-to. I think there is one more strand that adds to his bond of commitment: the "reluctant-to."[2] Before I explain this strand, let's start with highlighting his deep love and desire for Olivia.

The Want-to of Commitment

No doubt, Ethan loved Olivia. In one session he brought a shoe box of cards, letters, and small gifts she had given him over the years. He did this in defense of the love he knew she had for him in the past. He would listen to her in dismay when she said that she wasn't sure if she ever loved him. She wasn't even sure who she was anymore, and when she looked back on her life, she now wondered if she had been suppressing some unhappiness with Ethan all along. I assured Ethan that I believed his story of their decade together and that it was not uncommon for a partner to radically alter the way they look back on a relationship (or even marriage) as a result of an emotional affair.

This first strand of commitment is made from passion, devotion, and resoluteness. It prompts personal sacrifices for the good of your partner. It holds your partner close to you even when you are apart and elevates his or her importance when you are together.

It is this aspect of commitment that also generates an identity in being a couple, not just individuals. You start to always think of yourself in connection with your partner. You know this aspect of commitment is growing when you are having a good time and think, "I sure do wish _____ were here with me. It's not the same without him (or her)."

When you are considering the commitment potential of a partner, the following are some of the first qualities you should consider (you should also ask these same questions about yourself):

- Does your partner seem to have a "we" attitude?
- Is this partner a good friend to you?
- Does this partner share?
- Does this partner like to give? Or is this partner selfish?

These questions gain even more depth when you combine them with the Trilogy of Consistency we covered at the end of Chapter 9. This test of genuineness suggested that you look at the consistency between the patterns of someone's family background, other relationships, and conscientiousness toward you. Inconsistencies are red flags. The most important question for any inconsistency is whether or not your partner has put the time and work into changing the detrimental pattern that he or she has in one of these three areas. When looking for signs of commitment potential, you should ask:

- How do your partner's family members, especially his or her parents, live out commitment?
- Do they make sacrifices for each other?
- Do they keep each other a priority?
- Where in your partner's upbringing did he or she learn commitment?

You should also look at your partner's track record with keeping commitments with friends and other past romantic partners. You should figure that the way that they have been treated will be similar to how your partner will treat you. If he or she has been able to establish and maintain sound commitments, then you can have greater confidence that this partner will become committed to you.

However, if your partner has treated others in ways you would never tolerate, then you need to find out when and how this partner changed. Be careful you don't convince yourself with some rationalization that justifies your partner's lack of commitment to others and assumes that you are in a different class from them. Although this may boost your romantic ego, it often backfires in the disappointing reality that your partner is no respecter of persons; what goes around does in fact come around.

- What are some examples of your partner's commitment to other people?
- Is your partner loyal to those who depend on him or her?
- Does your partner make other people a priority, especially when he or she has taken on some responsibility?

What about your partner's conscience? How would you describe your partner's conscience toward you? A commitment will only be as strong as the conscience that upholds it.

- Does your partner make contact with you while you two are separated?
- How does your partner handle feelings of guilt when he or she has let you down?
- Does your partner initiate apologies and resolutions?
- Does this partner make sacrifices for you?
- Does this partner make you a priority in his or her daily schedule?

Ethan scored fairly high in the Trilogy of Consistency test, having grown up in a family that was religiously conservative and fairly vocal about their strong beliefs of family values, integrity, and finishing what you start.

Ethan's stability and seriousness had been the qualities that Olivia had been most drawn to. She had grown up in a chaotic home with constant bickering and fighting. Ethan's home had become her haven, and she often remarked how much she loved to be there.

Ironically, some of these characteristics were the very issues that Olivia now raised with him. She complained that he was no fun, that she grew up too fast, and that she needed more excitement and freedom before she settled down. However, she now has regular fights with her newfound love, is more stressed out than ever, has lost too much weight, and looks more like she has fallen back into her family of origin than moved up to true love. Ethan humorously asked if someone could be having a midlife crisis at the age of twenty-seven.

A commitment will only be as strong as the conscience that upholds it.

The Reluctant-to of Commitment

So why didn't Ethan just break it off with Olivia? She treated him coldly. She hardly ever talked to him. She acted like she didn't love him anymore. She even told him she was seeing someone else. So why wouldn't Ethan just face the facts and call it quits?

The answer lies partly with Ethan's continued love of Olivia (his want-to) and partly with Ethan's strong conviction to never quit (his have-to). But for the most part, it was because he had invested so much of himself into Olivia over the past eleven years that he was *reluctant to* go through all of that pain—the pain of breaking up, the ripping of family relationships, the reaction of friends, and the letting go of so many memories and experiences together. This is the reluctant-to strand in the bond of commitment.

This aspect of commitment is frequently left out of the common, "on the street" definition of commitment. For most, commitment is the want-to and the have-to. But it is very important that you understand this third force of commitment. This strand is made up of many threads. As you invest time and experiences in your relationship with your partner, it is as though you sew more stitches with this thread of commitment. Each stitch connects you and your partner a little more. The more meaningful your experiences, the deeper your talks, the wider your circle of friends and family, and the longer you spend together all become threads joining your lives together.

> The same force of commitment can also cause you to compromise what you want in a relationship so you don't lose what you've got.

Ethan was willing to stay in a hurtful relationship, compromise his pride, and wait to see if Olivia would return to being the woman and lover he once knew her to be—primarily because of the years of threads entwining his very soul with Olivia's. This strand of commitment says, "I am so very reluctant to let go, say good-bye, hurt my family, start over, be alone, never have anything better, and never get back what I put into our relationship," and this strand becomes more and more influential over the course of your relationship.

Enduring or Entrapping

This strand of commitment kept Ethan tied to Olivia while she sorted through her personal crisis. It empowered him to endure his feelings of betrayal. Although they broke up, Ethan continued to wait. He did not feel like dating anyone else, and he knew that he was far from over his feelings for Olivia.

It had been four months since they last talked when she sent him a text message asking how he was doing. She had broken off her relationship with her coworker and found herself reflecting on the good times she had with Ethan. Olivia felt like she was waking up from a dream as her feelings for Ethan returned. The same threads that bound Ethan to Olivia were now pulling Olivia back to Ethan.

This strand of commitment is a powerful source that holds a couple together when love and devotion are challenged or lacking. However, you need to be warned that the same force of commitment can also cause you to compromise what you want in a relationship so you don't lose what you've got. You can become entrapped by your fear of losing your partner, starting over, being alone, or not having the support you feel you need. All of these "investments" give you a staying power while the rocky times get better, but you need to be sure that they are not making you too dependent, too forgiving, and too enabling to a partner who is only getting worse.

A Stitch in Time

There is an old saying about sewing, "A stitch in time saves nine." This saying means that if there is a tear in the fabric that requires one stitch, take care of it immediately or it will grow and end up requiring nine. So for you and your partner, pay attention to the fabric of your relationship and deal with problems immediately.

Periodically take inventory of the strands of your commitment. For instance, jot down the want-to's you have for your partner; then on a different sheet of paper, write down the reluctant-to's. On the former list, include what you love about your partner, how your partner makes you feel loved and accepted, how your partner shows you respect, and what you are most attracted to in your partner. On the latter list, be sure to write down any forces that cause reluctance or insecurity about pulling away from this partner. Include any pressure and involvement from friends and family, apprehensions about going through a breakup, ways you have invested in your relationship with this partner, experiences you have shared together, the extent of openness you have achieved, ways you depend on this partner, and any apprehensions you have about no longer being in a relationship.

Now, on a third piece of paper, write down the things you do not like about your partner. Try to distinguish between minor characteristics and trivial incidences that you would naturally minimize, and patterns and habits that will both continue and get worse.

Hopefully, most of your reluctant-to's are tied in with the want-to's and consequently are positive (e.g., "I love his family and how he makes me feel a part of them—I would hate to lose them" or "I have been able to share things with her that I never talked with anyone about, because she is so understanding").

You don't want to have many of these reluctant-to's compensating for things you dislike in your partner or in the relationship (e.g., "I love his family and don't want to lose them even though he ignores me when we are together" or "I really want to break it off with her, but I don't want to go through all the heartache and emotion of breaking up").[3]

Obviously, you should have many more want-to's than negatives. Step back to take a global look at your relationship. Make sure you are not staying with a partner primarily because of the reluctant-to's (see Figure 12.1). Overall, you want to have significantly more positive want-to's that have created your reluctant-to's than want-to's that come from any of your dislikes of this partner.

I Can't Stand Being Alone

The RAM portrays two ways that commitment can become out of balance with the rest of your relationship. If you are someone who can't stand to be alone and become completely depressed when you are not in a relationship, then you are vulnerable to establishing a commitment prior to building a proven trust and reliance on a partner. What you long for is the security of feeling "at home" with a partner—the assurance that you belong to someone who loves you and that this person belongs to you. Although this is a natural desire that many have, it needs to be held in check while you build your trust in your partner (see Figure 12.2).

Pacing your relationship can be especially difficult if you already have this longing for a partner. The beginning of a relationship can feel so perfect that you would swear you already know, trust, and rely on your partner. Getting to know what a partner is really like and testing out your trust and reliance, however, takes at least *three* months. Therefore, it is important to guard your heart during this time so you do not place your-

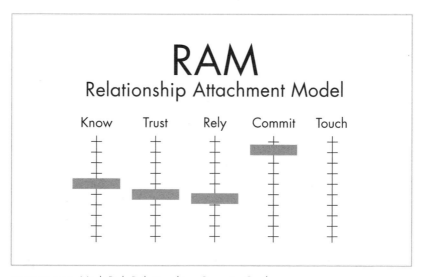

FIGURE 12.1 High-Risk Relationship: Security Seeker

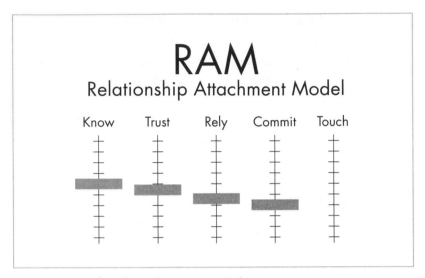

FIGURE 12.2 Safe Relationship: Security Achiever

self in the hands of a partner that later you realize was not the person you had believed him or her to be.

The Have-to of Commitment

The last strand in the bond of commitment is the have-to component and refers to the beliefs of responsibility and obligation that you or your partner associates with everything from your first meeting to marriage.

Moral responsibilities are encased within every commitment. No matter what kind of commitment you imagine, there are always responsibilities. If you say, "I am committed to my job," then you are acknowledging a responsibility, a set of obligations that come with the position.

The level of this have-to strand of commitment in a relationship corresponds with the degree to which you feel responsible to maintain that relationship. In a new relationship, for instance, you would have a small number of responsibilities. These may include such things as an obligation to keep in touch, call when you said you would, and initiate times to get together. If you had been exclusively involved with a partner for a year, then you would have a much greater set of responsibilities for maintaining that relationship.

The responsibilities of a commitment to a partner therefore increases incrementally from the lowest level in the beginning of a relationship to the highest level in marriage. Although you may think that this is obvious, it has become more complex with the rapidly rising number of couples who live together outside of marriage. This is often referred to as premarital cohabitation for those who are considering marriage in the future, and nonmarital cohabitation for those who see this arrangement as an alternative to marriage.

Commitment and Cohabitation

In the last few decades, there have been radical changes in the ethical obligations romantic partners believe they have toward each other. The results of these social shifts have contributed to a widespread crisis in this relationship dynamic of commitment. Although it is not entirely clear where these changes are leading, some startling facts should be considered as you chart your path toward marriage.

More than half of all marriages are now preceded with couples residing together before their wedding.[4] This is an enormous change from what it was just thirty years ago—in 1974, the number of couples who cohabitated before marriage was only 10 percent.

You will face decisions about living together outside of marriage (if you have not already). The facts and figures that have been collected in the past fifty years raise many questions about the way that cohabitation impacts a future marriage. Let me review the major changes that have transpired and the influences they have had on marriage and commitment.

There are two common reasons most couples give for living together before marriage: practicality and preparation. Practicality includes reasons such as saving on the expenses of running two households, convenience, spending more time together, and having a more emotionally and sexually intimate relationship without all of the obligations of marriage. Because one-third of those who cohabitate have children, some couples express additional reasons of supporting each other that involve the responsibilities of child care.

Preparation for marriage is the second common explanation for moving in together. Some of the frequently cited reasons for this explanation include making sure that you and your partner are compatible, getting to know each other more deeply, and testing out the ways that you and your partner work together in a 24–7 living arrangement.

In a recent national survey, 62 percent of young adults agreed that living with someone before marriage was a good way to avoid eventual divorce. However, all of the evidence contradicts this widespread belief. In fact, the likelihood of divorce increases dramatically for those who have lived with just one person other than the one they marry![5] Check out some of these well-established statistics on the results of couples living together outside of marriage:

- About 14 percent of those who lived together have stayed together but did not marry. In other words, they chose cohabitation as an alternative to marriage. This left 86 percent who either broke up or married.
- About 40 percent of the couples who lived together ended up splitting up.
- About 46 percent of those who lived together ended up marrying. However, their divorce rate is much higher than the average; in fact, it is just as high as the divorce rate for second marriages (around 66 percent).[6]
- In fact, for those who lived together with just one person other than the one they eventually married, they had

significantly lower satisfaction and *lower romance* in their marriage and a much higher divorce rate when compared to the average—and it worsened proportionally with each increase in the number of partners.[7]

- Depression among cohabitating couples is three times higher than that among married couples.
- About 40 percent of those who lived together now have children. Three-quarters of these children will watch their parents split up before their sixteenth birthday. This statistic for children born to married parents is only 34 percent.

These statistics are counterintuitive for most of you, especially if you are in your twenties and thirties. I have talked with many who hear these figures and immediately dismiss them as if they are completely unrelated to the trends that are happening.

It is not as though we stopped believing in marriage or wanting to get married. In a national survey, 88 percent of singles stated that they believed there is "a special person, a soul mate, waiting for you somewhere out there," and the same number agreed with the statement that they will find that special someone when they marry. Nine out of ten also concurred that the divorce rate was too high and that marriage requires hard work.[8]

Yet the trial method of noncontractual living arrangements has not resulted in better preparation for marriage. The real question we need to answer is why are those who "practice marriage" by premarital cohabitation actually doing no better, and in the majority of cases doing much worse, at making marriage work than those who follow a different path to the altar?

The Conditions of Unconditional Commitment

The vow of staying with a partner *for the rest of your life* has been central to the act of marriage since its conception. The vows that are frequently stated during the ceremony sound unconditional:

"for better, for worse; for richer, for poorer; in sickness and in health; till death do us part." This promise was considered a spiritual covenant by many in their respective faiths. *Everyone* considered it a contract that was not to be broken.

Over the last several decades there has been a greater emphasis on having a quality relationship in marriage. Everywhere you look, you read and hear experts talking about good and bad relationships, and what we need to do to make them better. But the *General Social Survey* discovered that since 1973 there has been a steady and moderate *decline* of both men and women who say they are "very happy" in their marriage![9]

We have seen that the trend to live together prior to marriage is considered as a way to improve the chances of having a satisfying marriage. So why are things getting worse? Why are the divorce rates climbing for those *practicing* marriage? It is quite the perplexing paradox that those who practice marriage by premarital cohabitation are actually less effective in marriage than those who take the leap of faith from singlehood into matrimony.

I believe that a major source of this paradox is found in the standoff between the personal longing for a quality relationship and the marital vow of unconditional commitment. It is to your credit that you want a relationship better than those that ended in divorce. Maybe you have grown up in a family where your parents divorced, or you have been divorced yourself and know firsthand the hurts and hardships that often occur with marital breakups. You are determined not to repeat the mistakes of the past, and you long for a better future.

You are very aware of the risk of failing in marriage, which does not just include the experience of a divorce. It would also include existing in an unhappy marriage where you felt trapped. You are reluctant to commit to a lifelong relationship that may not fulfill your ideals of love, partnership, and intimacy. More than half of all adults and an even larger percentage of young adults agree that one of their biggest concerns about getting married is the possibility that it will end in divorce.[10]

Yet the vows of marriage are unconditional. That is, in marriage you are promising to stay with a partner *no matter what*—even if that partner no longer fulfills your ideals. This contradicts the primary goal that most of you have to make sure you are in an emotionally fulfilling relationship. Therefore, if few of you would stay in a marriage for the long term if it continued to be unfulfilling, then what really does the promise of unconditional commitment mean?

Can you now see the standoff between a personal commitment to quality and a marital commitment to no conditions? Marriage commitment becomes redefined as an unconditional commitment *with* conditions!

Limited Investments Yield Limited Returns

At first glance, testing a relationship by living together sounds like a great idea. After all, this book does emphasize the need to fully get to know your partner before becoming too attached. So why wouldn't I endorse testing a relationship through cohabitation? Consider the following scenario.

Kate and Justin met in high school, although they didn't start dating until after college. Kate moved to a city about sixty minutes away from where Justin lived and worked at his family's business. After dating for about a year, Justin moved to the city to live with Kate and commuted an hour each way to work during the week.

Seven years later, Kate and Justin are still together. They are happy, although Kate is restless. Seven Valentine's Days, Christmases, birthdays, and every other holiday that creates potential for a proposal have passed and still no proposal for marriage.

Kate has wondered for some time if Justin will ever take the plunge and ask for her hand—so have the rest of their friends and family. She commonly can be overheard explaining how she thinks, "This is *our* year, I just know it," although *their* year has never actually come. Justin, apparently oblivious of Kate's expectancy of a proposal, claims he is satisfied just living together and sees no need to marry when they already are happy sharing a life together.

When I talked to Kate privately about her relationship with Justin, she described how over the years she has become increasingly more insecure in their relationship, especially because Justin is apathetic toward the idea of marriage. "He has seemed to become less interested in me altogether," she complained.

In the beginning of their relationship, Justin would dream with Kate about their future life together as husband and wife and the beautiful family they would create. But now Justin won't even discuss the idea of marriage. His ambivalence toward marriage and even their relationship has left Kate wondering if he still thinks of her as the one he wants to spend the rest of his life with. After all, if Justin had every intention of living with her for the rest of their lives, what is the big deal if they just get married? What is his hang-up? Does he want an easy way out? Does he have other interests? Is he worried about missing out on someone better?

> *Marital commitment, by definition, includes faith and risk.*

After all of these years without a firm commitment, it is no surprise that Kate questions Justin's intentions for their future. Kate is involved in a marriagelike relationship—*without* the commitment of marriage. In other words, she has ended up with a conditional-commitment relationship.

The Seal of Commitment

The conundrum you face is that you want a high-quality, stable marriage in a society where broken marriages are pervasive. This has created the dilemma where you hold high expectations for marriage in the face of increased apprehensions. In light of this predicament, it seems natural for you to feel a need to test your relationship to make sure it is ideal and suitable for marriage. While it is essential to take time to build a healthy relationship, however, there are limits on how far you should go in creating a marriagelike relationship without the commitment of marriage.

Marital commitment, by definition, includes faith and risk. You cannot practice or test this type of commitment. Premarital cohabitation is an attempt to retain a high level of personal commitment to a partner while minimizing the legal or financial risks. In reality, this arrangement actually compromises the level of personal commitment because your finances, possessions, and legal obligations *are* personal. You do value these things, and by placing yourself and all you own in a joint relationship with a partner, you are putting commitment into action.

The RAM can depict an imbalanced relationship in which you deeply know, trust, and rely on your partner, but lack essential elements in your commitment (see Figure 12.3 on the next page). This may be acceptable for a time, but eventually it diminishes the commitment that is there and strains the trust and reliance, pulling all levels of your relationship down toward the underdeveloped commitment.

By attempting to practice marital commitment through cohabitation, you actually practice a conditional commitment and diminish the security of belonging to your partner. When there is no "seal" of commitment from a marriage, there is the risk that a slow leak of security will develop.

When you know your partner is fully committed to you, this produces a security that deepens your sense of oneness and belonging. This enhances the emotional bond and broadens your experience of closeness, intimacy, and romance. Marriage, not premarital cohabitation, provides a structure that is extensive enough for the pledge and practice of a full commitment.

Obviously, some people have broken their commitments while married, or at least did not fulfill the promises they made to each other. But they had the *potential* within the structure of their marriage to have a full commitment. On the other hand,

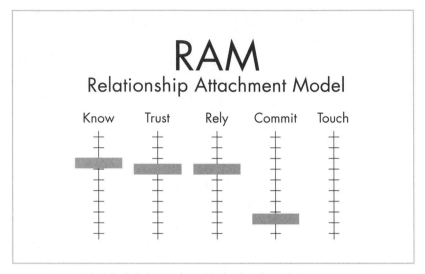

FIGURE 12.3 High-Risk Relationship: Underdeveloped Commitment

some people have made very deep commitments in a cohabitating relationship. However, this does not appear to be the case with the majority, and the structure of the living arrangement lacks the requirements that the marital structure places on a couple.

The final step of making a commitment to marry does involve risk and require greater responsibility, but it must be taken to gain a greater sense of security and oneness in the quality of your relationship. This is why most research clearly establishes that a larger percentage of couples who are married describe their relationship as achieving high levels of romance, sexual enjoyment, and personal satisfaction than the percentage of couples who cohabitate.[11]

In fact, one fascinating study from Cornell University found that couples who were married reported higher levels of overall well-being than those who were together for the same amount of time but not married. "Compared with other forms of romantic relationships," these researchers concluded, "marriage involves a higher level of commitment from partners and a stronger future orientation. . . . For these reasons, marriage is likely to have a particularly prominent role in shaping people's identities and sense of self. The institutional nature of marriage, therefore, combined with the long-term nature of marital bonds, may account for the especially favorable state of well-being among spouses."[12]

Practicing Marriage or Practicing Divorce

If and when a cohabiting relationship ends, the effects of the breakup extend far beyond that of just a dating relationship. Therefore, if cohabitation is practicing marriage, then breaking up is practicing divorce. This idea can account for the explanation why those who cohabitate with one or more partners have similar divorce rates as those who were actually married and then divorced (around a 66 percent divorce rate, 12 to 15 percent higher than first-time marriages).

It is necessary to acknowledge the cases of those who have "done everything wrong" but their relationship turned out great, and those who have "done everything right" but their relationship turned out poorly. But if we apply the law of averages, research shows no support for the notion that those who cohabitate have a greater likelihood of marital success. However, it does strongly imply that cohabitating

If cohabitation is practicing marriage, then breaking up is practicing divorce.

creates inherent dangers to your future marriage because living together seems to affect your relationship and specifically, your commitment.

Rethinking Your Position

If 60 percent of those who marry first live together, then probably at least half of you who are reading this book have either lived with a partner or are planning on it. That makes me particularly aware that some people may feel skeptical of reconsidering living together before marriage regardless of what studies have found. I would simply ask you to give some more thought to what you have read and the way that your commitment may be diminished by alternative arrangements, especially if it does not work out and you end up living together with more than one partner before marriage. If you are still uncertain, don't slip into apathy. Check out the research for yourself, and make a well-informed decision about how to best prepare for marriage based on what you conclude from what you read.

I am also acutely aware that some of you may wonder if your chances in marriage have been decreased by choices you have made in the past to live with a partner. No one can say for certain how your past relationships will affect your future, but I know that you can only benefit by strengthening your understanding and value of the unique commitment within marriage. Raising this commitment to heights beyond those of other arrangements will carry over into your future marriage relationship, sealing it with a more serious vow of unconditional promise.

Rethinking our socially acceptable approach to marriage today is warranted. The number of studies alone that portray more negatives than positives in the way that cohabiting carries over into marriage is compelling. You do not need to feel uncertain about whether you can get to know a dating partner deeply without first living together. The five areas to explore in a partner will reveal what could easily stay hidden even when you live together. Perhaps even more important, marital commitment is more than a legal document or just another living arrangement. It is a dynamic bond that seems to produce the strongest weld between you and your partner when it involves a distinctive step of faith from a dating relationship into a permanent union.

DON'T FORGET

- The heart of commitment is an abiding spirit of belonging to each other.

- Commitment is the intertwining of three strands: the feeling of "I want to," "I have to," and "I am reluctant to."

- Strong commitments can carry you through challenging times, but they can also cause you to compromise what you want in a relationship so you don't lose what you've got.

- The level of your commitment indicates the degree of responsibility you have to maintain that relationship.

- The final step of an unconditional marriage commitment is necessary to gain the security of belonging to your partner.

13

How to Have Great Sex

RAM Dynamic 5: Should We Have Sex?

Unfortunately, there is no one manual that you can use in your dating relationships to help you decide if and when to have sex. In the last couple of decades, however, much research has provided guidelines for achieving a satisfying sexual relationship in marriage. In a national study conducted among singles ages twenty-one to twenty-nine, researchers attempted to categorize the many sexual attitudes and practices and found that two types, or trends, of sexual involvement covered the majority of sexual practices.[1]

Everybody's Doing It

The first trend of sexual activity they referred to, *relational sex*, is the commonly understood practice of two people being attracted to each other, building a relationship, and becoming sexually involved in their romantic relationship. This assumes you have a relationship with a growing commitment. According to this type, respondents stated that they expected sex to be postponed until they knew their partner well enough to feel there is something more than sexual attraction between them. I will discuss this type of sexual relationship in the latter half of this chapter.

The second widespread type of sexual involvement was referred to as *recreational sex*, or "hooking up." This trend of sexual activity is based on the belief that sex does not have to occur only in relationships—it can also be a fun and pleasurable activity of simply being single. This type of sex required no commitment beyond the sexual encounter. It could be a one-night stand, a series of engagements, or even a friends-with-benefits type of arrangement. But in every case, it was considered a physical act that had no emotional strings attached.

The current practice of hooking up is based on the popular belief that sex can take place without emotional involvement. The idea of recreational sex has moved past the old stereotype that men can engage in a sexual encounter without emotional investments, to now include women, suggesting that there is a way for all people to experience the sexual act without any further involvement or commitment.

Sex Is More than Physical

The problem with the view that sex can be a physical act without any other ramifications is that it has no supporting evidence either in anecdotal surveys or scientific research. In fact, both bodies of evidence consistently tell us just the opposite: *sex is always relational*. Even if you have convinced yourself that you can have sexual relations with someone and it means nothing, it *still* is relational. This is true for both women and men, debunking the stereotype that men can have sex with no emotional or relational consequences.

The primary reason why sex is always relational is because you cannot separate your body from the rest of who you are; therefore, what your body does, you do. Sex and self are inextricably linked, and during a sexual encounter something happens that is more than just a physical act.

Tiffany became involved in a casual sex relationship with Derrick. Her friends warned her that she was setting herself up for an emotional disaster. Of course, she disagreed.

She and Derrick had been engaging in sex without a relationship for about two months, when she began noticing a trend. Derrick would not return her phone calls and would only call her when he wanted to have sex. When he saw her in public, he would ignore her. On top of all that, he was never available when she tried to reach him, although whenever he needed anything, she was there for him.

Sex is always relational.

Tiffany's friends could see right through him. They argued that he was just using her. Tiffany retorted that she was using him, that she was in it just for the sex, and that he couldn't hurt her feelings because her feelings weren't involved. Then she complained about the way he acted when she saw him at a party. When her friends tried to point out the way her reaction revealed her emotional investment, she seemed to be completely unable to understand what they were explaining.

Tiffany's rendezvous with Derrick lasted close to a year. Her complaints to her friends were always the same: "Why doesn't he call?" "Why can't he just invite me out with him?" "Why does he only want to see me when he wants sex?" The advice from her friends also was always the same: "You are doing more than an exercise routine when you have sex with Derrick—you want the guy to like you because you like the guy."

Finally, Tiffany and Derrick had a falling out and stopped meeting altogether. Although it is two years later, Tiffany still talks about her anger toward Derrick. She still resents his lack of attention and interest in her, as well as the vulnerable feeling she had when she saw him outside of their intimate meetings.

Sex Changes a Relationship

Sex intensifies your experience of closeness, whether in a committed relationship or not. Sex cannot be severed from emotional involvement. While Tiffany may argue that her sexual experiences with Derrick, or anyone else, did not affect her thoughts and feelings for Derrick, evidence from research suggests otherwise.

Some researchers have studied the changes, if any, that occur with the first act of intercourse in a relationship with a partner. What they found was that one act of sex ignited a chain reaction of several other relationship activities. Because of this domino effect, they referred to the first sexual encounter in a relationship as the "passion turning point."[2]

First, this "turning point" changed the overall feelings and activities in a relationship. For instance, when couples were interviewed and asked about major turning points in their relationship, the first sexual act together was the most frequently remembered. It was also among the most commonly commemorated by couples in their yearly schedule.

For some of you, the following may sound very familiar: the singles in this national study talked about additional changes that accompanied the time of their first sexual act in their relationships. They described several relationship activites that launched after they had sex for the first time together, significantly increasing mixed feelings and thoughts about their relationship.

When couples were interviewed and asked about major turning points in their relationship, the first sexual act together was the most frequently remembered.

One of the activities was a stronger desire to open up and feel closer. At the same time, this was countered by an equally strong feeling of being more vulnerable to getting hurt by the partner, and an apprehension about letting down your guard. This feeling of vulnerability was even more heightened when the first sex act occurred before certain shows of love and desire had been expressed. It made the couples wonder what was expected of them now in the relationship. This uneasiness and vulnerability, which was caused from the increased inclination to share more of oneself with a partner while feeling unsure of whether the partner can be trusted, fits with what we have seen in the RAM's portrayal of emotionally unsafe relationships (see Figures 13.1 and 13.2 on the next page).

Whenever you have allowed a relationship dynamic to become significantly more developed than a previous dynamic, as represented in the RAM, then you put yourself at risk. Whatever is true for you when you place more trust in a person than what you know about that person, depend on a partner much more than you trust that person, or become overly committed to someone who consistently isn't there for you (reliance) or hasn't earned your respect (trust) is *equally* true when your sexual involvement is greater than any of the relationship dynamics that precede it in the RAM, and your risk of getting emotionally burned is significantly increased.

Unsafe sex has been discussed more than ever in the last several decades, especially since the drive to educate the public about AIDS and venereal diseases. In addition to these obvious physical risks, there are other risks. First, if you are a woman, you place yourself at risk of being raped. Date rapes make up 78 percent of the reported rapes.[3] Date rape is an extreme violation of trust that never should be excused or justified for any reason. Yet there are ways you can put yourself in sexually vulnerable situations with someone who has not earned your trust. It is dangerous to let down your guard with a partner whom you are familiar with but have not known long enough to prove his or her character. We all can admit that it is easy to fill in the gaps of our trust-pictures when we know someone just a little, only to realize later that this person is grossly different than what we had at first imagined (we saw this in Chapter 10).

When you become sexually involved without the other bonding dynamics being equally involved in your relationship,

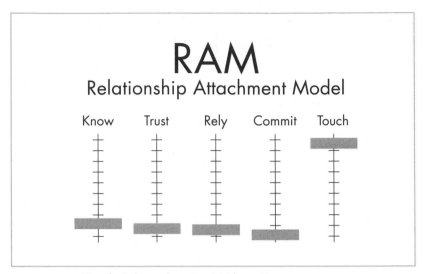

FIGURE 13.1 Unsafe Relationship: Sex Without Commitment

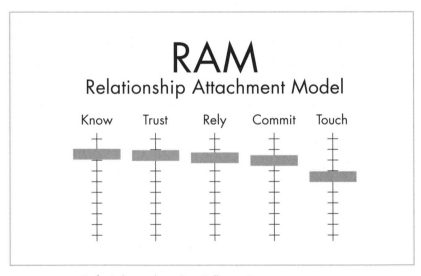

FIGURE 13.2 Safe Relationship: Sex Follows Commitment

then you create vulnerabilities for yourself. Another reason this happens is because your sexual involvement tugs on your trust and reliance so that you want more in your relationship than what was promised. Even though Tiffany did not admit it, she wanted to be able to rely on Derrick for something more than just a one-night stand.

Each time she had sex, it caused a turning point, prompting her to rely on Derrick, to be more open, and to desire stronger connections. Yet she knew he could not be trusted for any further investment than his sexual availability. This left her feeling confused, frustrated, and vulnerable. This explained why she was distraught when she would see him at parties or in other social settings and he would ignore her.

This increase in Tiffany's feelings of connection with Derrick is another relationship change that researchers discovered occurred with the passion turning point after the first sexual act in a relationship. The description of this feeling of connection sounded a lot like my description of the reliance dynamic on the RAM. They stated that one or both partners felt an increase in the overall need for the other partner, wanting to spend time with each other and do more together.

Just like the first change of wanting to open up more, this change also had its counterpart. The respondents apparently felt more vulnerable to being hurt and wanted to protect themselves by keeping a measure of independence. It was as though they felt pulled toward dependency but not fully sure they were ready for it. This created additional tension in the relationship, leaving the partners unsure of what each expected of the other.

I Was Too Drunk to Remember

By now you should understand that sexual involvement alters the dynamics in a relationship. Your primary struggle is to figure out *when* you should increase your degree of sexual intimacy (and maybe how to stop yourself from going too far too soon). I address this next, but before I do, let me add one more sobering fact to those who were too drunk with passion (or any other intoxicating influence) to remember.

Some people still think that sex doesn't matter when it is outside of a relationship. "If both are consenting adults, then what difference does it make?" they ask. "How can a meaningless sexual act be relational, especially if you can't even remember it happening?" I must admit that I have wondered these same things. However, I have been amazed by the astonishing facts established by numerous studies and surveys that directly oppose the widespread belief that hooking up between two consenting adults is harmless. These studies have been replicated over and over and need to be brought to the forefront because of how they challenge our contemporary dating beliefs.

More Premarital Sex Equals Fewer Lasting Marriages

First, the greater the number of sexual partners you have while dating, the fewer your chances of staying faithful when married. Jay Teachman, from Western Washington University, studied more than 6,500 women who were married between 1970 and 1995 from the National Survey of Family Growth and found an indisputable connection between the number of sexual partners they had before marriage and their likelihood of getting divorced.[4] Sexual involvement with a partner other than the one a person marries significantly increased that person's odds of divorce. In fact, when sex and cohabitation were compared, the sexual involvement seemed to have the bigger impact on the future marriage.

Teachman wanted to ensure no underlying characteristics or background experiences contributed to his finding. He wanted to be sure that the number of premarital sexual partners was the only reason that this group of sexually active women had higher rates of divorce. So he took into account the similarities and differences of family background, socioeconomic characteristics, age, religion, race, culture, number of siblings, and many more characteristics. Still, involvement with just one sexual partner other

Marriage acts like a magnifying glass, making the characteristics and practices of your premarital lifestyle more pronounced.

than her husband during the dating years raised a woman's risk of divorce *three times higher* than that of the woman who had sex with only her husband.

More Premarital Sex Equals Fewer Faithful Marriages

A second way that your premarital sexual patterns can affect your future marriage is that the more sexual partners you have, the lower your ability to stay faithful in marriage. Several U.S. and European studies have established this, but one study in particular looked at the link between sexual experiences in the dating years and sexual practices in marriage among more than 3,000 men in four countries.[5] Basically what they found was that the higher the number of sexual partners during dating, the greater the chances of having an extramarital affair during marriage. In fact, this rate was proportional, which means that as the number of sexual partners increased, so did the likelihood of infidelity. Other studies in both the United States and Europe have found similar results for not only men, but also women.

It doesn't take a genius to figure out that what you marry is what you get. Marriage acts like a magnifying glass, making the characteristics and practices of your premarital lifestyle more pronounced.

Both Tiffany and Derrick would have argued that their sexual experiences would not affect their future marriages. But the evidence from research suggests otherwise. Tiffany was trying to make herself engage in an unnatural type of relationship—sex with no other meaning. Deep down she wanted more, but she was determined to separate sex from love. What we have seen from research casts her sexual practices in a dangerous light. It seems that both men and women who separate sex from love risk damaging their ability to form lasting bonds. They reinforce an unnatural break between the bonding of sex and the building of a relationship. As a result, they find it more difficult in the future to maintain fidelity in their marriages. They have programmed themselves to find sexual fulfillment apart from a loving and committed bond.

The reason the effects of "meaningless sex" are not obvious at the time the sex occurs is because more relationships are affected than just the present relationship. Your most meaningful relationship—your future marriage—is also jeopardized by the meaningless sexual acts in your dating years.

Do You Do as You Believe?

Eighty-three percent agreed with the following statement on a national survey: "The things I do in my relationships today will affect my future marriage."[6] However, when these participants were further interviewed, they admitted that their actions contradicted this belief. In other words, they knew their future marriage would be impacted by their current dating practices, but that did not change their decisions.

Researchers were both intrigued and dismayed at the circular reasoning that many of the singles engaged in as they talked about the contradiction between their belief that "my present behaviors will affect my future marriage" and their chosen dating lifestyle. For instance, one college student who had agreed with the statement on the survey stated, "I think hooking up with different people and seeing what you like and don't like is a good idea. Because eventually you're going to have to . . . marry someone, and I'd just like to know that I experienced everything."[7]

This student represented those who ignore the inconsistencies between what they believe on the one hand and what they practice on the other. When you continue to practice a lifestyle that contradicts your beliefs, you will inevitably compromise those beliefs. That is what the researchers found with many of those who said they believed that their marriage would be affected by their dating experiences. As they continued to make choices in their dating relationships that directly opposed this belief, they became wishy-washy about this belief, pushing it farther back among their personal priorities. They illustrated the point that when you don't practice what you believe, you end up resolving the tension by changing those very beliefs, clouding them with rationalizations.

This is a truth of life: beliefs change behavior, and behavior changes beliefs. Try to maintain a belief that you refuse to follow in your behavior, and eventually one will win out. Either you will curb your behavior to match your belief, or you will alter your belief to allow exceptions for your behavior.

Some have claimed that it is not a person's *behavior* in dating that alters the state of that person's future marriage, but instead it is some preexisting *belief* that actually results in both. I think this is "the chicken or the egg" argument. Which is it? Has your sexual behavior resulted in detrimental consequences to your future marriage? Or is it that you hold certain beliefs that led to your sexual behavior during dating *and* the problems in your future marriage—in other words, a common underlying cause for both.

The choices you now make will shape the beliefs you someday hold.

My opinion is . . . it doesn't matter! According to our best research available, either way, you are at risk of ending up in a worse position in marriage if you are in the group who has made certain sexual choices in dating. Anyway, both are true. Your *genuine* beliefs will be clearly seen in your life because they will alter your behavior, and when your choices of behavior counter one of your beliefs, it will also reshape your belief to justify your behavior. Your choices are the judge and jury of the sincerity of your beliefs.

What this means to you is that the choices you now make will shape the beliefs you someday hold. If you have strong, deep-seated beliefs, then they will influence the choices you make and become reinforced over time. However, if your beliefs are not well thought out, then you are likely to contradict them in your behavior, which will result in rethinking and rationalizing that belief. Eventually, you will believe differently.

It is crucial that you have accurate information upon which to base your beliefs and ultimately your behavior. I have found few singles who were aware of the facts from these studies. Such people lack credible evidence to back up their belief that their present practices will affect their future marriage. This may be a primary reason that so many struggle to practice this belief. However, there is proof that your belief *does* have validity and that self-restraint in pacing sexual involvement *does* pay off in your future marriage.

The freedoms from the sexual revolution of the last fifty years need to be brought into balance with the requirements of self-restraint and personal investment that are needed to produce lasting and satisfying marriages. You have a sound and rational basis for slowing down your sexual pace in your dating relationships. The choices about sex belong to you and no one else. But know that your sexual choices impact your present relationship in nonsexual ways, and they also make an investment in your future marriage, for better or for worse.

Less Is More

So what do you gain from pacing your sexual involvement in balance with the other relationship dynamics represented by the RAM? I will be the first one to admit this, but the gains are definitely counterintuitive. The first major gain is a heightened, long-lasting love and romance in your future marriage.

John Cunningham and John Antill, relationship researchers from the Macquarie University in Australia who have researched relationships since the 1970s, conducted a project examining love and romance in couples outside of a college campus. They compared those living together but not married (cohabitators) with those who were married. They discovered that regardless of how long a couple had been together, those who were married stated that they had the highest feelings of romance within their relationship. They found that

1. Cohabitators who had been married previously had the *lowest* romance.
2. Cohabitators who had never been previously married were next.
3. Among those dating but not living together, those who had previous sexual partners reported less romantic feelings than those who had not been sexually experienced outside of that relationship.
4. Daters who were exclusive or engaged to be married had much higher romantic feelings than those who were not.
5. In every group there was a direct relationship between the number of sexual partners and the enjoyment of romantic feelings: every additional past sexual partner brought about a corresponding decrease in their present experience of romance.
6. In every group the overall relationship happiness and sexual satisfaction was directly related to their romantic feelings—better romance, better sex.
7. Those who had the fewest past sexual partners, did not cohabitate with their partner or any previous partners, and were married scored the *highest* on their ratings of love, satisfaction, sexual fulfillment, and romantic feelings.[8]

What becomes clear from this study and the many others like it is that sex, love, and marriage are definitely linked together. Marriage seals the depth of commitment, which is necessary for the security of love, which in turn enriches the fulfillment and satisfaction of sex and romance. Breaking this trio apart leaves the remaining two lacking the other essential piece. Think about it: marriage without sex or commitment, commitment without marriage or sex, and sex without marriage or commitment—all three pairs are inadequate to provide the full experience of intimacy and personal fulfillment that can come from a free and open sexual experience in the security of a committed and loving marriage.

You'll Go Blind

There is a second major gain from following the "less is more" approach to sex in dating: you will be able to use better judgment in your choice of a partner.

Jeffry Simpson from Texas A&M University and Steven Gangestad from the University of New Mexico have published numerous studies on relationships over the past several decades. They wondered if men and women who were sexually active in their dating relationships chose the same type of partners as those who were saving sex for marriage. They set out to answer their questions in a series of three related experiments. They discovered that there were, in fact, clear differences between these two groups of singles.

The first study asked the singles to fill out two questionnaires, one requiring them to describe their own sexual practices, the other inquiring about the most important qualities they look for in a partner.

The second study presented the singles with two written descriptions of two very different partners. The first partner was described as confident, somewhat arrogant, physically attractive, and sexy but with a habit of engaging in short and sometimes unfaithful relationships. The second partner was portrayed as physically average but known to be a caring, faithful partner who would likely be a good parent someday. The singles were then asked to choose the partner to whom they were most attracted.

The third study examined the qualities of the dating partners. Simpson and Gangestad wanted to see if singles chose partners similar to the partners they said they were attracted to from the descriptions in the second study.

Clear differences separated two groups of daters. Singles in the group who were having sex in their dating relationships (called the "unrestricted" group) were much more likely to overlook the sordid histories of their partners, including a track record of unfaithfulness, in order to have a partner they felt was sexy. Singles in the group who were referred to as the "restricted" (those who were saving sex for marriage) were determined to choose partners who had the characteristics necessary for being a faithful and caring partner. They were willing to compromise some of the outward appearance to gain inward quality. Interestingly, both groups actually chose partners who were similar to the types with whom they had been attracted.

A vital principle rises to the surface from this study: *the values you use influence the partner you choose.* Practice values that keep sex, love, and marriage linked together, and you will more likely choose a partner who also values these ideals. Raise the bar for your standards of dating, and you will be inclined to choose a partner who holds higher standards. You can improve your selection of a partner by adjusting your boundaries in dating.

This study, like the others I referred to before, reinforces the theory that what you believe and what you do are inseparably connected. Both are vital to the making of a fulfilling relationship and a lasting marriage. Marriage does not begin at your wedding; marriage begins with your ideals and values about love, sex, and marriage. The extent of the consistency between your dating relationships and these ideals further ensures that you will make better partner choices in your dating and establish better relationship patterns for your future marriage.

Stopping Points

Anyone who has a normal sex drive and an attraction to a partner will struggle with stopping points. I have found that older singles, especially single-again adults, feel that it is juvenile to set personal limits on the extent of sexual touch in their dating relationships. They feel embarrassed to discuss this with their dating partners and have come to accept that this is just the way that dating is done.

My hope is that the RAM and the research that backs it up offer a legitimate and explainable platform for those who wish to discuss with confidence sexual boundaries in their dating relationships. We have already seen that some issues in marriage have their roots in the sexual practices during dating. Therefore, you should feel justified in bringing up these topics with a partner with whom you have built a decent rapport. If your dating partner initiates sex very early on and you have not even had the chance to bring it up, don't be embarrassed to explain your value of first deepening what you know about each other and securing a trust before you go any further. Even if others dismiss it, deny it, or simply don't believe it, the preponderance of research remains, showing that the building of trust, reliance, and especially commitment before sexual involvement results in happier and more lasting marriages.

Sexual passion is easy to turn on but hard to turn off. If you choose to pace the extent of how far you will go in sexual touch, then you need to predetermine your stopping points. This is done by knowing what you can handle and what makes you lose control. Figure out the degree of sexual intimacy you are going to allow yourself. Knowing your zone enables you to stop thinking and enjoy the passion.

True passion disengages the mind. The nature of passion is that the more sexually aroused you are, the more you lose yourself in the feeling. That is how it is supposed to be. In marriage counseling, for example, a common source of sexual dysfunction occurs when one partner cannot turn his or her mind off and simply relax. We work on developing ways to help that partner release the rushing thoughts of the day and move into the physical and emotional sensation. In many ways, then, you could say that good sex is mindless.

Since this is the case, you easily can see how difficult it is to figure out how far you want to go with a partner while you are actually engaging in any kind of sexual touch. Many times I have heard singles explain that they will "just know" when to take that next step sexually. However, there is an intrinsic conflict of interests between the mind and the body during sexual interaction. Your mind may think one thing while your body tells you another. *The stronger your arousal, the less engaged your mind will be.* Therefore, it is very difficult to keep your mind clear so that you can determine where to stop when the very act you are involved in keeps shutting down the mind! It makes much more sense to address these issues outside of your sexual activity while you are thinking clearly about what you want and why. Then you can relax and enjoy your passionate times within your predetermined boundaries.

You may want to make it a personal rule to never alter your thought-out stopping point in the heat of the moment. Whatever the extent of the sexual intimacy in your dating relationship, you will always want to go a little further. This is also part of the nature of passion—the decreased feeling of satisfaction over time with each level of involvement, which prompts you to move to the next. Sexual arousal always wants to extend the horizon of physical activity beyond that which was previously set. So whatever sexual intimacy you experience in your relationship today won't seem to do it for you the next time; you will want to take it further. But there are benefits of maintaining a stopping point and staying within a specific zone of sexual contact. For instance, many couples have mastered passionate kissing during their dating because they refused to go any further.

The greatest experiences of sexual pleasure ultimately require a blend of self-restraint and self-fulfillment. During the sexual act, both are needed to gain the fullest enjoyment. Any sex therapist will tell you that good sex has times of holding back on some things, building anticipation and excitation. Lingering in the kissing, for instance, can heighten the arousal and build toward climax.

Staying within a certain zone during dating will not hurt your future sex life, although it will most likely test you, strengthening your sense of self-control. Think about it: you will always need to practice sexual self-control in different relationships the rest of your life. If pacing the extent of your sexual touch during dating further develops your ability to control your sex drive, then isn't that another gain for your marriage? This may be one of the reasons why those who hold off sexually during dating end up having significantly lower rates of extramarital affairs. They have learned the discipline and value of keeping their sexual interests in check with their overall values, they have not severed sex from love and marriage, and they have practiced their belief that no matter how recreational and enjoyable the sexual act is, it is still always relational.

Sexual Compatibility

While interviewing with a reporter about this subject, she challenged the practicality of these studies on love, sex, and marriage by questioning how a couple would ever determine their sexual compatibility if they were not to have sex. She further explained that it makes more sense to have sex before your relationship gets going. That way you figure out your compatibility fit and don't waste your time building a relationship with someone with whom you are not sexually compatible.

While this sounds logical, this reasoning has inherent flaws. First, there are many who had great sex while dating only to have it all change when they married. If sex during dating determines a couple's compatibility, then why does it change so drastically with some couples soon after they marry? I have seen this many times when doing a history with couples who sought counseling for problems in their sex life. They never had one argument about frequency until they married. After they married, something seemed to change.

A second inherent flaw in this reasoning is uncovered by another common problem that occurs when married couples have conflicts in their sex life. As I inquire about other areas of their relationship, it seems that unresolved issues in those other areas end up diminishing the enjoyment and sometimes even the interest in their sexual relationship. Once a couple is married, sex is clearly relational. This does not mean, by the way, that sex is never recreational or playful. But the dynamics of the relationship are intertwined with the overall satisfaction of the sexual experience. This is why so many married couples have problems in their sexual relationship—the other aspects of their marriage have not been resolved, overshadowing their sex life.

Therefore, becoming sexually involved during the dating relationship, especially in the beginning of the relationship, can result in extremely misleading expectations of what your sexual relationship will be like in marriage. This is also because the dating relationship has an agenda that marriage does not. For example, there is a lot of pressure to win over a partner, which causes a person to consciously or unconsciously please that partner in ways that may be very temporary. Finally, there is an exhilaration within a new relationship that, if the truth be known, predominantly comes from the initial attraction and sexual tension.

Without the development of the other areas of the relationship (represented by the first four dynamics of the RAM), a person can never be sure what the long-term sexual relationship will really be like. In a marriage, sex does not exist independently of everything else in the relationship. However, in *dating*, the sex can become a substitute for intimacy, creating a temporary euphoric feeling that everything is perfect. This not only backfires when hidden problems begin to surface, but it also dampens the very sexual fire that lit up the relationship in the beginning.

There are some better alternatives to solving the question of sexual compatibility. First, make sure you have good chemistry with your partner. We talked about how vital it is to have a vibrant chemistry in Chapter 5. Attraction to your partner is equally important to the sex life of a couple. I have counseled clients who never felt a strong sexual attraction to their partners. In most cases they stayed with their partners; however, they always felt something was missing.

During the dating period, you should hesitate moving forward in a relationship that lacks mutual chemistry and attraction. It is just as important for your partner to be attracted to you as it is for you to be attracted to your partner. In the studies on sex and romance, it was found that feeling attracted to your partner was consistently ranked as one of the most important qualities in a long-term relationship. Chemistry did not automatically result in a great sex life or a great marriage, but it was an essential piece for most couples. Therefore, if you've got chemistry, you tend to keep it. But know that if you don't, you may never get it. If you do eventually get it, it most likely will have taken a long time, growing when the accumulation of other bonding experiences filled in the gaps.

Second, do what couples in counseling do to improve their sex life: talk. As your relationship grows and becomes increasingly serious, you should be able to talk about sex and marriage. If this seems awkward, then step back and think: if it is too awkward to *talk* about sex, then maybe it is also too early to engage in sex.

I have found that most couples who seek counseling for sexual incompatibility are really disagreeing over the frequency of their sexual relations. Most of these couples greatly misunderstand each other, becoming polarized in hurt, anger, and frustration. The first step of helping improve their sex life is to get them to clarify to each other what they want. It is not unusual for these couples to have had a good sexual relationship during their dating years, without ever talking about crucial issues of sexual relating that come

> *During the dating period, you should hesitate moving forward in a relationship that lacks mutual chemistry and attraction.*

with the territory of a long-term relationship. As a counselor guides them in talking through their expectations, their sexual relationship often improves, once again showing the importance of being on the same page mentally about sex in order to achieve compatibility in their experience of sex.

Sex is as much mental as it is physical. This is why the compatibility of the act of sex ultimately requires more than just the compatibility of drives. Many couples have different sex drives. To be realistic, over time numerous changes can alter your sex drive (or your partner's). Therefore, talking about what you want in your sexual relationship in marriage, what to do when you and your partner disagree over timing, and your openness to grow and try new things in this area is just as important, if not more, as the matching of similar interests and drives.

No Regrets

Some of you may be reading this chapter thinking, "Let's see—I didn't do that right . . . nor that . . . been there, done that wrong . . . that too." If you fit in the high-risk categories cited in these studies, then you need to know one more very important point. Change your present perspective and change what you think and do, and you can change your future. You are not a slave to your past. Your present situation may be the result of some of the decisions you made in your past, but your future will be the result of the decisions you make now.

Some people regularly have had sex with partners they have dated and are skeptical about changing their lifestyle. I hope that this chapter has provided food for thought and has presented some new angles to look at the age-old subject of sex and love. The longer I have lived, the more I believe that sex, love, and marriage do go together like a horse and carriage. All three find a sense of security from belonging, a sense of belonging from commitment, a sense of commitment from sacrifice, and a sense of sacrifice from a deep-seated security.

The best sex occurs when you and your partner are in tune with each other, willing to please each other, committed to making each other happy even when it requires sacrifice, and fully secure in your feelings of belonging together. Sex, in this kind of relationship, is truly making love.

DON'T FORGET

- The idea behind recreational sex is the untrue belief that sex can be just a physical act that has no emotional strings attached.

- Sex creates a turning point in the relationship, intensifying the desire for closeness and commitment.

- Sexual intimacy that exceeds the level of commitment causes an emotionally unsafe state in a relationship.

- Research has found premarital sex to be associated with higher divorce rates and infidelity rates in people's future marriages.

- Your beliefs shape your choices, but your choices also shape your beliefs.

- Sexual compatibility can be more accurately determined by chemistry and talk than by the act of premarital sex.

Conclusion

What the World Needs Now Is
Pacemakers *and* Trendsetters

We have now come full circle. Your desire to find your best friend, soul mate, lifelong lover, and spouse does not have to be a random, haphazard, blind pursuit. Instead, you can follow a plan that guides both your head and heart as you journey toward love. No longer are social and family forces prominent in guiding you to that partner with whom you will have a harmonious fit. For the most part, you are on your own. But you are not without a road map.

The need for a personal plan has been evident ever since romantic love became emancipated from the long-standing arrangements used to bring two people together in marriage. Some people recognized this need years ago but did not know how to fill it. Read what one well-known scholar wrote:

> *The research findings . . . on the factors making for and against success in marriage have been presented. The reaction of many readers doubtless will be: "What of it? Will (single) people pay any attention to them? What chance is there that in the affairs of the heart they will use their heads?"*[1]

When do you think that quote was written? Let me provide you with a little more and see if you can guess the year:

Now that marriage has become essentially personal, with companionship as its goal, selecting a mate is a much more complicated and complex undertaking. It requires that . . . (singles) learn what they like and need in a companion of the opposite sex. The objective is no longer to marry someone of the desired social status, but someone who is compatible in temperament, congenial in interests, whose ideas and values are similar to one's own. . . . These profound changes in the nature of marriage and courtship are often confusing and bewildering. . . . There have been few sources where (singles) . . . could find help in understanding the bewildering, changing world, or in grappling with the personal problems it has evoked for them . . . they have to find their own way as best they could.

Fifty-three years have passed since these words were first penned by one of the greatest sociologists and family researchers of the twentieth century, Ernest Burgess. He had just stepped out of the 1940s and was aware that he was witnessing one of the greatest social revolutions in history. Dating around, as you know it today, began in the forties. Prior to that, if you liked someone, you immediately went steady. And prior to that, families and communities assisted in arranging marriages between singles. In 1931, more than 50 percent of the marriages in the United States took place between neighbors within five blocks of each other![2] The questions about compatibility were almost nonexistent because it was built into the system. You grew up with the person you married, attended the same school, knew the same friends, and shared similar family backgrounds, religious views, and traditions.

Burgess could see the erosion of the social and family banks that channeled the stream of singles into marriage but felt helpless to know what to do about it. What would he have thought if he could have looked into a crystal ball and seen the diversity of our world, our cyber- and telecommunication connections and the drastic changes in our attitudes toward sex, gender, marriage, and cohabitation?

Burgess was like a prophet who could identify the problems but didn't know the solutions. Although some still live in a similar, highly structured world of choosing a partner, the majority of people can never go back. And I, for one, don't want to. I love our diversity, individualism, and social revolutions that have busted us out of traditional norms and embraced new expressions of culture, art, and thought. I am grateful that there is less of a generation gap because there is a greater acceptance of change. Yet I appreciate the tension that is inevitable when differing views are respected.

I think there is an answer to the increasingly complex process of choosing a partner in the context of all of this freedom: provide a plan to singles that can be used as a road map, a guideline, and a plan for balancing one's heart with one's head.

So here we are, ending at the same place where we began. No one chooses your partner but you. You are on your own. You must know what to look for and how to get it. You must be able to ask the right questions while recognizing the right answers. You must be a lover, a detective, and a psychologist—all rolled up in one.

There was a lot of good in the way that families and society assisted singles in choosing a partner in the past. The practices that were beneficial will stand the test of time. I have attempted to provide you with the best of the lessons from the past with the latest in our research from the present.

I want to see another revolution—a pick-a-partner revolution, a social tidal wave that carries the belief that singles need and can learn vital skills that can be used in building a relationship and choosing a partner, that love is not a random force that mindlessly guides a person to the perfect partner, and that a person is responsible for using one's head in the interests of one's heart. I want this revolution to empower you with a plan to make decisions about your partners based upon universal laws of relationships—like the order and balance of the bonding dynamics of the RAM, and the revealing nature of family background, other relationship patterns, and the inner-workings of the conscience. I want the RAM to provide you with the best of both worlds by compensating for the changes and losses that occurred when our society shifted from collective guidance in choosing a marriage partner to an individualized aloneness where you are on your own in this massive venture.

Dating should be fun, safe, and effective. It should profit your future marriage, not damage it. Yes, I believe that choosing a partner is complex. The instant-formula approach will never work, because it defies the very goal that dating is attempting to gain: high-quality, loving, romantic, and lasting marriages.

I also believe that the complexity is nothing to despair about, because you can be a pacemaker in your romantic relationships. You can set a pace that gives you enough time to explore those five crucial areas that will clearly reveal what your partner is like. You have a visual in the RAM that can enable you to sort through your periodic mixed feelings, while helping you feel more safe and confident.

The world needs trendsetters who will step forward to be the pacemakers in their dating relationships. I believe that now is the time for a new, more systematic approach for you to use with those powerful and wonderful feelings of love as you journey toward marriage.

Notes

Chapter 1

1. Whitehead, B. D., & Popenoe, D. (2000). Sex without strings, relationships without rings. *The state of our unions, 2000* (pp. 6–20). Piscataway, NJ: The National Marriage Project, Rutgers University Press.
2. De Rougemont, D. (1959). The crisis of the modern couple. In R. N. Anshen (Ed.), *The family: Its function and destiny.* NY: Harper Brothers.
3. Burgess, E. W. (1926). The romantic impulse and family disorganization. *Survey, 57,* 290–294.

Chapter 2

1. Science proves that love is blind. *BBC news report* on article from NeuroImage [Television broadcast]. 2004, June 14. http://news.bbc.co.uk/1/hi/health/3804545.stm

Chapter 3

1. Harlow, H. F., & Zimmermann, R. (1996). Affectional responses in the infant monkey. In L. D. Houck, L. C. Drickamer, et al. (Eds.), *Foundations of animal behavior: Classic papers with commentaries* (pp. 376–387). Chicago, IL: The University of Chicago Press.

Chapter 4

1. Whitehead, B. D., & Popenoe, D. (2000). Sex without strings, relationships without rings. *The state of our unions, 2000* (pp. 6–20). Piscataway, NJ: The National Marriage Project, Rutgers University Press. The results were derived from a study of not-yet-been-married heterosexual men and women, ages twenty-one to twenty-nine, in five metropolitan areas: northern New Jersey, Atlanta, Dallas, Chicago, and Los Angeles. They had a variety of religious and ethnic backgrounds, generally representative of their geographic area.
2. Ibid., 10.
3. Ibid., 11.
4. Huston, T., Surra, C., Fitzgerald, N., & Cate, R. (1981). From courtship to marriage: Mate selection as an interpersonal process. In S. Duck & R. Gilmour (Eds.), *Personal relationships, 2: Developing personal relationships* (pp. 53–90). London: Academic Press.

5. Grover, K. J., Russell, C. S., Schumm, W. R., & Paff-Bergen, L. A. (1985, July). Mate selection processes and marital satisfaction. *Family Relations, 34*(3), 383–386.
6. Fletcher, G. J. O., Simpson, J. A., & Thomas, G. (2000). Ideals, perceptions and evaluations in early relationship development. *Journal of Personality and Social Psychology, 79*, 933–940. In this study it was found that about half of all dating relationships break up within the first three months. This suggests that the initial attraction is significantly altered by some newly found characteristic within a three-month period—significantly enough to result in the breakup of half of the relationships. Therefore, many initially hidden patterns seem to become evident within the first three months.

Chapter 5

1. Baxter, L. A., & West, L. (2003). Couple perceptions of their similarities and differences: A dialectical perspective. *Journal of Social and Personal Relationships, 20*(4), 491–514.
2. Buss, D. M., Abbott, M., Angeleitner, A., Biaggio, A., Blanco-Villasenor, A., Schweitzer, M., et al. (1990). International preferences in selecting mates: A study of 37 cultures. *Journal of Cross-Cultural Psychology, 21*, 5–47. This study was conducted with married adults who freely chose a mate and were not married by arrangement. For a comparison of the priorities of arranged versus free-choice marriages, see Myers, J. E., Madathil, J., & Tingle, L. R. (2005, Spring). Marriage satisfaction and wellness in India and the United States: A preliminary comparison of arranged marriages and marriages of choice. *Journal of Counseling and Development, 83*, 183–190.
3. Pennebaker, J. W., Dyer, M. A., Caulkins, R. S., Litowitz, D. L., Ackreman, P. L., Anderson, D. B., & McGraw, K. M. (1979). Don't the girls get prettier at closing time: A country and western application to psychology. *Personality and Social Psychology Bulletin, 5*(1), 122–125. Knight, B. (1975). "Don't the girls all get prettier at closing time?" [Recorded by M. Gilley]. On *The best of Mickey Gilley, Volume 2* [CD]. New York: Columbia Records. (1975). Unfortunately, the music world is not always politically correct. Any quotations using "girls" should read as "members of the opposite sex."
4. Huston, T., Surra, C., Fitzgerald, N., & Cate, R. (1981). From courtship to marriage: Mate selection as an interpersonal process. In S. Duck & R. Gilmour (Eds.), *Personal relationships, 2: Developing personal relationships* (pp. 53–90). London: Academic Press. Patz, A. (2000, January). Will your marriage last? *Psychology Today, 33*(1), 58–65.
5. Whitehead, B. D., & Popenoe, D. (2000). Sex without strings, relationships without rings. *The state of our unions, 2000* (pp. 6–20). Piscataway, NJ: The National Marriage Project, Rutgers University Press.

6. Kenny, D. A., & Acitelli, L. K. (1994). Measuring similarity in couples. *Journal of Family Psychology, 8*(4), 417–431.
7. Miller, P., Caughlin, J., & Huston, T. (2003). Trait expressiveness and marital satisfaction: The role of idealization processes. *Journal of Marriage and Family, 65*, 978–995.
8. Buss, D. M., Abbott, M., Angeleitner, A., Biaggio, A., Blanco-Villasenor, A., Schweitzer, M., et al. (1990). International preferences in selecting mates: A study of 37 cultures. *Journal of Cross-Cultural Psychology, 21*, 5–47.
9. Lauer, J., & Lauer, R. (1986). *Til death do us part: A study and guide to long-term marriage.* New York: Harrington Park. See also Ziv, A., & Gadish, O. (1989). Humor and marital satisfaction. *The Journal of Social Psychology, 129*(6), 759–768. Priest, R., & Theirn, M. (2003). Humor appreciation in marriage: Spousal similarity, assortative mating and disaffection. *Humor, 16*(1), 63–78. Fraley, B., & Aron, A. (2004). The effect of a shared humorous experience on the closeness in initial encounters. *Personal Relationships, 11*, 61–78. See also Sprecher, S., & Regan, P. (2002). Liking some things (in some people) more than others: Partner preferences in romantic relationships and friendships. *Journal of Social and Personal Relationships, 19*(4), 463–481.
10. Lauer, R., Lauer, J., & Kerr, S. (1990). The long-term marriage: Perceptions of stability and satisfaction. *International Journal of Aging and Human Development, 31*, 189.
11. Some of these values are discussed in greater detail in subsequent chapters and will be mentioned but not elaborated in this section. I will also note the chapters where they will be further described when I identify them.
12. Wilson, J., & Musick, M. (1996). Religion and marital dependency. *Journal for the Scientific Study of Religion, 35*, 30–40.
13. Houts, R., Robins, E., & Huston, T. (1996). Compatibility and the development of premarital relationships. *Journal of Marriage and the Family, 58*, 7–20.
14. Larsen, A. S., & Olson, D. H. (1989). Predicting marital satisfaction using PREPARE: A replication study. *Journal of Marital and Family Therapy, 15*(3), 311–312.
15. Olson, D. H., & DeFrain, J. (1997). *Marriage and the family: Diversity and strengths.* (2nd ed.) Mountain View, CA: Mayfield Publishing.
16. Flora, J., & Segrin, C. Joint leisure time in friendship and romantic relationships: The role of activity type, social skills, and positivity. *Journal of Social and Personal Relationships, 15*(5), 711–718.

Chapter 6

1. Geiss, S. K., & O'Leary, K. D. (1981). Therapist ratings of frequency and severity of marital problems: Implications for research. *Journal of Marriage and Family Therapy, 7*, 515–520.

2. Cordova, J. V., Gee, C. B., & Warren, L. Z. (2005). Emotional skillfulness in marriage: Intimacy as a mediator of the relationship between emotional skillfulness and marital satisfaction. *Journal of Social and Clinical Psychology, 24*(2), 218–235.
3. Gottman, J. M. (1994). *What predicts divorce?* Hillsdale, NJ: Erlbaum.
4. See the Couple Communication Program as an example of a program for developing better communication skills at couplecommunication.com.

Chapter 7

1. Darley, J. M., & Batson, C. D. (1973). From Jerusalem to Jericho: A study of situational and dispositional variables in helping behavior. *Journal of Personality and Social Psychology, 27*, 100–108.
2. Midlarsky, E., Fagin Jones, S., & Corley, R. (2005). Personality correlates of heroic rescue during the Holocaust. *Journal of Personality, 73*(4), 907–934.
3. Huston, T., Surra, C., Fitzgerald, N., & Cate, R. (1981). From courtship to marriage: Mate selection as an interpersonal process. In S. Duck & R. Gilmour (Eds.), *Personal relationships, 2: Developing personal relationships* (pp. 53–90). London: Academic Press. See also Elder, G. H. (1999). *Children of the Great Depression.* Boulder, CO: Westview Press.

Chapter 9

1. Birchler, G. R., Weiss, R. L., & Vincent, J. P. (1975, February). Multimethod analysis of social reinforcement exchange between maritally distressed and nondistressed spouse and stranger dyads. *Journal of Personality and Social Psychology, 31*(2), 349–360. Dindia, K. (1988). Communication with spouses and others. In P. Noller & M. Fitzpatrick (Eds.), *Perspectives on marital interaction* (pp. 273–293). Clevedon, England: Multilingual Matters, Ltd.
2. Mischel, W. (1967). Waiting for rewards and punishments: Effects of time and probability on choice. *Journal of Personality and Social Psychology, 5*(1), 24–31.
3. McCrae, R. R., & Oliver, J. P. (1992). An introduction to the five-factor model and its applications. *Journal of Personality, 60*(2), 175–215.
4. Ibid. The five factors and their descriptions are
    1. Extraversion (E)—talkative, skilled in play, humor, rapid personal tempo, facially and gesturally expressive, behaves assertively, and gregarious
    2. Agreeableness (A)—not critical or skeptical, behaves in a giving way, sympathetic, considerate, arouses liking, warm, compassionate, and basically trustful
    3. Conscientiousness (C)—dependable, responsible, productive, able to delay gratification, not self-indulgent, behaves ethically, and has high aspiration level

4. Neuroticism (N)—thin-skinned, brittle ego defenses, basically anxious, concerned with adequacy, and fluctuating moods
5. Openness (O)—wide range of interests, introspective, unusual thought processes, values intellectual matters, judges in unconventional terms, and aesthetically reactive

5. Botwin, M. D., Buss, D. M., & Shackelford, T. K. (1997). Personality and mate preference: Five factors in mate selection and marital satisfaction. *Journal of Personality, 65*(1), 107–136.
6. Nemechek, S., & Olson, K. R. (1999). Five-factor personality similarity and marital adjustment. *Social Behavior and Personality, 27*(3), 309–318.
7. Tucker, J. S., Friedman, H. S., Wingard, D. L., & Schwartz, J. E. (2006). Marital history at midlife as a predictor of longevity: Alternative explanations to the protective effect of marriage. *Health Psychology, 15*(2), 94–101. See also Friedman, H. S., Tucker, J. S., Schwartz, J. E., Martin, L. R., Tomlinson-Keasey, C., Wingard, D. L., & Criqui, M. H. (1995). Childhood conscientiousness and longevity: Health behaviors and cause of death. *Journal of Personality and Social Psychology, 68*(4), 696–703.
8. Terman, L. M., & Oden, M. H. (1947). *Genetic studies of genius: IV. The gifted child grows up: Twenty-five years follow-up.* Stanford, CA: Stanford University Press.
9. Waite, L. J., & Gallagher, M. (2000). *The case for marriage: Why married people are happier, healthier, and better off financially.* New York: Doubleday. Waite and Gallagher present a thorough review of the statistics on marriage and its protective benefits.
10. Ibid.
11. Friedman, H. S., Tucker, J. S., Tomlinson-Keasey, C., Schwartz, J. E., Wingard, D. L., & Criqui, M. H. (1993). Does childhood personality predict longevity? *Journal of Personality and Social Psychology, 65*(1), 176–185.
12. Goleman, D. (1995). *Emotional intelligence.* New York: Bantam.
13. Cordova, J. V., Gee, C. B., & Warren, L. Z. (2005). Emotional skillfulness in marriage: Intimacy as a mediator of the relationship between emotional skillfulness and marital satisfaction. *Journal of Social and Clinical Psychology, 24*(2), 218–235.
14. Halberstadt, A. G., Denham, S. A., & Dunsmore, J. C. (2001). Affective social competence. *Social Development, 10*(1), 79–119.
15. Miller, P., Caughlin, J., & Huston, T. (2003). Trait expressiveness and marital satisfaction: The role of idealization processes. *Journal of Marriage and Family, 65*, 978–995.

Chapter 10

1. Kaslow, F., & Robinson, J. A. (1996). Long-term satisfying marriages: Perceptions of contributing factors. *The American Journal of Family Therapy, 24*, 153–168.

Chapter 11

1. Matt. 10:39. (New International Version). (1984). International Bible Society.
2. Utne, M., Hatfield, E., Traupmann, J., & Greenbeger, D. (1984). Equity, marital satisfaction, and stability. *Journal of Social and Personal Relationships, 1,* 323–332.

Chapter 12

1. Whitehead, B. D., & Popenoe, D. (2001). Who wants to marry a soul mate? *The state of our unions, 2001.* Piscataway, NJ: The National Marriage Project, Rutgers University Press.
2. Michael Johnson, from Pennsylvania State University, has conceptualized three components in commitment in the theoretical research model he designed originally in 1973. Johnson, M. (1973). Commitment: A conceptual structure and empirical application. *Sociological Quarterly, 14,* 395–406. Since then, other researchers have revised and borrowed his constructs to devise similar theoretical models. The three areas I describe are an attempt to organize and consolidate the many research studies on commitment and its varying components.
3. Rate the positive and negative forces operating to keep you in this relationship. You could use a number scale (1 through 10 for positives; −1 through −10 for the negatives, with −10 being the most disliked quality), add up the totals, and compare them. You can also divide each total by the number of characteristics you added up. This would give you the average number on the positive and negative scales. You can use these two numbers to compare your two averages. The totals reflect the number of positive or negative characteristics you see in your partner, and the averages reflect the extent and intensity of your feelings about the positive and negative characteristics.
4. Larson, J. (2001, January). The verdict on cohabitation vs. marriage. *Marriage & Families,* 7–12.
5. Whitehead, B. D., & Popenoe, D. (2002). Why men won't commit. *The state of our unions, 2002.* Piscataway, NJ: The National Marriage Project, Rutgers University Press. Teachman, J. (2003). Premarital sex, premarital cohabitation, and the risk of subsequent marital dissolution among women. *Journal of Marriage and Family, 65*(2), 444–455.
6. Waite, L. J., & Gallagher, M. (2000). *The case for marriage.* New York: Doubleday. For current trends, see the yearly published review of statistics in the current *The state of our unions,* The National Marriage Project, Rutgers University. See also Stack, S., & Eshleman, J. R. (1998). Marital status and happiness: A 17-nation study. *Journal of Marriage and the Family, 60,* 527–536.
7. Teachman, J. (2003). Premarital sex, premarital cohabitation, and the risk of subsequent marital dissolution among women. *Journal of Marriage and Family, 65*(2), 444–455. Teachman found that those who

have sex with only the partner they eventually marry do not have better-than-average chances of succeeding in marriage, but their odds are not any worse either.

8. Whitehead, B. D., & Popenoe, D. (2001). Who wants to marry a soul mate? *The state of our unions, 2001.* Piscataway, NJ: The National Marriage Project, Rutgers University Press.

9. Conducted by the National Opinion Research Center of the University of Chicago: they used a nationally representative sample of an English-speaking 18 and over population. Also, Stacy Rogers and Paul Amato used a different data set and found that between 1980 and 1992, there was a decline in marital interaction and an increase in marital conflicts and problems. Rogers, S. J., & Amato, P. (1997). Is marital quality declining? The evidence from two generations. *Social Forces, 75,* 1089.

10. Whitehead, B. D., & Popenoe, D. (2001). Who wants to marry a soul mate? *The state of our unions, 2001.* Piscataway, NJ: The National Marriage Project, Rutgers University Press.

11. Teachman, J. (2003). Premarital sex, premarital cohabitation, and the risk of subsequent marital dissolution among women. *Journal of Marriage and Family, 65*(2), 444–455.

12. Camp Dush, C. M., & Amato, P. R. (2005). Consequences of relationship status and quality for subjective well-being. *Journal of Social and Personal Relationships, 22*(5), 607–627.

Chapter 13

1. Whitehead, B. D., & Popenoe, D. (2001). Who wants to marry a soul mate? *The state of our unions, 2001.* Piscataway, NJ: The National Marriage Project, Rutgers University Press.

2. Baxter, L., & Bullis, C. (1986). Turning points in developing romantic relationships. *Human Communication Research, 12,* 469–493. Metts, S. (2004). First sexual involvement in romantic relationships: An empirical investigation of communicative framing, romantic beliefs, and attachment orientation in the passion turning point. In J. H. Harvey, A. Wenzel, & S. Sprecher, (Eds.), *The handbook of sexuality in close relationships,* (pp. 135–158). Mahwah, NJ: Lawrence Erlbaum Associates.

3. Rape statistic, 1992. teenadvice.about.com.

4. Teachman, J. (2003). Premarital sex, premarital cohabitation, and the risk of subsequent marital dissolution among women. *Journal of Marriage and Family, 65*(2), 444–455.

5. White, R., Cleland, J., & Carael, M. (2000). Links between premarital sexual behaviour and extramarital intercourse: A multi-site analysis. *AIDS 2000, 14,* 2323–2331.

6. Whitehead, B. D., & Popenoe, D. (2001). Who wants to marry a soul mate? *The state of our unions, 2001.* Piscataway, NJ: The National Marriage Project, Rutgers University Press.

7. Ibid.

8. Cunningham, J. D., & Antill, J. K. (1981). Love in developing romantic relationships. In S. Duck & R. Gilmour (Eds.), *Personal relationships, 2: Developing personal relationships* (pp. 27–51). London: Academic Press.

Conclusion

1. Burgess, E. W., & Wallin, P., with Shultz, G. D. (1953). *Courtship, engagement and marriage.* Philadelphia and New York: J.B. Lippincott Co.
2. Bossard, J. H. S. (1932). Residential propinquity as a factor in marriage selection. *American Journal of Sociology, 38*, 219–224.

Index